Reading and Writing with Understanding

COMPREHENSION IN FOURTH AND FIFTH GRADES

Sally Hampton

Lauren B. Resnick

NEW STANDARDS®

INTERNATIONAL Reading Association

The International Reading Association attempts, through its publications, to provide a forum for a wide spectrum of opinions on reading. This policy permits divergent viewpoints without implying the endorsement of the Association.

Executive Editor, Books	Corinne M. Mooney
Developmental Editor	Charlene M. Nichols
Developmental Editor	Tori Mello Bachman
Developmental Editor	Stacey L. Reid
Editorial Production Manager	Shannon T. Fortner
Design and Composition Manager	Anette Schuetz
Design and Production	Progressive Information Technologies

Cover photos: © 2008 Jupiterimages Corporation

The publisher would appreciate notification where errors occur so that they may be corrected in subsequent printings or editions.

Library of Congress Cataloging-in-Publication Data

Hampton, Sally.
  Reading and writing with understanding : comprehension in fourth and fifth grades / Sally Hampton, Lauren B. Resnick.
      p. cm.
  Includes bibliographical references.
  ISBN 978-0-87207-767-6
1. Language arts (Elementary). 2. English language—Composition and exercises—Study and teaching (Elementary). 3. Reading comprehension. 4. Fourth grade (Education). 5. Fifth grade (Education). I. Resnick, Lauren B. II. New Standards (Organization). III. Title.
  LB1576.H2331715 2009
  372.6'044—dc22
                                                                      2008032667

Contents

Contributors

Sally Hampton is a Senior Fellow for America's Choice, Inc., in Fort Worth, Texas, USA. Previously she served as Director of English Language Arts and Deputy Director of Research and Development for New Standards.

Lauren B. Resnick is a Professor and Director of the Learning Research and Development Center at the University of Pittsburgh, Pennsylvania, USA. With Marc S. Tucker, she codirected the New Standards project.

ADVISORY COMMITTEE

Phil Daro, cochair
America's Choice, Inc.
Washington, D.C.

Sally Hampton, cochair
America's Choice, Inc.
Fort Worth, Texas

Lauren Resnick, cochair
University of Pittsburgh
Pittsburgh, Pennsylvania

Diane August
Center for Applied Linguistics
Washington, D.C.

Kathryn Bomer
Consultant
Austin, Texas

Lucy Calkins
Columbia University
New York, New York

Courtney Cazden
Harvard University
Cambridge, Massachusetts

Michele W. De Bellis
Consultant
Austin, Texas

Janice Dole
University of Utah
Salt Lake City, Utah

Susana Dutro
California Reading and Literature Project 2
Santa Cruz, California

Lily Wong Fillmore
University of California–Berkeley
Berkeley, California

John T. Guthrie
University of Maryland
College Park, Maryland

Georgia Heard
Consultant
Palm Beach County, Florida

Phyllis Hunter
Consultant
Houston, Texas

George Kamberelis
Bennington College
Bennington, Vermont

Walter Kintsch
University of Colorado
Boulder, Colorado

Margaret G. McKeown
University of Pittsburgh
Pittsburgh, Pennsylvania

Mary McMackin
Lesley University
Cambridge, Massachusetts

Sandy Murphy
University of California–Oakland
Oakland, California

Martin Nystrand
University of Wisconsin
Madison, Wisconsin

P. David Pearson
University of California–Berkeley
Berkeley, California

Edgar H. Schuster
Consultant
Melrose Park, Pennsylvania

Lillie Sipp
University of Pittsburgh
Pittsburgh, Pennsylvania

Catherine E. Snow
Harvard University
Cambridge, Massachusetts

Joan Stewart
Consultant
Queenscliff, Victoria, Australia

Dorothy Strickland
Rutgers University
New Brunswick, New Jersey

COMMITTEE CONSULTANTS

Peter Afflerbach
University of Maryland
College Park, Maryland

Jo Anne Eresh
Achieve, Inc.
Washington, D.C.

Andrés Henríquez
Carnegie Corporation of New York
New York, New York

Gaea Leinhardt
University of Pittsburgh
Pittsburgh, Pennsylvania

G. Reid Lyon
National Institute of Child Health and Human
Development
Bethesda, Maryland

Sara Michaels
Clark University
Worcester, Massachusetts

Helen Min
University of California–Berkeley
Berkeley, California

Senta Raizen
WestEd
San Francisco, California

Bruce VanSledright
University of Maryland
College Park, Maryland

Monica Yoo
University of California–Berkeley
Berkeley, California

About New Standards®

New Standards is a joint project of the Learning Research and Development Center at the University of Pittsburgh (Pennsylvania, USA) and The National Center on Education and the Economy (Washington, D.C., USA). From its beginning in 1991, New Standards was a leader in standards-based reform efforts. New Standards, heading a consortium of 26 U.S. states and 6 school districts, developed the New Standards® Performance Standards, a set of internationally competitive performance standards in English language arts, mathematics, science, and applied learning in grades 4, 8, and 10. New Standards also pioneered standards-based performance assessment, developing the New Standards® reference examinations and a portfolio assessment system to measure student achievement against the performance standards.

With support from the U.S. Department of Education, New Standards produced a collection of publications addressing literacy development, including the award-winning *Reading and Writing Grade by Grade*, as well as *Reading and Writing With Understanding*, *Speaking and Listening for Preschool Through Third Grade*, and a series on *Using Rubrics to Improve Student Writing* for kindergarten through fifth grade.

Acknowledgments

Reading and Writing With Understanding reflects the shared knowledge of an advisory committee of highly regarded literacy experts, each of whom shaped this book's vision of comprehending and composing. We wish to thank all the members of that committee, whose names appear on pages v to vi, for the time and commitment they brought to this project. We also wish to acknowledge the contributions of the committee consultants listed on page vi.

Special thanks goes to the following committee members for particular contributions. Lily Fillmore provided the insightful analysis of the role that language knowledge plays in reading comprehension captured in Chapter 2. John Guthrie shared with us the design of Concept Oriented Reading Instruction (CORI), in order to make clear the relationship between science learning and reading comprehension. Diane August provided information, highlighted in sidebars throughout the text, on working with English learners. Sandra Murphy edited and commented on the many drafts of this book and collaborated on the performance commentaries in Chapter 7. Phil Daro wrote the mathematics and science sections in Chapter 6. Staff developers Kathryn Bomer, Lillie Sipp, Joan Stewart, and Michele W. De Bellis kept us honest as we translated theory into practice.

And, especially, we thank Walter Kintsch for contributing his model of reading comprehension.

In addition, we wish to acknowledge certain individuals without whose efforts this document could not have been written. Helen Min and Monica Yoo worked with David Pearson in creating the reading probes, conducting the interviews, and drafting the commentaries that accompany the transcripts in Chapter 7. Martha Vockley offered organizational skills and work in translating abstract concepts into reader-friendly prose. Margaret Lowry negotiated the various perspectives on genre. Sunni Johnson continually updated the citations and bibliography and tracked the progress of this project. Lucy Hidalgo planned and organized our meetings, maintained the file of student samples, and kept the work on schedule.

Understanding Reading and Writing

Once students enter fourth grade, most of them are on their way to becoming readers and writers. They are still novices, of course, with much to learn about language and the power of literacy. What's next, then? What do fourth and fifth graders need in these upper elementary grades to become stronger readers and more effective writers? What can teachers of every academic subject do to prepare these students for the reading and writing requirements of middle and high school?

This book provides answers to these questions for teachers, administrators, and policymakers. Understanding the particular challenges that may arise in fourth and fifth grades, when many students begin to encounter more difficult reading material and different reading and writing expectations in major school subjects, will help educators anticipate potential obstacles, address individual needs, and improve student achievement.

To that end, this book brings together scholarly research, classroom applications, student performances, and commentaries on student work to create a vivid, richly textured picture of the habits of mind that engage young people in comprehending and composing meaning. The significance of this book is threefold:

● First, we present **a thoughtful vision of comprehension**, based on 20 years of research from the fields of cognitive science and reading, which defines comprehension as a dynamic thinking process in which readers actively and simultaneously mine the text for meaning and build meaning in their own minds.

This meaning-making process is intertwined with learning: Readers who make sense of text remember the information, ideas, and issues they encounter, which are stored in their memories as knowledge. This is why reading makes people smarter: Readers have stores of knowledge to draw on to make sense of new texts, experiences, and ideas—and to keep learning increasingly challenging content as they get older.

Yet comprehension is not an automatic result of reading. Instead, "comprehension is itself typically a product of instruction rather than a spontaneous accomplishment. Among the many factors influencing the macro-development of comprehension, it is instruction that is probably the most important for most students" (Sweet & Snow, 2003).

There is substantial research about the mental processes involved in comprehending texts. We will unpack this research, showing just what it means to read with comprehension, in an effort to bring improvements to reading instruction.

- Second, we offer **a balanced perspective on writing** that draws from effective teaching and learning approaches to form a comprehensive model. We take the best practices from programs that emphasize the writing process and incorporate the habits of successful writers. We balance these practices with a strong focus on text structures and discipline-specific expectations to prepare students to write effectively in the major school subjects of English language arts, history, science, and mathematics.

- Third, we provide **student performances** with commentaries that are designed to illustrate the

WHAT WE MEAN BY COMPREHENSION

There is a commonly held belief about reading: Grades 1 through 3 are about learning to read; grades 4 and above are about reading to learn. This widely accepted "truism" is actually problematic. Students in all grades read to learn, and students in all grades learn to read. That is, as they grapple with word skills, the youngest students pay attention to meaning. And as they progress through the grades, students hone their reading abilities while they work to understand more complex forms of text.

The U.S. National Reading Panel has summarized research that finds the early stages of reading include developing phonemic awareness, understanding phonics, becoming fluent as a reader, enlarging vocabulary, and understanding text (National Institute of Child Health and Human Development [NICHD], 2000). As a result, primary teachers work to help their students with these fundamental reading skills; the instructional focus is on making sure that every reader becomes increasingly skilled in the reading process.

By fourth grade, if their schooling has gone well, students should be sufficiently skilled as readers that the instructional focus can change somewhat. No longer is the teacher's central concern building fundamental reading skills and developing students' proficiency with the reading process; instead, the focus increasingly becomes helping students understand the content that they should take away from their reading. This instructional shift is essential if students are to develop an increasing understanding of the content in the complex texts they will encounter as they progress through school.

Third graders, of course, are expected to make sense of what they read, just as fourth graders are expected to handle phonemic awareness, phonics, vocabulary, and fluency. However, at fourth grade, reading is about digging into texts and *comprehending* them in the deepest sense of the word. By comprehending, we mean understanding to the degree that the information in the texts becomes part of the reader's storehouse of knowledge, retrievable at some time distant, significant beyond the moment.

The content area books that students encounter in school are, by design, outside a reader's domain of expertise, according to cognitive scientist Walter Kintsch (1998). They contain new information that readers must grapple with so that they can internalize it and add it to their growing knowledge base. Such reading goes beyond getting the gist of the text. Instead, readers must develop what Kintsch calls a "model of the situation," often referred to as a mental model. Developing a mental model fuses the information in the text with other kinds of relevant knowledge that the reader has so that this new knowledge can be stored in memory and readily retrieved on future occasions.

This is what we mean by comprehension: an understanding of the text integrated with the reader's knowledge, available for the reader to use again and again.

"But isn't this learning?" you may ask. Yes and no. Reading is central to academic learning, true; but learning encompasses more than comprehending text. In school, learning also encompasses discussion, instruction, and hands-on experience and writing. All of this learning is supplemented by comprehending content from reading. In this book, our view of comprehension exists as part of the learning experience. This is the sort of comprehension teachers assume when they ask students to read text, be it a story or a science text, to complement other in-class learning experiences.

elements of reading comprehension and writing presented in this book.

Additionally, in this book we present

- A view of the demands made to comprehend and compose in the different subject areas
- Targeted information on word knowledge
- Suggestions for instructional practice
- An exploration of the relationship between reading and writing

States and school districts can use the ideas in this book to improve existing literacy expectations—and make classroom teaching and learning more rigorous, relevant, and rewarding in the crucial fourth- and fifth-grade years. They also can use this book to illustrate how to recognize adequate performance in writing and reading comprehension.

About This Book

This book builds on previous, influential books about literacy from the New Standards project:

- *New Standards Performance Standards*, published in 1997, which sets content-specific end-of-year standards for students in English language arts, math, science, and applied learning at grades 4, 8, and 10.

- *Reading and Writing Grade by Grade*, originally published in 1999 with a revised edition appearing in 2008, which spells out fair and rigorous literacy expectations for students in kindergarten through third grade.

- *Speaking and Listening for Preschool Through Third Grade*, published in 2001 with a revised edition in 2008, which lays out oral language expectations for children in preschool through third grade.

- *From Spanish to English*, published in 2003, which provides guidance on helping English-language learners meet literacy expectations in English.

- The six grade-level–specific titles in the *Using Rubrics to Improve Student Writing* collection, also available in 2008 revised editions, which address specific elements that should be emphasized in an elementary writing program from kindergarten through grade 5.

Like the New Standards' earlier books, this book synthesizes the research evidence about reading and writing with the wisdom and guidance of a distinguished group of educators and researchers who have enlightened the field with their insights into students' literacy development.

Literacy Habits and Practices

I remember well one of my older brothers reading to me in my early childhood. My mother and father both read to me, but J., who was more than ten years older than I, was the one whose reading particularly delighted me. There has always been a bond of understanding between us which exists to this day. (Anonymous)

————G. ROBERT CARLSEN AND ANNE SHERRILL, *Voices of Readers: How We Come to Love Books*

[Writers don't] count metaphors or similes or dependent clauses or gerundive phrases as we write. We simply work hard at the most felicitous telling, hoping the reader will indeed fall through the words into the story.

————JANE YOLEN, Foreword to *Adventuring With Books: A Booklist for Pre-K–Grade 6*

To become successful readers and writers, students must have a thorough grounding in those literacy habits and practices that contribute to strong reading and effective writing. In this chapter, we examine the habits of mind and the everyday practices that matter for fourth and fifth graders as they learn to read and write with increasing proficiency.

Fourth and fifth graders are expected to take on increasingly complex reading and writing challenges. They are still children, true, yet they are now old enough for more mature conversations, sophisticated learning, and sustained inquiry into academic topics. Further, they are at the right age for solidifying their literacy habits and practices.

This chapter frames the presentation of reading and writing throughout this book. The information here should provide a useful and relevant context for understanding reading comprehension and writing for fourth and fifth graders.

First, though, we begin with a brief but important exploration of why we read and write in the first place. Reading and writing are more than skills: They are sustenance for well-being in life. This book honors that point of view.

Why Do We Read?

Learning to read is a rite of passage into the world, and our first associations with books can carry us through a lifetime of reading. Young children, adolescents, and adults alike all read for escape, solace, shared personal experiences, discovery, aesthetic pleasure, and to immerse themselves in authors' craft.

Reading feeds the life of the mind with insights into humanity, the world, and the way things work. Reading gives people important ideas to think about, shaping people into who they are and illuminating models for whom they can become.

People who live their lives without reading miss out on the riches of the mind that result from sustained attention to texts. Books can cause people to pause and ponder, to connect the obvious with the obscure, to make grand leaps of imagination, and to deepen understanding of their inner beings and the world around them.

Reading is also a cultural experience that creates an entrée into shared communities. Educated people read. There are recognized bodies of knowledge and classic works of literature that are shared across generations, cultures, and boundaries. Reading enables people to explore the accumulated wisdom and provocative expressions of the ages—and the emerging ideas that come to life constantly in dynamic societies.

Reading is a prerequisite for joining knowledgeable communities and participating fully in democratic societies. People must read critically if they are to weigh the validity of the claims made by the media, political candidates, and advertisers. Effective democracies depend on educated citizens. After all,

READING FOR PLEASURE AND FOR LEARNING

One of the most important reasons that both children and adults read is for pleasure (Guthrie & Wigfield, 2000). Fourth and fifth graders should spend a lot of time reading texts they like—just for fun. Their diet might start with jokes, riddles, comic books, and graphic novels, but it should extend to stories and informational texts, texts about hobbies and interests, mystery stories, fantasies, poems, magazines, newspapers, websites—wherever their interests take them.

Students should pursue their interests; live vicariously in books and other texts; revel in real places, people, and times; or escape into imaginary worlds. Students should immerse themselves in exploring topics they're wild about, such as racecars or horses or athletes—topics that may not make it into the curriculum but that hook children on reading and learning. They should unearth new favorites and reread old favorites.

If reading is not a pleasurable activity, students will not pursue it. They will not develop the habit of reading or the staying power that comes with it. And reading is a powerful way for students to learn, both in school and out of school. Students should be pursuing information and knowledge about topics that interest them in texts, where they will find far more depth, nuance, and detail than anywhere else. And they should be discovering new topics of interest and acquiring knowledge as a matter of course in their reading.

people have a responsibility to understand the issues that undergird elections and community life. Finding and validating information about such issues requires reading competence. Moreover, students who have high motivation to read and well-developed reading interests gain reading comprehension much faster than do less motivated readers (Guthrie et al., 2006).

Why Do We Write?

Writing is a powerful way for people to develop an understanding of themselves and their world. Self-expression and exploration of personal identity are the stuff of writings that range from diaries, poems, and stories to narrative accounts, travel journals, and memoirs.

WRITING FOR PLEASURE AND FOR LEARNING

Just as we want students to read for pleasure, we want them to write for pleasure. Writing personal notes, letters, stories, diaries, journals, poems, and pieces on topics of interest can satisfy students' urge to express themselves.

Such writing takes place without the pressure of a deadline or a grade or public scrutiny. Hence, it is safe, and students can stretch their abilities without fear of getting things wrong. It is primarily through explorations in personal writing that students gain confidence in their ability to create prose.

That said, it is important to realize that students will be called upon as they progress through school to write classroom papers. Students should be taught how to write so they are equipped with the knowledge and skills they need to succeed academically. They need adequate practice to write in all their academic subjects in order to meet school writing expectations with certainty—and, perhaps, with pleasure.

And writing about topics beyond the self helps writers to add information to their existing knowledge.

The self-focused writing that characterizes the early elementary years continues to be important to students throughout their lives. At all ages, people write to make sense of what they are feeling and thinking; in fact, many writers believe that only by writing can a person really think deeply about feelings and systematically about ideas. Writing clarifies thinking.

All types of writing are good preparation for the writing that students are expected to do in school and in life. Developing a habit of writing prepares students to approach a blank page or digital screen with anticipation and a sense of purpose. It helps students realize that knowledge of their subject matter keeps their ideas flowing and their reasoning cogent. By pondering over just the right word, students learn to be nimble with language. And by considering the reader—a teacher, parent, friend, or themselves—they learn to shape the writing for specific audiences and purposes.

Writing is a craft and an art that requires people to have something to say and to say it well with words that capture nuances of meaning. The act of writing, in fact, is a concentrated act of making feeling, perception, and thinking visible, permanent, and important.

Writing is as valuable as reading both in school and beyond. The art and craft of writing to express personal and public ideas, writing to learn and communicate knowledge, and writing to accomplish important purposes are marks of educated people. Moreover, writing is increasingly important for success in middle school and high school, higher education, and the workplace, where communicating effectively with colleagues in writing is essential at every rung of the career ladder.

Reading and Writing Habits

Becoming a strong reader and an effective writer takes practice. Students have a lot to learn about reading and writing—not just in English language arts classes, but also in all their other school subjects. Students need time to read texts, write texts, talk about texts, and use technologies to read and write.

In this section, we take a closer look at the habits students should develop to strengthen their literacy knowledge and skills:

● Read and write different kinds of texts

● Read and write purposefully

CLASSROOM APPLICATION

Teachers should talk to students about what it means to be a reader and about the habits that characterize readers. They should encourage students to establish these habits as goals. Such habits include the following:

● Read daily at home and at school.
● Choose books that are just right for you as a reader.
● Think about the book you are reading and be willing to recommend it (or not) to another reader.
● Pay attention to the kinds of books you especially like to read and the authors whose books you think are good—have favorite books and favorite authors.
● When you finish reading a book in a series, decide whether to read another.
● Try to read both fiction and nonfiction.

In this school we don't just teach reading. We teach students to become readers.

—Ann Marie Carrillo, former principal, PS 116, New York City

- Read and write daily
- Talk about reading and writing
- Make good use of knowledge to read and write
- Use technology to read and write

Read and Write Different Kinds of Texts

Fourth and fifth graders should be reading and writing widely and deeply on their own and in school. They should read many different kinds of texts and many authors. They should be familiar with both fiction and nonfiction. They should read feature stories, biographies, memoirs, poetry, and plays. They should read books, magazines, newspapers, and websites.

BENEFITS FOR ENGLISH LEARNERS OF READING TEXTS IN THEIR FIRST LANGUAGE

Language-minority students who are literate in their first language benefit from reading literary and informational texts in that language. Reading in their first language allows them to build world knowledge, topical knowledge, and disciplinary knowledge and strengthen their first-language literacy skills (August & Hakuta, 1997). But second-language skills also benefit. Studies have demonstrated that language-minority students instructed in their native language as well as their second language perform better on second-language reading measures (August & Shanahan, 2006). This is the case at both the elementary and secondary levels.

It may be that cross-language relationships exist in word reading, cognate vocabulary, comprehension, and reading strategies (August & Shanahan, 2006). For example, in the area of reading strategies, most studies find that bilingual students who read strategically in one language also read strategically in their other language (subject to proficiency level and other influences). In general, strategic reading skills do not need to be relearned as second-language acquisition proceeds because they are not language specific. Other studies show that aspects of writing skills, both emergent and higher order, developed in one language can be accessed for writing in the other.

Reading and writing different kinds of texts helps students understand that there are many ways of organizing information, making meaning, presenting a point of view, or stating a case—differences that are appropriate for different circumstances, purposes, or audiences.

On their own, students should be able to choose books and other reading materials that interest them. They should develop favorites, such as books about sports or space exploration or famous Americans or people from their native cultures, or authors who write historical narratives, mystery stories, fantasies, or poems. It's perfectly fine for them to read 15 mysteries in a row if mysteries are their preference, but students also should be encouraged to explore new genres and challenging topics.

Students at this age continue to benefit from hearing texts read aloud to develop an ear for language—and also for sheer enjoyment.

Students should read texts at two challenge levels:

- Texts that they can read comfortably on their own with ease, which will give them pleasure and a sense of accomplishment and confidence
- Texts that they can read and understand with instruction, that challenge them or push them cognitively and linguistically

Similarly, fourth and fifth graders should produce many different kinds of writing that are meaningful to them and that are appropriate in all of their academic subjects. In these grades, students should be learning more about the different genres they typically will be required to write in specific school subjects. (We'll talk more about these different kinds of text types throughout this book.)

Students should write for personal and public purposes:

- Texts that are meant for themselves, such as notes about language, ideas, and issues they encounter in and out of school
- Texts that are meant to be shared with others for different purposes, such as school assignments, that may take a good deal of knowledge, planning, time, and effort to produce

Read and Write Purposefully

Fourth and fifth graders should read and write with specific purposes in mind. They should know what

THE CASE FOR LITERARY TEXTS

Literature is central to the English language arts curriculum, serving as a focus for reading and discussion. Teachers should help students grapple with the ideas, themes, language structures, genres, and authorial techniques of good children's literature.

There are many reasons to incorporate literary texts into classroom reading collections, curriculum, and instruction:

- Reading good literature inspires effective writing.
- Reading well-crafted prose exposes students to rich language, including metaphors, similes, and other kinds of figurative language.
- Well-developed characters and plots help students reflect on their own lives and begin to understand the human condition.
- Reading good literature prepares students to understand important literary themes.
- Reading good poetry and other literary forms enhances aesthetic appreciation.

THE CASE FOR INFORMATIONAL TEXTS

Students should have diverse reading experiences. Many texts, in many genres, at different reading levels should be readily available to students in classrooms and libraries, including trade books, magazines, newspapers, Web texts, and so on. Among these materials should be a wide variety of informational texts.

There are good reasons to incorporate informational texts into classroom and school libraries and to use them for instruction:

- Informational texts are key to success in later schooling.
- Informational texts are ubiquitous in society.
- Informational texts are the preferred reading material for some children.
- Informational texts often address children's interests and questions.
- Informational texts build knowledge of the natural and social world.
- Informational texts help build vocabulary and other kinds of literacy knowledge.

There are many high-quality informational texts that are appropriate for fourth and fifth graders. Further, student achievement in reading and writing improves when informational texts are incorporated into classroom teaching and learning (Duke & Bennett-Armistead, 2003; Kamberelis, 1999; Martin & Rothery, 1980; Newkirk, 2005).

they're trying to get out of their reading. They should also have something to say when they write. Further, readers and writers should have opportunities to generate their own purposes, which will shape how they go about their work.

Readers who are engaged and self-directed are more likely to be motivated to read than are those who have no clear purposes in mind. When students are interested in a story or a topic, or when a text is so good that it gets them interested, they are more likely to persist, to believe they can succeed, and to choose more difficult texts. Moreover, they will put forth the effort to comprehend and persevere in their reading—even when texts are challenging. According to Guthrie and colleagues (2004), students are more likely to read purposefully if they can

- **Choose texts that are rich in content and that reflect their interests.** Many fourth and fifth graders will develop burning interests when they are exposed to interesting topics. There is a high correlation between the desire to know more about a topic and interest in reading.

- **Collaborate with other students.** Working with other students fosters interests and aids comprehension.

Collaboration also fosters communities of readers and learners—the kinds of communities that schools strive to become.

DiPardo and Freedman (1988) suggest that students are more likely to write purposefully if they are self-directed and if they can

- **Select genres that help them shape their writings.** Students are more likely to write purposefully if they have a working knowledge of the genre options that are appropriate for communicating effectively for particular circumstances, audiences, and effects.

- **Choose writing topics independently.** Students should be given frequent opportunities to choose their own topics because a personal interest in the topic is motivational.

- **Collaborate with other students.** Students should read other students' writing and offer and receive comments about writing from others. Collaboration gives students targeted assistance for improving their work and also lets them know that their work is valued.

Read and Write Daily

Reading and writing every day makes reading and writing part of students' lives. The cumulative experiences of frequent reading and writing build students' knowledge and capacity to learn. The more reading and writing they do, the more comfortable and confident they will become at taking on more challenging texts and more complex pieces of writing. Students at this age should begin to initiate daily reading and writing activities on their own.

Fourth and fifth graders should be expected to read a sufficient number of books to put them on track to add at least 1,000 new words to their vocabulary every year. This is the range of vocabulary development that students need to be successful in school. (For more on vocabulary development, see the section beginning on page 46.)

Similarly, students should write daily with the aim of integrating writing into their lives. They should write to track their thinking, express their feelings, explain topics, explore ideas, ask questions, and get things done. Students should realize that they must "roll up their sleeves" and work hard at writing. They should take pride in their work and their progress.

Students also should engage in sustained writing, working on pieces that take several days or weeks to revise, refine, and complete. Students of this age should be expected to write an adequate number of "polished"—fully revised, edited, and produced—pieces every year.

Talk About Reading and Writing

Reading and writing are inherently *social* activities despite the iconic images of the lone reader with her nose tucked in a book or the solitary writer lost in thought over a piece of paper. Reading scholar Alan C. Purves argued that it takes two to read a book—every reader benefits from access to another reader in order to negotiate comprehension.

Engaged readers don't just read the words, they try to "read" the author and sometimes the narrator, the characters, or the sources of information. They interrogate these invisible others to try to make sense of the text in front of them: What is this about? What is he trying to tell me? Why did she use that word? Who's talking now? Should I trust this writer?

Classroom talk brings out the social dimensions of reading and writing. Talking about texts gives students opportunities to voice the thinking, questioning, probing, and comprehending processes that are running through their minds as they read and after they read. Discussions open up and expand these meaning-making processes, allowing students and teachers to share their different insights about texts, learn from one another, and build meaning together. Routine classroom talk, whole-class book discussions, small-group literature circles, and one-on-one conversations with the teacher or other students all provide interactive forums for students to understand, interpret, and explore texts together.

In talking about texts, students and teachers should first focus on comprehension—making certain what has been read has been understood. Discussions may take place after a sentence or passage or a few chapters to build a coherent understanding of the text so far. Talking about texts makes the process of comprehension public, giving students the chance to practice in an arena where they receive feedback and support.

Classroom talk about texts is important in every academic subject, not just English language arts. In mathematics, for example, teachers and students should attend to the language and meaning of word problems, which may puzzle even the most competent readers. Likewise, teachers and students should discuss difficult, complex, or ambiguous text passages in history and science.

Classroom talk is a habit that provides a window into comprehension and knowledge, allowing teachers to monitor how well students understand what they read and offer guidance when they experience difficulty. Classroom talk also gives teachers the opportunity to model effective habits, practices, and strategies for comprehending and interacting with texts. Classroom talk makes it possible for students to learn from hearing, considering, and responding to the interpretations and ideas of their peers.

Once comprehension is well developed, classroom talk should move to the deeper questions and the big ideas—the interpretation of a character's motives, perhaps, or the perspective of a historical document. This

THE IMPORTANCE OF SCAFFOLDING FOR SECOND-LANGUAGE LEARNERS

As we note in this chapter, in talking about texts, students and teachers should first focus on comprehension—making sure students understand what they read. This is especially the case for students who are reading in a second language and may lack the proficiency necessary to understand grade-level text in English.

Research indicates that teachers can support students' comprehension through scaffolding, such as in the use of instructional conversation. Goldenberg (1991) defined instructional conversation as

> first, interesting and engaging. It is about an idea or a concept that has meaning and relevance for students. It has a focus that, while it might shift as the discussion evolves, remains discernible throughout. There is a high level of participation, without undue domination by any one individual, particularly the teacher.... Teachers and students are responsive to what others say, so that each statement or contribution builds upon, challenges, or extends pervious ones. Topics are picked up, developed, elaborated.... Strategically, the teacher (or discussion leader) questions, prods, challenges, coaxes—keeps quiet. He or she clarifies and instructs when necessary, but does so efficiently, without wasting time or words. The teacher assures that the discussion proceeds at an appropriate pace—neither too fast to prohibit the development of ideas, nor too slowly to maintain interest and momentum. The teacher knows when to bear down and draw out a student's ideas and when to ease up, allowing thought and reflection to take over. Perhaps most important, the teacher manages to keep everyone engaged in a substantive and extended conversation, weaving individual participants' comments into a larger tapestry of meaning. (pp. 3–4)

Saunders and Goldenberg (1999) found that for upper elementary school students who were English-language learners, instructional conversation as well as discussion plus writing groups outperformed writing-only groups and control groups who read a story and completed worksheets but did not discuss the text. In a related study, instructional conversations were one component of enhanced instruction that found significant effects for students who participated in this instruction compared with students in control groups (Calderón et al., 2005; Saunders, 1999).

An interesting finding is that instructional conversations were equally effective with native English speakers (Saunders, 1999; Saunders & Goldenberg, 1999). Research is needed to understand whether there are certain aspects of instructional conversations that enhance literacy more or are required for second-language learners with very limited proficiency compared with more proficient second-language learners and monolingual speakers.

A second method of scaffolding entails previewing information in students' first language prior to teaching it in their second language. Fung et al. (2003) described a modified reciprocal teaching method in which Chinese and English reciprocal teaching occurred on alternate days, with new information presented in Chinese first. On each day prior to the first language assisted reciprocal teaching procedure (for the first 12 days), there was a 15-minute session of teacher-directed strategy instruction. The language used for the direct instruction was the same as the language used for reciprocal teaching on that day. The strategies taught included questioning, summarizing, clarifying, and predicting. As a result of the intervention, students made significant gains on standardized and researcher-developed tests of reading comprehension.

kind of discussion may take place while students are reading or after they have finished reading a text once or even several times. Students should have something substantive—words and ideas from the text—to talk about in classroom discussions.

Sometimes students see connections between the text and their own life experiences. When this happens spontaneously, discussion about those connections can be effective. But classroom talk should help students move toward a deeper understanding of the text, not simply push them to make a personal connection or to make a connection that may be forced or irrelevant.

Classroom talk about writing will cover much of the same ground as it does in reading. When they read, reflect upon, and discuss another student's writing, students should focus on many of the same kinds of questions as they would with a trade book or a textbook: What is this text about? What is it trying to tell me? Why did the author use that word?

Students often discuss their writing as works in progress, not necessarily as finalized pieces. Students may talk through their topics with the teacher or other students even before they begin writing. Verbalizing their ideas, plans, or outlines and listening to others' helpful reactions may spur them to investigate their topics further, consider a new angle, or simply get their creative juices flowing.

Classroom talk about written drafts can provide constructive comments to writers, who can then use these comments to revise. Such conversations should

---

GROUND RULES FOR CLASSROOM TALK

It is important for students to have some ground rules for classroom talk about texts. One school of thought, known as Accountable Talk, emphasizes that classroom talk should be academically productive (Michaels & O'Connor, 2002). In other words, students must talk about the text at hand, not veer off on tangents. The text and the topic should drive the discussion.

Several researchers have investigated how classroom interaction patterns relate to classroom engagement. They maintain that attributes of teaching that are culturally compatible promote the academic achievement of young minority students (Au, 1980, p. 112). For example, Au and Mason (1981) found that when Hawaiian students could speak freely and spontaneously without waiting for teacher permission—an interaction pattern similar to that at home—students' achievement-related behaviors (defined as academic engagement, topical and correct responses, number of idea units expressed, and logical inferences) all increased during the reading lesson. These are potentially important outcomes, since research does suggest that academic engagement and other achievement-related behaviors are associated with measured achievement (see, e.g., the review in Wang & Walberg, 1983, and, more recently, Fredericks, Blumenfeld, & Parks, 2004).

Further, classroom talk about texts should be accountable at three levels:

- **Accountable to the community.** Students should listen to their classmates, consider their points, and build on what they have to say or choose to disagree with them, taking their turn and staying on topic. Politeness is important in any classroom talk, of course. It is not an end in itself, however, but rather a foundation for substantive academic talk about words and ideas.

- **Accountable to knowledge.** Students should keep their facts straight, accurately and explicitly referring to the text. Classroom talk about texts requires students to ground their remarks in the ideas they believe the text presents. Students should be prepared to defend their remarks with evidence from the text and to ask others, "Where does the text say that?"

- **Accountable to rigorous thinking.** Students should use acceptable standards of reasoning within a given academic subject. For example, a good argument in analyzing a poem would not be a good argument in analyzing a history text: With a poem students may be focused on imagery, whereas with a history text, they would be more likely to talk about perspective.

With these ground rules in mind, students can attend to questions rooted in the text. Here are some questions that can initiate classroom talk and help students comprehend texts (Beck, McKeown, Hamilton, & Kucan, 1997):

- What's happening now?
- What is the author trying to tell you?
- Why is the author telling you that?
- Does the author say it clearly?
- How does this connect with what the author told us earlier?
- How does this fit with what we know (about an event, topic, or character) in the text?
- How could the author have said things more clearly?
- What would you say instead?
- What positions, interests, or values are presented in the text?
- How does the text do its work through specific language and text features?

address questions such as these: Is the text well structured, the information well organized? Is this an effective opening? Is the writing interesting? Are the words well chosen? Is there anything missing? Can you see the character with the details provided? Does the ending make sense? Does the writer guide the reader through the text with appropriate headings, transitions, and other aids?

As effective as it is for students to articulate their thinking about reading and writing, setting expectations for classroom talk can be problematic. It is difficult to assess an individual student's performance in a discussion because each student's participation is very dependent on group dynamics.

Make Good Use of Knowledge to Read and Write

Cognitive research has established knowledge as a prerequisite to and key component of comprehension. This is irrefutable. We cannot get very far in a serious examination of reading comprehension, which is the topic of Chapter 2, without focusing on both the knowledge students bring to the printed page and the knowledge they take away from it. Students must learn to make good use of the knowledge they have to help them make sense of texts.

Competent fourth and fifth graders who are reading in familiar domains with adequate knowledge process text automatically, fluently, and effortlessly. Many fourth and fifth graders, however, do not have well-developed knowledge of many of the topics they will be reading about—nor are they expected to. Especially with more challenging chapter books, textbooks, and informational materials that are introduced in these grades, fourth and fifth graders often find themselves reading in unfamiliar domains about which they know very little. Students need to exert specific and deliberate effort to keep moving through these challenging texts successfully.

Likewise, writing requires students to have something to say—something to write *about*. Other things being equal, students who know a good deal about a topic generate more text, and more coherent text, than students with only a vague or superficial understanding. Knowledgeable writers also can use their ideas to organize their texts, develop more insights, and incorporate more details. Again, though, lack of knowledge does not mean that students should not be expected to write about unfamiliar topics. In

fact, having to write about a topic can be a powerful impetus for students to learn more about it, often by reading books and articles. It is at this age that we begin to expect students to be able to "compose from sources," such as books, articles, encyclopedias, and the Internet.

In this section, we take a closer look at the specific knowledge that helps students comprehend texts and write effectively:

- World knowledge
- Topical knowledge
- Disciplinary knowledge

WORLD KNOWLEDGE:
UNDERSTANDING FROM EVERYDAY LIFE

A general understanding of the world that comes from personal experience, reading and other media, and talking to other people is fundamental to comprehending and creating text.

Everyday life, relationships, and events at home, at school, and in their communities give students a wealth of memories, personal experiences, and insights. Reading, watching television, listening to music, playing electronic games, exploring the Web, and other interactions with media also provide students with knowledge of the world. Conversations with family members, caregivers, teachers, and peers over the years add to this growing store of knowledge about how the world works.

READING ABOUT WHAT YOU KNOW

Several studies converge in suggesting that language-minority students' reading comprehension performance improves when they read culturally familiar materials (see, for example, Abu-Rabia, 1995, 1996, 1998a, 1998b; Hannon & McNally, 1986; Jiménez, 1997; Kenner, 1999, 2000; Lasisi, Falodun, & Onyehalu, 1988; McCarty, 1993). For example, Abu-Rabia (1998a, 1998b) found that Arab students received higher comprehension scores when reading stories with Arabic cultural content. However, it is important to note that across the studies, text language appears to be a stronger influence on reading performance: Students perform better when they read or use material in the language they know better.

All students come to school with some sociocultural knowledge that they can use when they read. A student who lives in an apartment in the Bronx can draw on her knowledge of city life when she reads about public transportation. A student who lives on an Iowa farm can draw on his knowledge of farm animals when he reads about the reproductive systems of mammals. And a student from the California coast can draw on her experience as a beachgoer when she reads about tides.

These same sources of knowledge can be put to work when reading unfamiliar text. The Bronx girl can use her knowledge of the New York subway to help her understand crosscountry railroad trips in China. The Iowa farm boy can draw on his knowledge of farm life to evaluate the environmental effects of factory farms. The California beach girl can use her knowledge about the plant and animal life in the tide pools along the coast to understand the growth of organisms in alpine lakes in the Swiss Alps. In short, even when students' knowledge is not perfect or completely relevant, it can still be a sufficiently good fit to be used in new and different domains.

However, knowledge is not always benevolent when it comes to schooling. Students can come to school with misinformation about the world. This misinformation can inhibit their comprehension of texts or detract from the accuracy of their writing. Therefore, it is important for teachers to check students' understanding by asking probing questions and fostering discussion about texts and topics.

Topical Knowledge:
Understanding From Inquiry and Interests

Knowledge about specific academic and nonacademic topics can help readers comprehend texts and write effectively. This knowledge comes primarily from learning in school and secondarily from investigating topics of interest outside of school. In-school knowledge can be as varied as expertise about insects or dinosaurs; out-of-school knowledge can be equally varied, such as expertise about skateboards or the care and training of dogs.

Students who know something about topics they meet in different academic subjects bring a great advantage to their reading and writing. The more specialized academic knowledge they have, the easier it is to comprehend and convey new information when they read and write.

For example, students may know about the Underground Railroad from reading memoirs or information books, visiting a museum, exploring historic sites, or browsing the Web. These students will have valuable topical knowledge to draw on when they read and write about the Civil War, reconstruction, or civil rights. Not every bit of information they encounter will be new; some of it will reside already in their memories, ready for them to activate and integrate with new knowledge. Likewise, learning about the Civil War in history can enhance comprehension and enjoyment of literature and other writings from and about that period.

Disciplinary Knowledge:
Understanding From Academic Subjects

Students who know something about the "big ideas," the organizing structures, and the language of typical texts in their academic subjects bring a special advantage to reading and writing in school. For most students, fourth and fifth grades mark the beginning of the real distinctions in the academic subjects. Disciplinary knowledge will help them to develop the skills they need to understand and write texts for English language arts, history, science, and mathematics.

Literary writers, historians, scientists, and mathematicians approach their work with very different kinds of knowledge, questions, and points of view about the world. They organize the knowledge in texts in distinct but predictable and conventional ways—for example, historians use evidence-based explanations; scientists describe, observe, hypothesize, experiment, and report results; and mathematicians solve problems and write proofs.

Literary writers, historians, scientists, and mathematicians also use highly specialized language, including discipline-specific vocabulary, that applies to topics. And they express themselves in distinct ways. In literature, for example, metaphorical and figurative language is commonplace, whereas such language plays a very different role in math. In literature, the characters cause action (which is usually expressed in active voice, as in "Henry berated John one too many times, and finally John had had enough. He lashed out like he never had before"). In contrast, the action in science is caused by natural-world phenomena (hence the prevalence of passive voice, as in "the molecules are broken up into...").

To write a science piece, for example, students must draw on their knowledge of the discipline's genres and specialized language *and* their knowledge of the subject. Here's an excerpt from "In the Grasslands," a piece written by a fifth grader:

A variety of animals live in the grasslands, for different reasons.

Some major animals in the prairie are prairie dogs, buffalo, deer, rabbits, owls, antelope, and mice. There are bigger animals that eat the smaller ones. Some of the bigger animals are foxes, coyotes, rattlesnakes, and even lizards! These animals live in a prairie instead of a steppe or savannah for different reasons, like the prairie dog for instance. He might live in the prairie because of the soil. The soil in the prairie might be easier to dig through than the steppe or the savanna soil since they live underground.

Some animals that live in a steppe are deer, oxpeckers, buffalo, squirrels, foxes, and coyotes. Most animals that live in a steppe are the same as the animals in a prairie mostly because the weather is pretty much the same in both grasslands.

Some animals that live in a savanna are lions, cheetahs, and other big, wild cats. All of the big cats are predators of other animals in the savanna such as zebras, giraffes, elephants, and antelopes. The big cats eat the other animals because they are the food and they aren't as fast. Also because the big cats are one of the highest on the food chain.

This end-of-unit writing demonstrates the student's knowledge and understanding of informational writing in science *and* the academic content of the unit. The controlling idea ("A variety of animals live in the grasslands, for different reasons") is expanded upon by an explanation (the prairie dog "might live in the prairie because of the soil. The soil in the prairie might be easier to dig through than the steppe or the savanna soil since they live underground").

This piece provides a wonderful example of how words like *because* and *since* are used in science explanations. The student also uses specialized vocabulary such as *steppe, savanna, food chain, predators,* and *soil.* The complete piece of student work includes diagrams and illustrations that clarify meaning, such as a map of the world that shows where the world's grasslands are located. The piece also demonstrates the student's understanding of science concepts such as biomes, survival, and interaction. (See Chapter 7 for more on this piece.)

Students perform better on writing assignments when they possess deep knowledge about the topic (Langer, 1984). Moreover, as they go through the process of writing such a piece, students further develop their knowledge of the genre and the content information they are learning (see pages 58–59).

In addition, the representational conventions of different academic subjects, such as diagrams, charts, tables, symbols, and references, can reinforce or aid comprehension and cue readers in to the big ideas—if students know how to use them.

We discuss disciplinary knowledge for each major academic subject in the chapters that follow.

Use Technology to Read and Write

Technology is a powerful tool for learning, for getting things done, and for being creative. Students should be using technology as a matter of course for their classroom work—to read and write and to *learn about* reading and writing. Technology can support and enhance literacy development.

Many fourth and fifth graders are savvy about technology. They use an array of digital devices in their daily lives to find information on the Web; communicate and collaborate with e-mail, chat, and instant messaging; and create texts and multimedia presentations. Technology can engage and motivate students to learn.

Research suggests that at least four education technologies can support students' reading skills: audio books; e-books and online texts; electronic talking books, which are texts embedded with speech; and

THE PROMISE OF TECHNOLOGY FOR ENGLISH LEARNERS

A recent review by Proctor, Dalton, and Grisham (2007) highlights the growing body of research suggesting the potential for hypertext, hypermedia, and computer-mediated text to support students' reading development. While relatively little is known about how supports might interact with learner characteristics for English-language learners, recent work by the authors of the review indicates these approaches are promising.

Thirty fourth-grade struggling readers, including Spanish-speaking English-language learners, read several narrative and informational hypertexts that provided embedded vocabulary and comprehension strategy supports, along with text-to-speech read-aloud functionality. The results indicate the students made use of the digitally embedded features in such a way as to promote both learning novel lexical items and effectively applying reading comprehension strategies.

programmed reading instruction (Holum & Gahala, 2001). Beers (2003) highlights the advantages of students reading a text and following along with an audio book, especially for reluctant or struggling readers.

Increasingly available to students are technologies that offer systematic instruction in reading and writing as well as short, discrete, just-in-time tutorials that focus on specific aspects of literacy. These tutorials, known as learning objects, can deliver interactive, multimedia lessons on topics such as summarizing, vocabulary, grammar, and punctuation. Learning objects, which may deliver an entire sequence of lessons or brief, two-minute snippets, are available from free or subscription repositories developed by universities, school districts, teachers, and commercial providers.

There is growing awareness that students need to be proficient with technology and to have the learning skills that will help them use technology effectively. The English and Communication Benchmarks from Achieve, Inc.'s American Diploma Project (see www. achieve.org) describe the facility with digital media that fourth and fifth graders should be able to demonstrate as follows:

- Present a clearly identifiable, explicit message using basic, straightforward visual, audio, and graphic effects.

- Use visual images, text, graphics, music and/or sound effects that relate to and support clear, explicit messages.

Further, the Programme for International Student Assessment (PISA) defines proficiency with technology as *information and communications technologies (ICT) literacy*, which is "the interest, attitude and ability of individuals to appropriately use digital and communications tools to access, manage, integrate and evaluate information, construct new knowledge, and communicate with others in order to participate effectively in society" (Partnership for 21st Century Skills, 2002). The International Reading Association (2002) adds that proficiency with the literacy of the Internet is essential to students' futures.

At the same time, there are special challenges to using technology for reading and writing. "Using computers and accessing the Internet make large demands on individuals' literacy skills; in some cases, this new technology requires readers to have novel literacy skills, and little is known about how to analyze or teach those skills" (Sweet & Snow, 2003).

The Internet, for example, presents students with environments and text formats that are different from the conventional places and texts traditionally used in school. The Internet presents nonlinear, interactive formats that require different methods of interacting with information as well. When students work with online text, many conventions are familiar, but others, such as hypertext, can present challenges. Teachers must explicitly teach students to understand and use strategies for navigating digital information.

Most school systems either use or have technology standards based on the National Education Technology Standards (NETS), the technology standards developed by the International Society for Technology in Education (ISTE) for teachers and students. These standards provide a clear picture of the types of engagements needed by students to be successful with the technology. According to NETS, students in fourth and fifth grades must understand the social, ethical, and human issues related to using technology in their daily lives and demonstrate responsible use of technology systems, information, and software. NETS advocate that students use technology tools to enhance learning; to increase productivity and creativity; to construct technology-enhanced models; and to prepare publications and produce other creative works. Building on productivity tools, students should collaborate, publish, and interact with peers, experts, and other audiences using telecommunications and media. Also, students are expected to use technology-based research tools to locate and collect information pertinent to the task, as well as evaluate and analyze information from a variety of sources.

Finally, despite the allure of the bells and whistles of technology to many students, it is important to remember that technology is not an end in itself but rather a means of supporting the needs, goals, and objectives for student achievement. Successful application of technology in the classroom means that it is transparently integrated into instructional practice. Also, because of the ever-changing nature of technology, students should be provided with tools that will help them keep up with the rich and dynamic possibilities for learning it affords.

Recommended Books for Fourth and Fifth Graders

Many books can be recommended to students in fourth and fifth grades. The following lists contain recommendations based on merit, awards, and content for English language arts, history, and science. Although this list is not comprehensive, it represents a good sampling of appropriate titles.

English Language Arts

Atwater, Richard, & Florence Atwater. *Mr. Popper's Penguins*. Boston: Little, Brown, 1938.

Blume, Judy. *Tales of a Fourth Grade Nothing*. Santa Barbara, CA: Cornerstone Books, 1972.

Clements, Andrew, & Brian Selznick. *Frindle*. New York: Simon & Schuster, 1996.

Coerr, Eleanor. *Sadako and the Thousand Paper Cranes*. New York: Putnam, 1977.

Creech, Sharon. *Granny Torrelli Makes Soup*. New York: Joanna Cotler Books, 2003.

Creech, Sharon. *Walk Two Moons*. New York: Joanna Cotler Books, 1994.

Curtis, Christopher Paul. *Bud, Not Buddy*. New York: Delacorte Press, 1999.

Curtis, Christopher Paul. *The Watsons Go to Birmingham—1963*. New York: Delacorte Press, 1995.

DiCamillo, Kate. *Because of Winn-Dixie*. Cambridge, MA: Candlewick Press, 2000.

DiCamillo, Kate. *The Tale of Despereaux: Being the Story of a Mouse, a Princess, Some Soup, and a Spool of Thread*. Cambridge, MA: Candlewick Press, 2003.

Estes, Eleanor. *Ginger Pye*. San Diego: Harcourt Brace Jovanovich, 1951.

Fleischman, Paul, and Judy Pedersen. *Seedfolks*. New York: HarperCollins, 1997.

Fleischman, Sid. *The Whipping Boy*. New York: HarperTrophy, 1986.

Fletcher, Ralph J. *Fig Pudding*. New York: Clarion Books, 1995.

Gantos, Jack. *Joey Pigza Swallowed the Key*. New York: Farrar, Straus & Giroux, 1998.

Gardiner, John Reynolds. *Stone Fox*. New York: Crowell, 1980.

Hesse, Karen. *Just Juice*. New York: Scholastic, 1998.

Jimenez, Francisco. *The Circuit: Stories From the Life of a Migrant Child*. Albuquerque: University of New Mexico Press, 1997.

Lord, Bette Bao. *In the Year of the Boar and Jackie Robinson*. New York: Harper & Row, 1984.

Lowry, Lois. *Number the Stars*. Boston: Houghton Mifflin, 1989.

Mead, Alice. *Crossing the Starlight Bridge*. New York: Bradbury Press, 1994.

O'Dell, Scott. *Island of the Blue Dolphins*. Boston: Houghton Mifflin, 1990.

Paulsen, Gary. *Hatchet*. Santa Barbara, CA: Cornerstone Books, 1989.

Ryan, Pam Muñoz. *Esperanza Rising*. New York: Scholastic, 2000.

Sachar, Louis. *Holes*. New York: Farrar, Straus & Giroux, 1998.

Sachar, Louis. *Sideways Stories From Wayside School*. New York: Morrow Junior Books, 1998.

Smith, Robert Kimmel. *The War With Grandpa*. New York: Delacorte Press, 1984.

Snicket, Lemony. *The Bad Beginning*. New York: HarperCollins, 1999.

Spinelli, Jerry. *Maniac Magee: A Novel*. Boston: Little, Brown, 1999.

RECOMMENDED TEXTS FOR SPANISH-SPEAKING CHILDREN

As described at the website of the Association for Library Service to Children, the Pura Belpré Award, established in 1996, is presented to a Latino/Latina writer and illustrator whose work best portrays, affirms, and celebrates the Latino cultural experience in an outstanding work of literature for children and youth. The award is named after the first Latina librarian from the New York Public Library. As a children's librarian, storyteller, and author, she enriched the lives of Puerto Rican children through her pioneering work of preserving and disseminating Puerto Rican folklore. Visit www.ala.org/ala/alsc/awardsscholarships/literaryawds/belpremedal/belprepast/belprmedalpast.htm for information about the award and past winners.

Other sources of information on outstanding books in Spanish include

- Books in Spanish from Spanish-speaking countries, www.ala.org/ala/booklist/specialists/specialistsandfeatures1/booksspanishspanishspeaking.htm
- Books in Spanish published in the United States, www.ala.org/ala/booklist/specialists/specialistsandfeatures1/SpanishBks.htm
- Barahona Center for the Study of Books in Spanish for Children and Adolescents, www.csusm.edu/csb/

Taylor, Mildred D. *Roll of Thunder, Hear My Cry*. New York: Dial Press, 1976.

Yep, Laurence. *The Star Fisher*. New York: Morrow Junior Books, 1991.

History

Ammon, Richard. *Conestoga Wagons*. New York: Holiday House, 2000.

Ancona, George. *Harvest*. New York: Marshall Cavendish, 2001.

Bial, Raymond. *One-Room School*. Boston: Houghton Mifflin, 1999.

Curlee, Lynn. *Capital*. New York: Atheneum Books for Young Readers, 2003.

Evans, Freddi Williams, and Shawn Costello. *A Bus of Our Own*. Morton Grove, IL: Albert Whitman, 2001.

Hoyt-Goldsmith, Diane, and Lawrence Migdale. *Celebrating a Quinceañera: A Latina's Fifteenth Birthday Celebration*. New York: Holiday House, 2002.

Ichord, Loretta Frances, and Jan Davey Ellis. *Skillet Bread, Sourdough, and Vinegar Pie: Cooking in Pioneer Days*. Brookfield, CT: Millbrook Press, 2003.

King, Wilma. *Children of the Emancipation*. Minneapolis, MN: Carolrhoda Books, 2000.

Krensky, Stephen, and Greg Harlin. *Paul Revere's Midnight Ride*. New York: HarperCollins, 2002.

Kurlansky, Mark. *The Cod's Tale*. New York: Putnam, 2001.

Maestro, Betsy, and Giulio Maestro. *Struggle for a Continent: The French and Indian Wars, 1689–1763*. New York: HarperCollins, 2000.

Miller, Debbie S., and Jon Van Zyle. *The Great Serum Race: Blazing the Iditarod Trail*. New York: Walker & Co., 2002.

Myers, Walter Dean. *Blues Journey*. New York: Holiday House, 2003.

Pinkney, Andrea Davis, and Stephen Alcorn. *Let It Shine: Stories of Black Women Freedom Fighters*. San Diego: Harcourt, 2000.

Podwal, Mark H. *A Sweet Year: A Taste of the Jewish Holidays*. New York: Random House Children's Books, 2003.

Savage, Candace. *Born to Be a Cowgirl: A Spirited Ride Through the Old West*. Vancouver: Greystone Books, 2001.

Schanzer, Rosalyn. *How We Crossed the West: The Adventures of Lewis & Clark*. Washington, DC: National Geographic Society, 1997.

Sneve, Virginia Driving Hawk, and Ronald Himler. *The Apaches*. New York: Holiday House, 1997.

Young, Robert. *A Personal Tour of Monticello*. Minneapolis, MN: Lerner Publications, 1999.

Science

Ashby, Ruth, and Robert Hunt. *Rocket Man: The Mercury Adventure of John Glenn*. Atlanta, GA: Peachtree, 2004.

Chorlton, Windsor. *Woolly Mammoth: Life, Death, and Rediscovery*. New York: Scholastic Reference, 2001.

Collard, Sneed B., and Michael Rothman. *Forest in the Clouds*. Watertown, MA: Charlesbridge, 2000.

Dewey, Jennifer. *Antarctic Journal: Four Months at the Bottom of the World*. New York: HarperCollins, 2001.

Garrison, David, Shannon Hunt, and Jude Isavella. *Fantastic Feats and Failures*. Toronto: Kids Can Press, 2004.

Hiscock, Bruce. *The Big Storm*. New York: Atheneum, 1993.

Knight, Tim. *Journey Into the Rainforest*. New York: Oxford University Press, 2001.

Koppes, Steven N. *Killer Rocks From Outer Space: Asteroids, Comets, and Meteorites*. Minneapolis, MN: Lerner Publications, 2004.

Marrin, Albert. *Dr. Jenner and the Speckled Monster: The Search for the Smallpox Vaccine*. New York: Dutton Children's Books, 2002.

Montgomery, Sy, and Nic Bishop. *The Tarantula Scientist, Scientists in the Field*. Boston: Houghton Mifflin, 2004.

Nagda, Ann Whitehead, and Cindy Bickel. *Tiger Math: Learning to Graph From a Baby Tiger*. New York: Henry Holt, 2000.

Pringle, Laurence P., and Meryl Henderson. *Snakes! Strange and Wonderful*. Honesdale, PA: Boyds Mills Press, 2004.

Ross, Michael Elsohn, and Wendy Smith. *Pond Watching With Ann Morgan*. Minneapolis, MN: Carolrhoda Books, 2000.

Sayre, April Pulley. *Secrets of Sound: Studying the Calls and Songs of Whales, Elephants, and Birds*. Boston: Houghton Mifflin, 2002.

Simon, Seymour. *Eyes and Ears*. New York: HarperCollins, 2003.

Sussman, Art, and Emiko Koike. *Dr. Art's Guide to Planet Earth: For Earthlings Ages 12 to 120*. White River Junction, VT: Chelsea Green, 2000.

Swinburne, Stephen R., and Jim Brandenburg. *Once a Wolf: How Wildlife Biologists Fought to Bring Back the Gray Wolf*. Boston: Houghton Mifflin, 1999.

Vanderwarker, Peter. *The Big Dig: Reshaping an American City*. Boston: Little, Brown, 2001.

Wenzel, Gregory C. *Feathered Dinosaurs of China*. Watertown, MA: Charlesbridge, 2004.

Zoehfeld, Kathleen Weidner, Paul Carrick, and Bruce Shillinglaw. *Dinosaur Parents, Dinosaur Young: Uncovering the Mystery of Dinosaur Families*. New York: Clarion Books, 2001.

2

Reading Comprehension

To read well is to acknowledge the relationship between the text and the reader. Our reading is directed not only by our responses to the text but also by the text itself.

————Donna Santman, *Shades of Meaning: Comprehension and Interpretation in Middle School*

There may be as many kinds of reading as there are books, each one demanding its own form and degree of active participation; our choices can depend on whether we relish the exertions of volleyball, as it were, or prefer a meandering round of croquet.

————Lynne Sharon Schwartz, *Ruined by Reading: A Life in Books*

Comprehension is the centerpiece of our reading expectations in fourth and fifth grades. Most students by these grades are able to decode with fluency and accuracy. They also should understand what they are reading. This is the ultimate goal and the core value of engaging with texts.

What does it mean to comprehend text? What should fourth and fifth graders be expected to do? How good is good enough?

This chapter draws on 20 years of research on reading comprehension from both the reading and cognitive science communities where there is substantial understanding about how people come to comprehend. We unpack a new model of reading comprehension and make suggestions for embedding this model in existing classroom instructional practices.

What Is Comprehension?

In years past, researchers studied comprehension by asking people what they remembered *after* they read. More recently, researchers have studied comprehension by tracking what people do *while* they read. This latest research has produced striking new insights into how our brains make sense of text as we read—*and* the evidence of deep understanding that builds and results from proficient reading.

We know that comprehension is a complex, highly interactive thinking process that cannot be defined in simple terms. As they make their way through a text, readers build understanding in their minds using the text *and* their own knowledge, experiences, and purposes. They synthesize the language, information, and ideas presented in the text with what they hold in their own minds.

Comprehension, then, is a dynamic cognitive process in which information from the text mingles and blends with information from the reader's mind. These conscious interactions (for struggling readers) and subconscious interactions (for strong readers) happen simultaneously, continually, and repeatedly during reading, phrase by phrase and moment by moment.

Drawing on the work of many researches (Graesser & Person, 2002; Kintsch, 1974, 1988, 1998; Kintsch & van Dijk, 1978; Perfetti, Rieben, & Fayol, 1997; Van Den Broek, Young, Tzeng, & Linderholm, 1999), we can examine the two fundamental components of reading comprehension: developing a textbase and building a mental model.

- **Developing a textbase: making connections within the text.** In this process, readers work with the information and ideas presented by the text. They develop a textbase, which is a network of ideas that links the meaning drawn from phrases, clauses, and sentences into larger ideas.

- **Building a mental model: making meaning from the text.** In this process, readers build a world or create an image in their minds of the situation described by the text, using the related knowledge, experiences, and purposes they already have. They build a *mental model*, which is a representation of the ideas in the textbase that is enriched by the reader's knowledge.

Readers move between developing a textbase and building a mental model simultaneously as they process text, shifting and adjusting their understanding in the act of reading. There is a dynamic interplay in the reader's mind between the textbase and the mental model. As they read, strong readers continually check their mental model against their textbase to make certain that the mental model accurately reflects what the text says and is consistent with their knowledge base.

The thinking processes of developing a textbase and building a mental model interact with and depend on each other. Neither stands alone or

BACKGROUND KNOWLEDGE AND THE ENGLISH LEARNER

Some second-language learners may find it difficult to build mental models because they lack background knowledge. This may result from the cumulative effect of schooling in a second language, since language learners do not have access to content knowledge when information is available in a language they do not fully understand.

Research indicates it takes second-language learners from three to five years to develop oral proficiency and four to seven years to develop academic proficiency commensurate with their monolingual peers (Hakuta, Butler, & Witt, 2000). In addition, some second-language learners arrive in the United States with limited or interrupted schooling in their first language and thus begin behind their better schooled peers. Finally, a large proportion of second-language learners are from low socioeconomic status (SES) backgrounds; half of school-age children of immigrants in the United States come from low-income families (Capps et al., 2005). Socioeconomic status is powerful in predicting English acquisition, with students from lower SES homes taking considerably longer to acquire English proficiency (Hakuta, Butler, & Witt, 2000).

The Construction–Integration Model of Comprehension

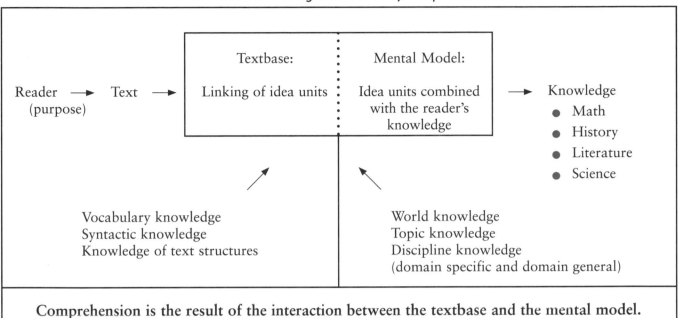

Comprehension is the result of the interaction between the textbase and the mental model.

happens without the other—they represent seamless, coordinated thinking in action. In the pages that follow, however, we will tease them apart and examine each in turn to show the distinctions and interactions between them and demonstrate the complexity of comprehension.

Developing a Textbase: Making Connections Within the Text

Understanding *what is in the text*—the information and ideas that the text presents—is the essential undergirding for understanding what it means. Readers must understand the meaning of the words, phrases, sentences, and paragraphs and link these ideas coherently.

As people read, phrases and sentences come into their minds one at a time. Readers need a way to hold onto the many pieces of ideas in the text and put them together into larger ideas. Short-term memory does not have enough capacity to hold them in storage as a long list. Instead, the reader's mind accomplishes this task by linking together the ideas in the phrases and sentences into a network called the textbase. The textbase is a representation in the mind of what is in the text.

When people are reading well, developing the textbase is likely to be automatic; they may not even be aware they are doing it.

Developing a textbase makes use of our knowledge of language, including

- The meanings of words
- Cues that signal connections—the logical, causal, and temporal relationships among ideas, such as

CLASSROOM APPLICATION

Teachers can help students comprehend text by modeling a close reading and then saying what the text means in their own words. This recasting of ideas (paragraph by paragraph or chunk by chunk) demonstrates that the reader has understood the ideas expressed in the writing. The teacher can then provide time for students to work in pairs and practice this strategy while she monitors their performances.

linking words (*and*, *so*, and *but*, for example), punctuation, pronouns, and other reference words

- Linking names, pronouns, nouns, phrases, and clauses to their referents (as in *Harry*, *he*, *him*, and *the guy who left the door open* all referring to the same person)

- The relationship between sentences, paragraphs, and larger structures of meaning

Students should begin fourth grade with a vast knowledge about written language, as we will discuss in Chapters 3 and 4. They can automatically—and simultaneously—process many of these aspects of written language as they read.

To develop a textbase, readers put together the pieces of the text for meaning. They link the meanings of smaller units of text—the words, phrases, and sentences (known as the *microstructure*)—to the larger organizational framework of headings, chapters, and sections (known as the *macrostructure*), which holds the meaning together.

Developing a textbase can happen in a variety of ways. Sometimes readers simply open a book and start reading. Sometimes they scan the titles, headings, subheads, and graphics to preview the text. Sometimes they read through some topic sentences to get an idea of what they can expect from a text. Developing a textbase, then, is not a top-down (macrostructure to microstructure) or bottom-up (microstructure to macrostructure) process. Often, it's a mix of both happening at once.

From the textbase they develop, readers can summarize or paraphrase a text, sticking very much with the text. Readers who build a good textbase can use the larger framework of the text to organize their understanding of the smaller units. For example, in reading Laura Ingalls Wilder's *Little House on the Prairie*, strong readers understand that this text is a narrative account of life on the prairie, organized by key events and periods in the heroine's life. They use this framework to organize their understanding of the smaller patterns of episodes. Each episode—an event or series of events that builds the plot—is developed through networks of phrases, clauses, sentences, and paragraphs.

As they read, strong readers think about or look back to previous sentences, pages, or concepts that they already have encountered to make sense of the new information in front of them. Readers process the logical, syntactic, and semantic relationships within and among sentences and sections of text. In other

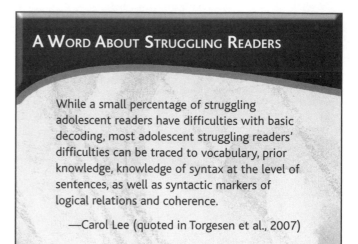

A WORD ABOUT STRUGGLING READERS

While a small percentage of struggling adolescent readers have difficulties with basic decoding, most adolescent struggling readers' difficulties can be traced to vocabulary, prior knowledge, knowledge of syntax at the level of sentences, as well as syntactic markers of logical relations and coherence.

—Carol Lee (quoted in Torgesen et al., 2007)

words, they recognize how one thought connects to another. They understand the cues that signal meaning in sentences, including reference words, connecting words, punctuation, and grammatical devices. They understand the meaning that these words and signals convey. We explore these topics in more detail in the next sections and in Chapters 3 and 4.

DEVELOPING A TEXTBASE FROM *HATCHET*

A good way to understand what it means to develop a textbase is to show how readers think their way through an actual text. Gary Paulsen's *Hatchet* exemplifies the kind of narratives that students should be able to read by the middle or end of fifth grade: It is at the appropriate level of challenge, and it appears on many respected reading lists across the country.

In this excerpt from the book, the words in brackets show the connections among words and ideas that readers must map out to develop a textbase.

Some of the quills were driven in [*into what? his leg*] deeper than others [*other what? quills*] and they [*the quills that were driven in deeper*] tore when they [*the deeper-in quills*] came out [*of his leg*]. He [*Brian*] breathed deeply twice, let half the breath out, and went back to work [*work on what? don't know yet; suspense; expect to find out in next sentence*]. Jerk, pause, jerk [*the work is jerking quills out*]—and three more times [*jerking quills out*] before he [*Brian*] lay back in the darkness, done [*all the quills jerked out*]. The pain filled his [*Brian's*] leg now, and with it [*the pain*] came new waves [*what were the old waves?*] of self-pity. Sitting alone in the dark, his [*Brian's*] leg aching, some mosquitoes finding him [*Brian*] again, he [*Brian*] started crying. It [*the whole situation Brian was in*] was all too much, just too much, and he [*Brian*] couldn't take it [*the situation*]. Not the way it [*the situation*] was [*what way was the situation? don't know yet; suspense; expect to find out in the next paragraph*].

I [*Brian*] can't take it [*the situation*] this way [*what way? still don't know; suspense*], alone with no fire and in the dark [*now we know "this way" means "alone with no fire and in the dark"*], and next time it [*the next situation*] might be something worse [*than this situation*], maybe a bear, and it [*the problem that will define the situation*] wouldn't be just quills in the leg, it [*the problem*] would be worse [*than quills in the leg*]. I [*Brian*] can't do this [*deal with the problem situation*], he [*Brian*] thought, again and again. I [*Brian*] can't [*deal with the problem situation*]. Brian pulled himself [*Brian*] up until he [*Brian*] was sitting upright back in the corner of the cave. He [*Brian*] put his [*Brian's*] head down on his [*Brian's*] arms across his [*Brian's*] knees, with stiffness taking his [*Brian's*] left leg, and cried until he [*Brian*] was cried out.

(Excerpts reprinted with the permission of Atheneum Books for Young Readers, an imprint of Simon & Schuster Children's Publishing Division from *Hatchet* by Gary Paulsen. Copyright © 1987 by Gary Paulsen.)

Most strong readers make these parenthetical inferences about words and sentences almost unconsciously. They also understand the shift in point of view from the first paragraph, narrated in the third person, to the use of the first person in the second paragraph. Writers, in fact, expect readers to catch these shifts and fill in the "blanks" in their texts, especially in terms of reference: who or what is being referred to in any given phrase or sentence.

Consider this sentence:

> Brian pulled himself up until he was sitting upright back in the corner of the cave.

Most strong readers understand intuitively by reading this sentence that *himself* and *he* refer to Brian. And it would be silly, unwieldy, and even confusing to eliminate these different words that refer to Brian. Without them, the sentence would read "Brian pulled Brian up until Brian was sitting upright back in the corner of the cave." We don't talk this way or think this way, so it wouldn't make sense to write this way. Imagine reading a whole passage or book that spelled everything out like this! It would be very long and dreadfully dull.

PARTICULAR CHALLENGES FOR ENGLISH LEARNERS IN DEVELOPING A TEXT BASE

For English-language learners, lack of proficiency in the areas of English vocabulary, meaning, language structure, background knowledge, and textual knowledge undermines the ability to comprehend text and develop a text base. In the excerpt from *Hatchet*, for example, English-language learners might struggle with meanings for words like *quills, tore, pain, pity, aching, next,* and *worse,* and for expressions such as *all to much, just too much,* and *can't take it.* They might know the meaning of the word *waves* as in "waves in the ocean," but not in the context of "waves of pain." Other difficulties for second-language learners include the extensive use of anaphora (e.g, *he* and *his* instead of *Brian*) and the use of first person combined with voice of the narrator.

Instead, writers know that readers can figure out that words such as *he, himself, his,* and *it* are references to people, things, and situations in the text. Sometimes these references refer back to named people, things, or situations introduced earlier in the text. Sometimes references are ambiguous, propelling readers forward by building suspense that will keep them reading to find out about the "it" that lurks ahead.

Here's another sentence from *Hatchet* that exemplifies the temporal and logical relationships that readers must figure out. In this passage, Brian is eating some berries, his second such attempt at easing his hunger:

> Soon, as before, his stomach was full, but now he had some sense and he did not gorge or cram down more.

In this sentence, readers must juggle between what is happening now and what happened earlier. A good experience of eating berries is taking place in the moment, which is signaled by the words *soon* and *now.* The phrase *as before,* though, tells readers to remember or refer back to Brian's earlier bad experience eating berries. And the word *but* tells readers that there is a logical, contrasting relationship between these two events. To fully understand this relationship, readers also would need to understand that the words *gorge* and *cram* denote rapid and careless eating.

CLASSROOM APPLICATION

- Teachers can make an overhead of a page of text that contains problematic pronoun references, substitute words, or connecting words. They can then ask students who or what is being referred to or what relationship is being signaled by the connecting word, and then draw arrows between the related words to illustrate that relationship. This is something Kylene Beers (2003) calls "syntax surgery."

- When a comprehension problem is caused by a lack of vocabulary knowledge, the problematic word should be defined during the reading and then returned to later so as not to disturb comprehension.

- Teachers can make a chart showing often-used connecting words and then ask students to add to the list as they encounter more connectives. For example,

  o Words that signal new information: *and, also, in addition, furthermore*

  o Words that signal contrasting information: *yet, but, however, although*

  o Words that signal causal relations: *because, so, hence*

  o Words that signal time sequence: *first, later, next, finally*

Building a Mental Model: Making Meaning From the Text

To fully understand what a text means, readers must build a mental model, or re-presentation, of the text in their minds. To do this, strong readers integrate the chunks of meaning "mined" from the text with relevant knowledge they already possess. In so doing, they enhance the meaning of the text.

Here are two examples that illustrate how readers put together a mental model:

- When they read a literary narrative, such as Judy Blume's *Tales of a Fourth Grade Nothing* or Phyllis Reynolds Naylor's *Shiloh* or Christopher Paul Curtis's *The Watson's Go to Birmingham— 1963,* strong readers fuse their understanding of

what the text presents with their own knowledge of life, people, and places to bring to mind a world peopled with characters who live in the context of motives, chronological events, time periods, and settings. This understanding is the mental model of the text.

- When they read an informational text on the life cycle of frogs, strong readers might envision the egg, tadpole, and mature frog—and egg again—as a "cycle" that recurs. They might even envision how each of these amphibian forms interacts with its environment. This understanding is the mental model. To build this mental model, readers would integrate the information drawn from the text with their general knowledge of ponds, tadpoles, or insects. They also would make use of knowledge from prior science learning—what a life cycle is or other examples of cycles in science. Depending on their academic sophistication, they might also draw on their topical knowledge of how species interact with the environment and their genre knowledge of informational texts that describe a natural process.

Strong readers bring the meaning of a text to life in their own minds: They literally create a vivid representation in their minds about the text, and they find a "home" in their memory for this idea by fusing it to existing knowledge. This constructed world of the mental model makes use of all the variety of knowledge and memory—sensory, emotional, spatial, logical, intentional, and experiential—and it is a direct response to the text.

To be valid, the mental model must be derived from the text and must make sense given the text at hand. It must be consistent with the facts presented in the text. The text is the foundation of the mental model. Just as surely, a mental model is accountable to one's knowledge base as well. Ideas that run counter to knowledge may be rejected or at least questioned.

Strong readers use knowledge they already have to make sense of the new information and ideas in the text. As previously noted, writers *expect* readers to fill in blanks, connect dots, and "read between the lines," inferring a motive for a character's action in a story, for example, or seeing the causal link in a history text between an action taken by one country and the reaction from a neighboring country. Filling in the blanks by making logical connections and using their

THE ROLE OF RELEVANT BACKGROUND KNOWLEDGE

Students are expected to learn from increasingly technical expository texts during adolescence, and their knowledge base must continue to grow in order to meet the demands of this text...students who do not keep pace with the increasing demands content area texts place on prior knowledge will fall further and further behind in their ability to construct the meaning of the text. (Torgesen et al., 2007)

While it is true that proficient reading and critical thinking are all-purpose activities, they are not content-independent formal skills at all but are based on concrete, relevant knowledge and cannot be exercised apart from what psychologists call "domain-specific" knowledge. (Hirsch, 2006)

own knowledge helps readers build a mental model of the text.

Readers who don't have the knowledge that the writer assumes they have can have trouble making sense of the text. They may fill in the blanks with knowledge the writer had not counted on—or, even more problematic, they won't fill in the blanks at all. Indeed, some students have difficulty accumulating the parts of a text into a coherent whole. Their reading is disjointed; they read as if the paragraphs, sections, or chapters have nothing to do with one another (Santman, 2005).

Sometimes readers' knowledge leads them astray. Their inferences, assumptions, and mental models may be plausible, given their experiences, but incorrect, given the actual text. Their understanding is flawed if it does not accurately reflect the information and ideas in the text. Such misreading may not greatly disrupt comprehension of narrative texts because with narratives, students often compensate for incorrect assumptions by drawing on their rich knowledge of story structure or human relations to help them understand the text. When the text contradicts their mental model, which continually changes as they keep reading, they may reread to make adequate adjustments. Narrative texts that play with time sequences or feature complex

characters or symbolism require a much more careful reading than those without such complexities.

Building a plausible but incorrect mental model can be particularly detrimental to students' comprehension of informational texts, especially when precise rather than just plausible understanding is called for. For example, a reader of the informational text about frogs may come to the faulty understanding that adult frogs raise their tadpoles if the text states that the mother frog lays the eggs and an illustration that accompanies the text shows tadpoles swimming together as if in one big family. Based on the text, the illustration, and prior knowledge about other young creatures that depend on their parents to survive, the reader may assume that adult frogs care for their young. This would represent a plausible but incorrect understanding of the situation described in the text.

Strong readers may build a mental model easily and automatically if they are reading a text within their comfort zone (with words they recognize easily and ideas that are at least relatively familiar). On the other hand, readers may need to work consciously, effortfully, and strategically when they are reading a challenging text or encountering an unfamiliar topic in order to succeed at understanding the text.

CLASSROOM APPLICATION

- Teachers can demonstrate how to construct a mental model by reading a section of text aloud and drawing connections between what they have just read and their relevant background knowledge.
- Teachers can ask students to write in response to what they are reading. The prompt should be specific enough to tap more than cursory understanding.
- Perhaps the best strategy for helping students to construct a valid and complete mental model is through discussion. Because all students in a class will not have the same or an equal amount of background knowledge, they will not form identical mental models. Discussion of the text—particularly discussion that encourages multiple perspectives such as occurs in collaborative reasoning (Reznitskaya et al., 2001)—will highlight differences in understanding and address readers' inadequacies or misconceptions.

Why is this cognitive process of building a mental model such a crucial aspect of comprehension? Here's why: *Building a mental model transforms new ideas and information into a form that can be added to memory, where it endures as knowledge that can be retrieved in the future. Unless readers build a mental model, the information they derive from the text is not likely to connect to their stored knowledge. The new information will be forgotten or lost.*

Having no mental model—in other words, failing to integrate the text with one's own knowledge—is not only a cause for forgetting. Even when the ideas and information are not forgotten, they may remain inert, unusable. Readers may be able to recall a text if they are asked, but if the information and ideas do not become part of the readers' knowledge, they are not available in new situations. They are rote memory, not knowledge.

"A Meeting of the Minds"

In *On Writing*, popular writer Stephen King describes the interaction between readers and writers as "an act of telepathy" that enables them to communicate across time and texts. Here's how he describes a reader building a mental model of a situation described in text:

> So let's assume that you're in your favorite receiving place just as I am in the place where I do my best transmitting. We'll have to perform our mentalist routine not just over distance but over time as well, yet that presents no real problem; if we can still read Dickens, Shakespeare, and (with the help of a footnote or two) Herodotus, I think we can manage the gap between 1997 and 2000. And here we go—actual telepathy in action. You'll notice I have nothing up my sleeves and that my lips never move. Neither, most likely, [do] yours.
>
> Look—here's a table covered with a red cloth. On it is a cage the size of a small fish aquarium. In the cage is a white rabbit with a pink nose and pink-rimmed eyes. In its front paws is a carrot-stub upon which it is contentedly munching. On its back, clearly marked in blue ink, is the numeral 8.
>
> Do we see the same thing? We'd have to get together and compare notes to make absolutely sure, but I think we do. There will be necessary variations, of course: some receivers will see a cloth which is turkey red, some will see one that's scarlet, while others may see still other shades. (To color-blind receivers, the red tablecloth is the dark gray of cigar ashes.) Some may see scalloped edges, some may see straight ones. Decorative souls may add a little lace, and welcome—my tablecloth is your tablecloth, knock yourself out.
>
> Likewise, the matter of the cage leaves quite a lot of room for individual interpretation. For one thing, it is described in terms of rough comparison, which is useful only if you and I see the world and measure the things in it with similar eyes. It's easy to become careless when making rough comparisons, but the alternative is a prissy attention to detail that takes all the fun out of writing. What am I going to say, "on the table is a cage three feet, six inches in length, two feet in width, and fourteen inches high"? That's not prose, that's an instruction manual. The paragraph also doesn't tell us what sort of material the cage is made of—wire mesh? steel rods? glass?—but does it really matter? We all understand the cage is a see-through medium; beyond that, we don't care. The most interesting thing here isn't even the carrot-munching rabbit in the cage, but the number on its back. Not a six, not a four, not nineteen-point-five. It's an eight. This is what we're looking at, and we all see it. I didn't tell you. You didn't ask me. I never opened my mouth and you never opened yours. We're not even in the same year together, let alone the same room... except we *are* together. We're close.
>
> We're having a meeting of the minds.

Comprehension, in the sense of building a mental model, is a crucial part of knowledge acquisition. Sometimes the reading fits with existing knowledge, so not much new learning occurs. At other times, the reading conflicts with existing knowledge, leaving the reader with unresolved questions—questions that open the door to learning. Ideally, these questions make hands-on work in science, discussion in history, and problem solving in mathematics all the more productive and meaningful.

BUILDING A MENTAL MODEL OF *HATCHET*

A good way to illustrate what we mean by building a mental model is to show how students make sense of a passage from a book appropriate for fifth graders. We return to *Hatchet* as an example.

The blurb from the jacket of *Hatchet* gives a preview of the book:

> Thirteen-year old Brian Robeson is on his way to visit his father when the single-engine plane in which he is flying crashes. Suddenly, Brian finds himself alone in the Canadian wilderness with nothing but his clothing, a tattered windbreaker and the hatchet his mother has given him as a present—and the dreadful secret that has been tearing him apart since his parents' divorce. But now Brian has no time for anger, self-pity or despair—it will take all his know-how and determination, and more courage than he knew he possessed, to survive.

After reading Chapters 1 through 7 of *Hatchet* and using background knowledge to make appropriate inferences about the meaning of the text, strong readers would know the following:

> Brian is stranded in the Canadian wilderness with a hatchet and his wits as his only tools for survival. He already has overcome several obstacles, including surviving a plane crash, building a small shelter, and finding food.

In Chapter 8, Brian awakens in the night to realize that there is an animal in his shelter. He throws his hatchet at the animal but misses. The hatchet makes sparks when it hits the wall of the cave. Brian then feels a pain in his leg. He sees the creature scuttle out of his shelter. Brian figures out that the animal was a porcupine because there are quills in his leg.

In addition to the information provided by the text itself, readers bring highly individual experience and knowledge to the text. Fifth graders might know

PATTERNS OF MISREADING

Students who have difficulty with reading comprehension may struggle with similar patterns of misreading. Classroom teacher Donna Santman (2005) discovered these common problems among her middle schools students:

- **Retelling as recitation.** Strong readers can retell a story or text passage from memory. Struggling readers may have to keep looking back at the text to recall it—and then almost recite the text verbatim rather than summarizing it in their own words.
- **Having problems with accumulating the story.** Strong readers build an understanding of the text from one section to the next. Struggling readers do not make connections among the parts.
- **Failing to question inconsistencies and ironies.** Strong readers pause and ponder over details in the text that seem odd or unconventional to them. Struggling readers do not question such oddities.
- **Changing the story to fit preconceived categories.** Many readers try to slot texts into familiar categories of texts they have encountered before. While this can be a smart approach for understanding texts, as we'll see in Chapter 3, it also may constrain some students from discovering new complexities and surprises in texts that don't fit the molds students want to impose on them.
- **Seeing books as an end rather than a beginning.** Many students seem to read as though getting to the end of a text—just finishing it—is the goal. Students who read like this close the book on their thinking, neglecting to consider whether the texts have something more to offer them.

SELF-MONITORING AND SELF-CORRECTING: COMPREHENSION REPAIR TACTICS

Throughout our discussion of the essence of comprehension, we highlight many kinds of cognitive "moves" that good readers make to comprehend texts. The underlying principle of reading is that students should comprehend well enough to achieve their purposes, meet school expectations, and organize new information in their minds as knowledge.

How will they know, though, if they are comprehending well enough? What can they do when comprehension breaks down? Students can get into the habit of checking their understanding as they read, which is known as self-monitoring, and then trigger repair, or self-correcting, skills or tactics when they are not reading well enough to meet their strategic purposes. Further, students benefit even more if they can tailor these skills or tactics to the text genre and academic subject in which they are reading. We talk more about this in later chapters.

Self-monitoring can be portrayed as a kind of mental dialogue between the student as reader and the student as learner. This internal comprehension checkup may be a web of unconscious processes, or it may be a conscious, deliberate effort. It becomes conscious when the text fails to make sense. These are the kinds of important questions students should learn to ask themselves as they read:

- Do I understand the text at this point? Do the words, sentences, and paragraphs make sense? Do I understand well enough to meet my purposes?
- Is my understanding complete? Is there something missing or suspenseful in the sentences or meaning that I need to figure out? What do I need to hold in my mind as I keep reading to understand the sentences and their meaning?
- Does this new information change my understanding of what I am reading? How do I need to revise my understanding now?
- Does this new information change what I know from other texts, my own knowledge, or personal experience?
- Do I want to keep reading this? Am I getting anything out of it?

When students encounter difficulties with these kinds of questions, there are literally hundreds of skills they can use to get back on track. Every reader is unique, however, deploying different skills in different circumstances.

Here are a few self-correcting tactics for which there is evidence of effectiveness in improving reading comprehension:

- **Summarizing.** Students identify the main ideas and occurrences in the text, starting with summarizing sentences and gradually learning to summarize paragraphs, pages, and then whole texts. Summarizing orally and in writing enables students to differentiate between the big ideas and the supporting details (Palincsar & Brown, 1983).
- **Asking questions.** Students generate big-picture questions about the text—good questions that teachers would ask. Creating good questions enables students to test their own knowledge of what is happening in the text (Palincsar & Brown, 1983).
- **Clarifying.** Students identify the cause of their comprehension problems, such as difficult vocabulary or concepts. Clarifying enables students to target their trouble spots, then to reread or ask for help with specific problems (Palincsar & Brown, 1983).
- **Predicting.** Students stop at various points when they are reading, using their knowledge of what is happening so far to predict what will happen next. Predicting enables students to think critically about how the information and ideas from the text they've read so far could develop (Palincsar & Brown, 1983).
- **Creating graphic organizers.** Students write, draw, or map out a visual explanation of the relationships among the big ideas or occurrences and the supporting details in the text. These graphic organizers enable students to see and remember these relationships and to organize this information in their minds.
- **Using text structure.** Students use the structure of the text to help them recall text content. Texts typically are organized in predictable patterns, which can help students remember the specific ideas and occurrences in what they are reading.
- **Answering questions.** Students answer targeted questions about texts from teachers or other students, which gives them immediate feedback on their comprehension. For more about answering questions, refer to Chapter 1, Talk About Reading and Writing, on pages 10–13.

things that bring the situation described in the text to life. They might know

- What sparks look like
- How it feels to be scared by an animal
- How big porcupines are
- You have to have food, water, and shelter to survive
- You have to be strong to survive

Here is a passage from Chapter 8 of *Hatchet* from which readers can further develop and refine their mental model of the text:

> Some of the quills were driven in deeper than others and they tore when they came out. He breathed deeply twice, let half the breath out, and went back to work. Jerk, pause, jerk—and three more times before he lay back in the darkness, done. The pain filled his leg now, and with it came new waves of self-pity. Sitting alone in the dark, his leg aching, some mosquitoes finding him again, he started crying. It was all too much, just too much, and he couldn't take it. Not the way it was.
>
> I can't take it this way, alone with no fire and in the dark, and next time it might be something worse, maybe a bear, and it wouldn't be just quills in the leg, it would be worse. I can't do this, he thought, again and again. I can't. Brian pulled himself up until he was sitting upright back in the corner of the cave. He put his head down on his arms across his knees, with stiffness taking his left leg, and cried until he was cried out.

Sam (a pseudonym), an end-of-year fifth grader in a regular classroom in a public school, has read *Hatchet* from the beginning through these two paragraphs. Here, in response to questioning, he discusses Chapter 8 of *Hatchet*, using language that reveals his developing mental model of the book:

> Okay. Um...in Chapter 8, he was asleep and he had just eaten a lot of raspberry, uh-huh, and he has fallen asleep happy because he found a good food source. And he woke up to a sound and he was, like, really scared because apparently he had watched a lot of scary movies and he thought of that. Uh-huh.
>
> He thought something was trying to kill him, and the sound was getting closer and he could smell it. So he got scared and, um, he, he like, like, kicked out, tried to like, uh, push the thing back. Uh-huh. Because it was...and uh, and immediately he felt this pain.

> Uh-huh. So he pulled his leg back and threw his hatchet uh-huh, um, at the wherever the sound was, but he hit the wall instead of the cave, uh-huh, and sparks showered from the wall. Uh-huh. Um, yeah, so in the, um, and he struggled back to the end of the cave and like, um, he was backed up against the wall and he, um, but then he could hear this littering and it was actually going away from him out of the cave. Uh-huh. So, and in the dim light of the moon he could see that it, it looked like a very low kind of, uh, shape that wasn't that big. And he, uh...and then he went closer to the edge of the cave and, uh, looked and there were like needles in, like needles this big, in his leg. And so from that, he figured that there were porcupines. Uh-huh. There was a porcupine. Uh-huh.
>
> Um, and he didn't want the wound to get infected, so he decided he had to pull them out and, um... So he like...when he touched one, it made the pain worse, but he forced himself to pull them out one by one. And, um yeah, and after that his leg got really stiff and, uh, you know, uh-huh, like it was swollen and it was bleeding... and he decided that if he left the needles in there, that it would get infected. Uh-huh. So he forced himself to yank 'em out. And when he was done yanking, his leg was like, in like, totally like burning, uh-huh, like on fire. And, um, he felt really sorry for himself, and he started crying....
>
> This part was when he was, like, really sad and he was crying. Uh-huh. But he...when he was done, crying didn't solve it. He was still, you know, there with his leg hurting without fire or anything. Uh-huh. So he decided then that crying for himself just really didn't work. Uh-huh. So he pretty much just, you know, grew up, grew up, you know, and got tougher in that situation.

The Text: The Foundation of Comprehension

In this book, we ground our discussion of comprehension in actual texts. Texts are, of course, the foundation of reading. Yet too often, students wander away from the words of the text as they try to understand them. They look outside the text—to their personal experiences and their own knowledge, even if it is incomplete or inaccurate knowledge—to try to make sense of what they read. Calling on their own knowledge can be valuable, of course, but not when incorrect knowledge replaces or contradicts the ideas in the text.

MAXIMIZING INSTRUCTION FOR ENGLISH LEARNERS

As is evident from the studies reviewed in August and Shanahan (2006), to provide maximum benefit to language-minority students, instruction must do more than develop a complex array of reading skills. It may be that what is needed is sound reading instruction combined with simultaneous efforts to increase the scope and sophistication of these students' language proficiency, including proficiency in comprehending text.

It should be noted that there are no experimental or quasi-experimental studies conducted with second-language learners that indicate teaching students strategies in a second language improves reading comprehension.

Writers make intentional decisions about what they say and how they say it. Misreading a phrase, a clause, or even a single word can make a fundamental difference in readers' comprehension. Here, mystery writer Christianna Brand explains why it is important for readers to attend carefully to the text:

I like to say that no two lines could be removed from any work of mine, whose removal would not leave somewhere else in the book, a gap, which those lines referred to. If I so much as say that a character "went wearily upstairs, cleaned his teeth and fell into bed"—you watch it! The "wearily" may catch your attention and so deflect from the apparently throwaway detail that he cleaned his teeth, which sounds like just a bit of "color". But no, no: the fact that his toothbrush is damp, and has evidently been recently used—that may be the important phrase, may be going to fit in somewhere later on. Nor will the "wearily" have been used only as a deflection of the reader's attention from the toothbrush; there will be a reason somewhere why the character was weary. You may even find that "he went upstairs" is the vital point: two pages ago he was in a ranch house—without your noticing it, he must have changed his scene, he was going to bed elsewhere. Three little, apparently unimportant phrases; but each of them germane to the plot, each of them possibly important to the plot and each of them—and for the author this is the tricky part—fitting in with *all* the actions of *all* the other people taking part in the plot.

3

Text Structures

An increasing emphasis on more advanced reading strategies is appropriate as students reach the 4th or 5th grade level of reading ability. Students who have not read a great deal often lag in their knowledge of genre, text structure, text organization, and literary devices.

———Louisa C. Moats, "When Older Students Can't Read"

Understanding how texts are put together helps students both comprehend the texts they read and communicate effectively in writing (Donovan & Smolkin, 2002; Freedman & Medway, 1994; Kamberelis & Bovino, 1999; Pappas & Brown, 1987; Wollman-Bonilla, 2000). By fourth grade, students know a good deal about texts. Moreover, they likely have had experience talking about texts.

In this chapter, we examine the knowledge of texts, text structures, and signal words that fourth and fifth graders should be learning in the course of interacting with and writing texts.

We start with a discussion of genres, the macrostructure of texts, that writers use to shape meaning. Then we consider midlevel structures of texts and, finally, connecting words that writers use to establish relationships.

Genres: Shaping Meaning

To comprehend and communicate effectively, students need to know how people shape texts and use language to create meaning in different circumstances.

Hence, genre knowledge is essential (Bakhtin, 1986; Bazerman, 1988; Berkenkotter & Huckin, 1995; Chapman, 1995; Kamberelis, 1999; Miller, 1984).

Genres are typical ways of accomplishing particular communicative purposes. Genres emerge from recurring situations in which these purposes are served. They follow general, predictable patterns in their structure, organization, and language. These predictable patterns provide savvy readers and writers with a common, shared set of assumptions about what to expect when they read and how to approach a particular writing task (Cope & Kalantzis, 1993; Freedman & Medway, 1994; Halliday & Hasan, 1989; Martin & Rothery, 1981; Nystrand, 1982, 1986; Pappas, Kiefer, & Levstik, 2006).

For example, fourth and fifth graders generally understand that the thrust of a mystery story is a crime or a secret or a puzzle to be solved. They expect to find suspects, motives, and clues. They expect to unravel the mystery—with the crime solved, the secret revealed, the puzzle put together—by the end of the story. They read with these assumptions and expectations in mind. Comprehension, then, is easier for students who can use their knowledge of mystery stories to anticipate the text, reading strategically for what they know they will find there. Further, wide reading of mysteries helps students create a mental model of the genre, which helps them understand other mysteries (Andersen, 1990; Hasan, 1989; Kintsch, 1982; Langer, 1986; Pappas et al., 2006).

Likewise, fourth and fifth graders who want to *write* a mystery story know that they might develop a plot filled with intrigue and suspense, create characters who are villains and sleuths, and create a sense of foreboding through language choice. Writing mystery stories, then, is easier for students who can use their command of the structure and content of mystery stories to shape their own pieces.

Yet these same students would have a different set of expectations about a chapter in a science text. Here, they would expect long explanations of processes, scientific vocabulary, headings, charts, diagrams, and graphs. They would expect the sentences and paragraphs to be full of information, most of it new to them. The typical pattern of a science text is very different from the pattern of a story. Savvy readers and writers will know about the differences. Knowledge of the typical pattern of a genre and how patterns differ among genres helps people to communicate effectively for different social purposes, audiences, and situations.

Genres give people flexible frameworks for understanding and creating texts, for genres are laden with meaning for readers and writers alike. Genres are not rigid formats but typical patterns of structure and language. Because the patterns are predictable, readers can recognize them and gauge whether they are effective for accomplishing a particular purpose. And writers can choose to use or adapt them to create original new texts of their own (Bakhtin, 1986; Donovan, 2001; Freadman, 1987; Freedman & Medway, 1994; Halliday & Martin, 1981; Kamberelis, 1999; Miller, 1984; Pappas et al., 2006).

Research suggests that even preschool children have an emergent awareness of written genres (such as lists and stories) (Donovan & Smolkin, 2002; Dyson, 1997; Kamberelis, 1999; Kamberelis & de la Luna, 2004; Newkirk, 1987; Pappas, 1993; Zecker, 1996). In school, students encounter—and learn to read and write—genres that are valued in school. Informational texts, for example, are useful for reporting facts, identifying the relationships among parts of a whole, categorizing pieces of information, and giving instructions. Arguments are useful for explaining ideas, writing persuasive essays or book reviews, or taking a stand on an issue. Narratives are useful not just for imaginary stories but also for telling the real-life stories of famous people, the remembrances of ordinary people, and the accounts of historic events. Poems are useful for expressing information, ideas, and emotions precisely, eloquently, and with controlled effect.

Readers and writers with an understanding of common genres have an immediate and explicit channel of communication open between them. There is a kind of solidarity between writers and readers who are "on the same page." For example, a casual note to a friend or an online message may be personal, lively, and filled with shared references. Students assume that their friends will understand common references and fill in the blanks with shared knowledge. On the other hand, students produce academic writing that is more explicit and formal to meet school expectations (Chapman, 1995; Gundlach, McLane, Stott, & McNamee, 1985; Kamberelis, 1999; Langer, 1986).

Fourth and fifth graders do not have a well-developed sense of audience, but because they are themselves readers, they can consider what a reader would find useful and interesting in making their writing more intelligible and readable (Britton, Burgess, Martin, McLeod, & Rosen, 1975). Who is this information for? What are the key points or events? What kind of organization will help readers understand my writing? What kinds of details do I need to build in for this audience? What is the reader supposed to think, feel, or do with this text?

CLASSROOM APPLICATION

- Teaching students about genre structures should be an ongoing enterprise. Whenever students are working with a text, teachers should help students identify organizing features, such as how the story or topic is introduced, how a topic or a plot is developed, how the writer brings closure.
- Genre studies, reading a collection of texts that are all cast in the same genre, are perhaps the best way to develop genre knowledge. There are many such studies available on the Internet and also many books that discuss text features and classify texts by genre.
- Teachers can have students write in the genre they are studying or can have students address the same topic in more than one genre—both a poem and a story about kindness, for example.

Reading and writing texts in a variety of genres introduces students to text structures, patterns of development, organizational choices, and language that will help them comprehend the texts they read and communicate effectively when they write (Chapman, 1995; Derewianka, 1990; Donovan, 2001; Kamberelis, 1999; Langer, 1986; Newkirk, 1989).

The broad categories of genres that fourth and fifth graders should be familiar with include

- Informational genres
- Argument genres
- Narrative genres
- Poetic genres
- Blended, or hybrid, genres

Within these broad categories are many different, specific genres and subgenres, as shown in the table below.

Understanding How Genres Work

We use five texts, each one about wolves, to illustrate broad categories of writing: informational, argument, narrative, poetic, and blended genres.

INFORMATIONAL GENRES

The purpose of informational texts is to *convey factual information about a topic* as a means of inviting readers to increase their knowledge. Informational texts address classification or type (What are the different kinds of bears? What are the differences between thunderstorms and tornadoes?); component parts (What are the parts of a fish? What planets orbit the sun?); and various other aspects (such as size, function, and behavior) (Derewianka, 1990; Halliday & Martin, 1981; Newkirk, 1989; Pappas et al., 2006). Informational texts also can provide an explanation of how something works (procedures).

Here is an example of informational text that classifies wolves and then lists wolf subspecies. It is an excerpt from Seymour Simon's *Wolves*, a nonfiction text for young readers that includes photographs of wolves:

> Wolves may look and act differently from each other, but most wolves belong to the same species, called *Canis lupus* (*canis* means dog and *lupus* means wolf). The wolf's closest relatives are the domestic dog, the coyote, the jackal, and a dog of Australia called the dingo.
>
> There are many subspecies of North American wolves and also lots of common names for the same kind of wolf. These include tundra (or arctic) wolves, gray (or timber) wolves, and lots of location names for wolves, such as the Mexican wolf, the Rocky mountain wolf, the eastern timber wolf, the Texas gray wolf, and the Great Plains wolf (also called the lobo or buffalo hunter). In colder locations, wolves usually have longer and thicker coats, smaller ears, and wider muzzles than do wolves that live in warmer regions.

(Copyright © 1993 by Seymour Simon. Used by permission of HarperCollins Publishers.)

Broad Categories of Genres	Examples of Specific Genres and Subgenres
Informational	Report, instructions, procedures, brochure
Argument	Explanation, literary essay, book review, position paper, letter to the editor, editorial
Narrative	Short story, mystery, fairy tale, biography, autobiography, science fiction book, folk tale, historical account
Poetic	Free verse, haiku, cinquain, rhyming couplets, epic, sonnet
Blended	Texts that contain features of more than one genre

Informational Texts

Purpose	Subgenres	Text Structure	Other Features	Academic Subjects
Provide facts and information about a topic	Report, instructions, procedure, brochure, and so on	Statement and supporting details (facts or steps); can include structures such as compare–contrast, cause–effect, problem–solution, and sequence	Specialized language; specific, accurate facts and information; timeless verbs; logical connectors; graphs, charts, and other illustrations; organized around topics/subtopics	Science, history

As this excerpt demonstrates, informational texts often are organized around a topic statement and include supporting details that describe or support the statement. The first sentence provides the controlling idea for the paragraphs (although different kinds of wolves have different appearances and behaviors, they belong to the same species), and the text that follows provides the supporting facts and information (subspecies of wolves and their features). In this excerpt, the first paragraph names the species and close relatives of the species. The second paragraph names and discusses the subspecies in North America. The piece uses timeless verbs, such as "wolves belong" and "wolves usually have," and describes wolves in general rather than focusing on a specific wolf. The writer also uses specialized content vocabulary, such as *Canis lupus*, *species*, *subspecies*, *tundra*, and *muzzle*. When terms and specialized vocabulary are used in such texts, they often include definitions that make use of conventions such as the appositive (a word or phrase that restates or modifies a noun preceding it, sometimes with an "or" construction, as in "tundra (or artic) wolves"), relative clauses, and so on.

Because the text structures of informational genres are more varied than those of narrative genres, and because informational texts often introduce new and difficult concepts, these genres can be challenging for students to comprehend.

Fourth and fifth graders encounter many different informational subgenres, including reports, instructions, procedures, and brochures (Britsch, 2002; Chall, Jacobs, & Baldwin, 1990; Donovan & Smolkin, 2002; Duke & Kays, 1998; Halliday & Martin, 1981; Langer, 1986; Martin & Rothery, 1981; Newkirk, 1989). Students usually read and write such texts in science and history.

ARGUMENT

Arguments usually begin with a problem or issue statement as the basis for discussion. Arguments *state a claim or take a position, provide evidence to support the claim, and give some reasoning* for why the evidence supports the claim, also known as the *warrant* (Derewianka, 1990; Newkirk, 1989; Toulmin, 2003). In *explanations*, writers use the claim–evidence–reasoning structure to make claims, using data and logic to tie the data to the claim. Writers also use the claim–evidence–reasoning structure in *position papers*, in which they take positions on issues and support these positions with evidence (such as data or experience). In *literary essays*, writers state a claim about a text or author, provide evidence from the text or author's life to support the claim, and give reasons, based on evidence, that link the claim and the text.

In this argument about wolves from the website of ProtectWolves.org, the writer argues that people's fears about wolves are based on misconceptions and that wolves should be protected because they are an essential part of their habitats and ecosystems:

People have false beliefs about the world. They continue to believe old folk tales and think the wolf is evil. The misconception that was created years and years ago needs to stop. People need to stop judging and start educating themselves with the truth. Wolves are NOT out to kill people or livestock. Wolves have few natural enemies and if given the chance, the wolf can fully recover....

There are many good things about wolves. They help us keep a healthy ecosystem. Wolves are at the top of the wild animal food chain and they help with the nature balance between predator and prey. Predators

Argument

Purpose	Subgenres	Text Structure	Other Features	Academic Subjects
Make a statement or take a position and support it with evidence	Explanation Literary essay, book review Position paper, letter to the editor, editorial	Claim–evidence–reasoning	Relevant and specific evidence to support the claim (kinds of evidence depends on the subject area); reasoning relevant to the subject area; emphasis on data and logic rather than emotion	Science, history English language arts English language arts, science, history

are important to the balance of nature. If wolves mostly eat the sick animals and not the healthy ones, the sick ones wouldn't pass on the sickness to the healthy ones. Wolves help control the population of deer and other large animals. Wolves reduce the number of coyotes by taking some of their food and maybe killing others. Coyotes are more likely to bother people's pets because they are more used to people. Wolves are also helpful to other animals. When they kill big prey, they leave some meat for coyotes, ravens, and other small animals. Once a wolf pack abandons their den, other animals can use it. When a wolf sheds his fur, birds use it to help build their nests and make them warm.

This piece supports wolf conservation and argues that wolves benefit—rather than harm—their surroundings. The writer states a claim, contending that wolves "help us keep a healthy ecosystem." The writer supports the claim with evidence about how wolves benefit the ecosystem, such as "Wolves help control the population of deer" and "When they kill big prey, they leave some meat for coyotes, ravens, and other small animals."

Students encounter argument genres in English language arts, history, mathematics, and science.

NARRATIVE

Narratives can be fiction (such as stories) or nonfiction (such as biographies and personal accounts). They typically focus on individuals at specific points in time. Generally, narratives create a context, establish a point of view, introduce and develop characters, organize events around time and causality, and provide some sort of closure. Some narratives feature a

conflict–resolution structure. Narratives use temporal (time) connectives, dialogue, description, and, frequently, metaphorical language (Derewianka, 1990; Hasan, 1989; Pappas at al., 2006).

Within the broad category of narrative, students encounter subgenres such as the short story, mystery, fairy tale, biography, autobiography, science fiction, folk tale, historical account, and so on. Obviously, there are differences among these narrative subgenres, though all share common characteristics.

Consider this excerpt from Laura Ingalls Wilder's *Little House in the Big Woods*, in which the narrator talks about wolves:

At night, when Laura lay awake in the trundle bed, she listened and could not hear anything except the sound of the trees whispering together. Sometimes, far away in the night, a wolf howled. Then he came nearer, and howled again.

It was a scary sound. Laura knew that wolves would eat little girls. But she was safe inside the solid log walls. Her father's gun hung over the door and good old Jack, the brindle bulldog, lay on guard before it. Her father would say:

"Go to sleep, Laura. Jack won't let the wolves in." So Laura snuggled under the covers of the trundle bed, close beside Mary, and went to sleep.

One night her father picked her up out of bed and carried her to the window so that she might see the wolves. There were two of them sitting in front of the house. They looked like shaggy dogs. They pointed their noses at the big, bright moon and howled.

(Text copyright © 1932, 1960 Little House Heritage Trust. Used by permission of HarperCollins Publishers.)

Narrative				
Purpose	**Subgenres**	**Text Structure**	**Other Features**	**Subject Areas**
Entertain or inform	Short story, mystery, fairy tale, biography, autobiography, science fiction, folk tale, historical account, and so on	Opening/orientation; chronology of events; closing; may include conflict/resolution	Metaphorical language; dialogue; character development; interior monologue; temporal words; description	English language arts, history, science, math

The excerpt appears at the beginning of the book when the author is describing the story's setting (the big woods). The passage includes words that indicate time and sequence, such as *at night*, *sometimes*, *then*, and *one night*. The piece includes dialogue between Laura and her father and metaphorical language: "the sound of the trees whispering together."

In school, students encounter narratives in English language arts, history, science, and mathematics.

POETIC GENRES

There are three main kinds of poetry: epic, narrative, and lyric. And there are two basic poetic forms: formal and free verse. Formal poetry has specific rules for line structure, stanza structure, and rhythm (for instance, haiku and cinquain). Free verse does not adhere to preestablished rules. All poetry is characterized by *precise language and attention to the craft of writing*. Line structure and the white space on the page play a role in all forms of poetry. Word choice, figurative language, and rhythm support and affect a poem's meaning (Friedrich, 1986; Friedrich & Dil, 1979; Heard, 2002a; Kamberelis, 1993, 2004).

Consider the poem "In the Company of Wolves" by WolfBard (D.J. Sylvis):

When the moon crests the hills
giving each tree a black pool-shadow
the wolves wade in the forest
wet themselves in the darkness
shake it from their fur
in clearings of light

their eyes are stars
their teeth comets their tails
galaxies they are
constellations of the night
they roam the universe

they run as Diana's companions
laugh as her silver arrows
and their iron teeth
harvest the hunt's bounty
they hide in her moon
cloud around her with breath

they are brave of soul
clear of eye and mind
they are strong of jaw
they are loyal-kind
they are keen to scent
quick to 'fend their kin
they are hot of blood
they are slow to sin

grey brown white black blonde
ear tail paw claw tongue
they play as a pack and they
melt together so that one
is part of all and all
become one

they prance through the forest
they track through the sky
they are noble in friendship
and single in thought
i join them in flight
i run in the company
of wolves

(Copyright © 2005 by D.J. Sylvis. Reprinted by permission of the author.)

"In the Company of Wolves" is about wolves' affinity for the night, about the character of wolves, and about the narrator's kinship with these animals. The poem is written in free verse from the narrator's perspective. The poem uses no punctuation and relies heavily on line breaks for rhythm. The poet creates various images of wolves: their melting into the "black pool-shadow[s]" of trees; their eyes "like stars"; their hunting skills and "iron teeth"; their loyalty and playfulness with their pack. The narrator characterizes these animals as brave, strong, and loyal, "quick to [de]fend their kin," "hot of blood," and "slow to sin." In the last three lines of the poem, the narrator aligns himself with these animals: "i join them in flight / i run in the company / of wolves."

The dramatic use of imagery in this poem and the poet's admiration of and kinship with wolves create within readers empathy for these animals and an understanding that although they are fierce hunters, their good qualities easily outweigh their bad.

Students encounter poetry in English language arts. The poems they write can address a range of topics or subjects they care about from both inside and outside of school learning.

BLENDED OR HYBRID TEXTS

Not all texts conform to specific genre conventions for organization and content. Texts that blend the features of more than one genre are called hybrid texts (Bakhtin, 1986; Dyson, 1997; Juzwik, 2004; Kamberelis, 1993, 1999). Students frequently encounter hybrid texts that mix genre features, such as the story about an animal that includes both narrative and informational strands; a website about endangered species that includes information about a species' role in its habitat, facts and graphs about endangered animals, stories of successful conservation efforts, and links to conservation websites; or a novel written in poetic form.

Scruffy: A Wolf Finds His Place in the Pack by Jim Brandenburg is a book about wolves that combines features of narrative and informational genres. The text opens like a story:

> Scruffy, a young white Arctic wolf, lives in a faraway frozen place called Ellesmere Island. He was born the year before I arrived, so he was no longer a pup. But he wasn't an adult member of the pack yet. If Scruffy had been human, he probably would have been called a teenager.

(Excerpts from *Scruffy* reprinted by arrangement with Walker Publishing Company.)

The text begins with an introduction of the main "characters": Scruffy and the narrator. Unlike WolfBard's "In the Company of Wolves," which discusses wolves in general, *Scruffy* tells the story of one wolf's life and the writer's experience observing this wolf's pack. The writer compares Scruffy to a human ("he probably would have been called a teenager")

and uses storybook language to describe Ellesmere Island ("a faraway frozen place").

The writer also uses content vocabulary to explain how the wolf pack is organized:

> The leader of a wolf pack is called the alpha male (or in some cases, the alpha female). On Ellesmere Island, the pack was led by a strong alpha pair. They were always the first to attack after a hunt and the first to eat after a kill.

Notice that the writer uses content vocabulary, such as *alpha male* and *alpha pair*, rather than storybook language.

Texts such as this one can be both engaging and confusing. By framing the information about wolves and wolf packs within the story of Scruffy and his "family," the writer presents information within a story structure that is familiar to young readers. On the other hand, the writer's personification of the wolves can hinder students' understanding of the science concepts he introduces.

For instance, in the sentence "[Scruffy] was hovering by Mom," the word *Mom* refers to the pack's alpha female. Describing the alpha female as Mom or Scruffy as the pack's babysitter can confuse students (for instance, if readers think that *Mom* refers to the author's mother rather than to the pack's alpha female or if students think the alpha female's role in the wolf pack is the same as "Mom's" role in the human family).

The *textbook* is yet another kind of hybrid text that students encounter in fourth and fifth grades—and one that often poses distinct challenges to students. In a textbook, students likely will encounter multiple genres and graphics, illustrations, sidebars, text boxes, section headings, a table of contents, a glossary, and specialized content vocabulary. These text features can support students' understanding if they know how to use them to make sense of the information they read. Yet textbooks are often hard for students to read and comprehend because they introduce new and difficult concepts and often contain academic language. (See page 47 for more information about academic language.)

Research also suggests that many textbooks fail to make explicit the connections between ideas, or they assume prior knowledge that students do not have, thus making it difficult for students to understand the text and concepts (Beck, McKeown, & Gromoll, 1989; Beck, McKeown, & Kucan, 2002; Beck, McKeown, Sinatra, & Loxterman, 1991; McKeown & Beck, 1990; McKeown, Beck, Sinatra, & Loxterman, 1992).

Midlevel Structures: Patterns of Development

Genres act as superordinate frameworks for structuring text. One level down—and frequently operating at more than one level—are *midlevel structures*, commonly referred to as patterns of organization (Kintsch & van Dijk, 1978; Meyer, 1975; Schank & Abelson, 1977). These include comparison and contrast, cause and effect, description, definition and example, and analysis and classification. When whole texts use these patterns of organization, the format for the piece is most frequently signaled in an opening paragraph. For example, if an opening paragraph states, "All good leaders share similar characteristics," it follows that readers would expect subsequent paragraphs to analyze the specific characteristics of good leaders. But if an introductory paragraph states, "The question of whether to buy a poodle or Labrador retriever is a complicated decision," readers would expect subsequent paragraphs to follow a comparison-and-contrast format (Kinneavy, 1980; Langer, 1986; Moffett, 1968; Newkirk, 1987; Pappas et al., 2006; Pearson & Fielding, 1991; Stein & Glenn, 1979).

Sometimes these patterns of development occur at the paragraph level or between sentences in a paragraph. In this case, the development flowing from the poodle/retriever dilemma might devote one whole paragraph to the benefits of owning a poodle followed by a paragraph that details the benefits of owning a Lab. Or the pattern could be developed at the sentence level, with each sentence focused on comparative differences between the dogs: "The question of whether to buy a poodle or a Labrador retriever is a complicated decision. On one hand, a poodle is a good choice because it has no body dander or odor. By contrast, a Labrador retriever has hair that sheds frequently and that sticks to clothing, upholstery, and carpet. The Lab, though, is the most popular breed in the United States and is prized as a family pet. The poodle, by contrast, is the national dog of France and is both athletic and an urbane companion...."

Then, too, midlevel structures frequently function within sentences: "Whereas the poodle is recognized for its intelligence, the Lab is known for its enthusiastic attitude toward life." The connecting word *whereas* sets up the contrast and helps readers to link the two propositions appropriately. However, sometimes the linking words are omitted, and readers must infer how the ideas should be linked.

Knowledge of midlevel structures helps readers make sense of text. Readers can understand the relevance of the parts to the whole and the principle behind the organization of the parts. Everything adds up; the ideas cohere.

Cohesive Devices: Structural Cues to Relationships

Just as sentences are not simply words strung together, well-formed texts are not just collections of sentences. In learning to deal with academic texts, students must do more than read and understand each sentence in turn as a stand alone; they must consider it in relation to what came before, interpret it in light of what they have already learned, and anticipate what might come next in the text. The coherence of any text depends on the use of cohesive devices for linking one part of a text to the other. Writers use a variety of structural devices, including signal words and coreferences, to signal relationships between sentences as well as between parts of texts (Biber, 1988; Derewianka, 1990; Halliday & Hasan, 1976, 1989; Pappas et al., 2006).

Signal Words: Cues for Making Meaning

Suppose students come across this sentence in a text: "Otherwise nobody would be interested in it, and their tax support would drop off." To interpret this sentence, readers would have to refer back to the previous sentence, "The people who run the space program know that they have to continue sending humans into space," and make use of the following cues:

Otherwise: If x didn't happen. (What's x?)

it: What's the thing people would lose interest in?

and: What two things are connected? What's the nature of the connection?

their: Who are they?

Only then could readers understand the sentence as meaning, "If the people who run the space program don't send humans into space, taxpayers will lose interest in the program, and Congress will not feel pressure to provide taxes to keep the program going." *Otherwise* is a signal word that ties together the two sentences.

Signal words, also called connectors or connection words, are logical linking structures that indicate contingencies between ideas, such as condition, result, cause, reason, and purpose. These relationships frequently are made specific by overt connector words such as *because, therefore, hence, although, but, if,* and *when,* and the relationships must be inferred from the juxtaposition of ideas. Signal words can be

- **Additive:** Words such as *and, also, furthermore,* and *likewise* signal new information being added to existing information

SPECIAL CONSIDERATIONS FOR ENGLISH LEARNERS

As for all students, it is important to help second-language learners understand how texts are put together, including building their understanding of genres, mid-level structures, and cohesive devices.

Schleppegrell and Colombi (2002) taught teachers how to use linguistic tools and text analysis to help students come to a better understanding of the meaning of history texts. For example, teachers were taught patterns of language in history textbooks such as accounts, discussion, and explanation as well as how to help students "chunk" sentences and use the chunking process to clarify text meaning. Results indicated that second-language learners instructed by these trained teachers outperformed students who were taught by teachers without this training.

However, second-language learners need to know more than the role that words play; they need to know the meaning of these words. They need to learn to make use of the cues that signal words provide, but they also need to know the meaning of those signal words.

Finally, it may be especially important to teach second-language learners how to interpret visual representations in text because these representations provide redundant information about the concepts covered in the text, and do so using a format that depends less on language.

- **Contrastive:** Words such as *yet, though, but, instead,* and *on the other hand* signal contrasting information being added to existing information
- **Causal:** Words such as *so, hence,* and *as a result* signal causal relationships
- **Temporal:** Words such as *then, next, finally,* and *in conclusion* signal time sequences

Sometimes the relationships are not explicitly signaled, and sometimes the relationships that writers expect readers to infer are many pages apart. Students might need to infer, for example, that an event that occurred in the protagonist's childhood serves as the motive for an action later in life, or that the 15 pages of prose describing the differences in the economies of the North and the South, in their attitudes toward colonialism, and in their views of states' rights all help explain why the Civil War broke out in 1861. Readers have two resources available

CHUNKING, COHERENCE, AND COHESION

Chunking is the process of organizing language into manageable units, or chunks. Chunking increases the amount of material that can be held in consciousness at any one time. So, instead of processing individual words, as in /the/child/was/lost/, we chunk the information into a single unit, the sentence "The child was lost." Likewise, /t/h/i/n/k/ becomes "think."

Chunking is another way that our brains consolidate, organize, and make sense of letters, letter strings, words, sentences, and paragraphs quickly and efficiently as we read:

> The nervous system seems to be organized in terms of levels. Higher levels of organization deal with the successively larger units that are the output of lower levels.... Each level in these hierarchies seems to do some processing which reduces the information load of subsequent levels. It is possible that the phenomena of chunking and organization in memory, and in various skilled performances such as reading, are realized in terms of a hierarchical arrangement of a similar sort. (Rozin & Gleitman, 1977)

Knowledge of mechanics, especially punctuation, is an important tool for chunking language. For instance, an initial capital letter and a terminal period signal a sentence. Indentation (paragraphing) is another important signal. Often, a paragraph indentation marks an especially large chunk of meaning, but sometimes it may isolate a small chunk that the writer wishes to emphasize.

Equally important for readers to grasp as relationships within sentences is the flow of ideas from sentence to sentence. When writing "flows" for readers—that is, when the information moves smoothly between one idea and the next—that writing is said to have cohesion. When all parts of the document fit together logically, the writing has coherence. Joseph Williams (2003) wrote, "Think of cohesion as the experience of seeing pairs of sentences fit neatly together, the way Lego pieces do. Think of coherence as the experience of recognizing what all the sentences in a piece of writing add up to, the way lots of Lego pieces add up to a building, bridge or boat." So cohesion is local and coherence is global.

VISUAL REPRESENTATIONS IN TEXTS

Graphic literacy—the ability to interpret and create visual messages accurately—becomes increasingly important as students move up through the grades. By fourth and fifth grades, most textbooks and nonfiction trade books use charts, graphs, maps, and other pictorial presentations to supplement prose. And in the world beyond school and on the Internet, the use of words and images together to convey meaning is ubiquitous.

Many benefits accrue to readers who can process visuals. First of all, whatever is represented visually is frequently of importance. So readers who read the prose and augment their understanding by "comprehending" the visual will have a deep understanding of an important concept, having processed the information in two different ways. Moreover, the spatial nature of an illustration offers a range of learning possibilities not available when language is used alone (Kress, 2003; Kress & Van Leeuwen, 2006; Levie & Lentz, 1982; Mirzoeff, 1999; New London Group, 1996; Paillotet, Semali, Rodenberg, Giles, & Macaul, 2000; Semali, 2002).

Second, visuals frequently make explicit the connections among relevant ideas in a text. This feature of visuals is captured in the phrase "a picture is worth a thousand words." Textbooks are filled with factual information to the extent that students may be overwhelmed with content knowledge for which no explicit conceptual linkages are made. Learning requires that facts be linked to concepts and concepts linked to one another. Visuals help readers do this work (Kress, 2003; Kress & Van Leeuwen, 2006; Levie & Lentz, 1982; Mirzoeff, 1999; New London Group, 1996; Paillotet et al., 2000; Semali, 2002).

Third, visuals can transmit information more rapidly than prose. Hence, the visually adept reader can either "read" the visual first or move back and forth between the visual and the connected text, using the visual as an organizer to extend his comprehension and lead him through the prose (Kress, 2003; Kress & Van Leeuwen, 2006; Levie & Lentz, 1982; Mirzoeff, 1999; New London Group, 1996; Paillotet et al., 2000; Semali, 2002).

Moreover, "humans are typically visually oriented and the retention of information presented in visual form usually exceeds the retention of information presented verbally" (Levie & Lentz, 1982).

to draw these sorts of inferences: their knowledge of particular topics or disciplines and their knowledge of genres (that is, knowing that in texts like the one they are reading, they often have to make these connections on their own).

Coreference: Multiple Words That Refer to the Same Concept

Ordinarily, writers try to avoid using the same words repeatedly in identifying a particular referent in successive mentions. Instead, after the first mention, the usual practice is to use a pronoun or a paraphrase instead. For example, here is a sentence from *Hatchet*:

> As he watched, a large bird—he thought it looked like a crow but it seemed larger—flew from the top, real forest, and the reflection-bird matched it, both flying out over the water.

Readers must recognize that the word *it*, used three times, identifies the large bird, while *both* refers to that large bird and its reflection. Here is another example of coreference, one that requires readers to keep track of referents across multiple sentences:

> Michael could not remember when he had last seen his dog, King. The animal had been missing since his last fit of barking occurred. Even as a puppy, however, King had run off, so Michael was not especially concerned about him.

In this example, readers understand that a variety of words, or referents, all mean or refer to Michael's dog: *dog*, *King*, *animal*, *his*, *puppy*, and *him*.

Benefiting From Knowledge of Text Structures

Readers who understand the macrostructures of genres as well as the role of midlevel structures and cohesive devices have an immediate advantage. They know that the text will conform in some ways organizationally, and they can recognize when a text shifts from one genre to another, as hybrid texts do (Nystrand, 1982, 1986).

Research shows that explicit instruction in text structures can also benefit students' reading comprehension (Pearson & Fielding, 1991; Pressley, 2006). For example, text structure knowledge helps students make sense of relationships between ideas in informational texts (such as distinguishing between the main idea and the supporting information), and it can also help students make sense of the different kinds of information (such as charts and graphs) that clarify ideas.

Like readers, writers who have knowledge of text structures have an advantage. Such structures provide writers with generative frameworks for their writing, which function as sets of options that writers can call upon to select and organize their thoughts when they write and speak for particular purposes (see, e.g., Nystrand, 1986). However, it is important to know that organizational structures are not prescriptive "formulas" for students' writing. Rather, students can learn to alter typical structures or change them to serve their own uses and purposes as writers. Learning about genres, midlevel structures, and cohesive devices helps students learn to write texts in particular ways and to create their own variations (Bazerman, 1988; Kamberelis, 1993, 1999; Pappas et al., 2006; Prior, 1998).

4

Syntax, Vocabulary, and Knowledge Structures

*Understanding the basics of how one's own language
works contributes to skillful reading and writing. Recognizing
the difference between nouns and verbs, consonants and vowels,
oral and literary forms is as basic for the liberally educated
human being as is knowledge about addition and subtraction,
evolution, or the solar system.*

——LILY WONG FILLMORE AND CATHERINE E. SNOW, *What Teachers Need to Know About Language*

We start this chapter with a discussion of language use at the sentence level. Knowledge of subjects and predicates, clauses, phrases, and other sentence components is important and unarguably should become part of every student's repertoire. In this chapter, though, we address only the two major sentence-level problems that most frequently lead readers astray: connections and references.

We also examine vocabulary and the relationship between reading comprehension and knowledge.

Syntax: Sentence Structures That Support Meaning

As has been pointed out previously, students in fourth grade and higher read texts that express increasingly complex ideas and the relationships among these ideas. In well-written texts, the sentence structure, or syntax, of the text supports the complexities of meaning; however, more complex sentences will likely confound unprepared readers.

At their most basic level, sentences in English are composed of a complete subject—a topic of some sort—and a complete predicate—a comment about the subject. Subjects usually take the form of a phrase headed by a noun, while predicates consist of a phrase headed by a verb. Each type of phrase—noun and verb phrases as well as the prepositional phrase, adverbial phrase, and adjective phrase (phrases headed by a preposition, an adverb, an adjective)—can have a variety of forms and can itself contain other types of phrases.

Each sentence contains one or more ideas or thoughts. To make sense of the thought in a sentence, readers must build a coherent representation of the idea units within that sentence. Moreover, almost every sentence relies on ideas in other sentences. The small ideas cohere into larger ideas. The relationships among sentences form the basic level of coherence in a text. To comprehend a text, readers must understand how each small idea connects to other ideas to form a coherent larger idea; they must consider each sentence in relation to what came before, interpret it in light of what they have already learned from the text, and anticipate what might come next.

How and Why Sentences Become Complex

A notable feature of academic English is especially apparent when we look at written language used in expository texts. Consider, for example, the following sentence that describes condensation, taken from the website of the Missouri Botanical Gardens. The language and construction are typical of academic English.

> Condensation is the opposite of evaporation. It occurs when a gas is changed into a liquid and the temperature of the vapor decreases.

By contrast, consider how the text might be rewritten for younger readers:

> Condensation is the opposite of evaporation. Condensation occurs when a gas is changed into a liquid. Condensation occurs when the temperature of the vapor decreases.

Efforts like this to keep texts simple or short can result in materials that have a choppy feel, and they are more difficult to process because grammatical elements that signal relationships among ideas are missing.

Furthermore, it is difficult to express complex ideas and information in simplified language. As we see in the following paragraph, also from the Missouri Botanical Gardens website, the writer cannot use simplified language given the complexity of the information being communicated:

> Energy cannot be created or destroyed. Then where does the energy come from that spins the turbines that generate the electricity that lights our homes? The turbines in this example are hydroelectric; they are turned by water rushing down from the dam. Gravity pulls the water downhill. The impact of the water rushing through the turbine spins its blades that turn the generator. The generator converts the rotation to electricity; one form of energy is converted into another.
>
> But how did the water get up so high on the mountain? It could not flow downhill unless it was uphill first. Where did the energy come from to lift so much water so high above sea level? The water fell as snow from clouds even higher than the mountain. It got up into clouds by evaporating from the ocean. The ocean is way down at sea level. The sun's energy heated the water, providing the energy to evaporate the water and lift it into clouds.
>
> The sun lights the sea and lifts the moisture into the weather that drops it high in the mountains as snow or rain. It runs into creeks and rivers as it flows downhill. We dam it and use it to generate our electricity. The water spills out from the turbines, joins the river again as the river runs on down to the sea. The light and heat from our bulbs spread out through our rooms, out the windows into the air and eventually out to space.

To comprehend a passage like the preceding requires comprehending the relationships among the individual ideas described; the comprehension challenge is in the connections among the ideas. (While many of the connections are between sentences, many are within.) It is the sentence structures that guide the reader through the connected ideas.

Vocabulary: Words Convey Meaning

In the early childhood years, children learn most of their vocabulary from the oral language of everyday interactions. By even the earliest elementary school years, however, there is not much more vocabulary

A Prerequisite for School Success: Academic English

There is no guarantee that students who are reading on grade level at the end of third grade will continue to do so in the upper elementary grades. Many lack the language skills of academic English that are essential for further success in school. This is true for English learners and native speakers of English alike. Academic English is learned at school and primarily through exposure to the language of written texts. Most children require instructional support in the form of frequent discussions of language in the classroom to acquire it. Empowering students with a mastery of academic English will enable them to be successful in school.

What precisely is academic English? It has been defined as reasoned discourse that is more precise in reference than ordinary spoken language and more dependent on text than on context for interpretation. In contrast to the more personal and informal language of everyday social discourse, academic English makes use of more complex syntax and more sophisticated and specialized vocabulary, which allow speakers and writers to express complex ideas in coherent and logical pieces of discourse.

The following is an example of a sentence written in academic English from the children's website of the Missouri Botanical Garden (mbgnet.mobot.org):

> When the temperature and atmospheric pressure are right, the small droplets of water in clouds form larger droplets and precipitation occurs.

In conversational English, a speaker might comment instead, "When it gets hot enough, the little drops of water in clouds grow bigger and then it starts to rain."

The practical reality is that academic English is necessary because it enables students to understand the written materials they must read and learn from in school, to participate in the conversations and experiences that characterize interactions in school settings, and to prepare for higher education and the workplaces in which such language structures will be expected and valued.

There is more than one variety of academic English because each academic subject has its own style of discourse, its own specialized vocabulary, and its own preferred approach for communicating information. Academic language reflects the knowledge structures of different subjects, such as math, science, literature, and history. This knowledge is formalized and systematized and is easily expressible in the academic register of that subject.

One of the most important tasks confronting students is to learn to understand more specialized, technical, and abstract language that is useful in the academic disciplines. This language is characterized by

- **Dense prose** (packing a lot of information into clauses or phrases), such as "Surface runoff is an important part of the water cycle because through surface runoff, much of the water returns again to the oceans, where a great deal of evaporation occurs."
- **Nominalization** (whereby verbs and adjectives are turned into nouns), such as "Hubble's *finding*, which was about the *expansion* of the galaxies, revolutionized our *understanding* of the universe and its origins" (Derewianka, 1990). Comparisons of various types of texts have revealed that nominalizations are very frequently used in academic English, far more so than in conversational English and even more so than in literary texts.
- **Complex noun phrases** (using various types of modifiers to pack as much information as necessary for interpretation into noun phrases), such as the following: "It [water] is *an odorless, tasteless, substance that covers more than three-fourths of the Earth surface.*" Here we see both adjectives as prenominal modifiers and a relative clause as a postnominal modifier for the head noun "substance."

Helping students gain mastery over academic English does not mean or suggest that schools and teachers should devalue or replace the everyday language of the home, community, and local culture. But all students, both English speakers and speakers of other languages or varieties of English, need access to the language of academic disciplines. And to practice the written and oral conversations of these disciplines, students must learn the language of schooling. We talk more about this topic in Chapter 6.

to learn in everyday conversations. By fourth and fifth grades, students need extensive interactions with texts and effective instruction—especially classroom talk about the words that students encounter in their reading—to develop their vocabularies.

The more words students know, and the more they know *about* words, the more they can learn. This works in several important ways. First, knowing more words allows students to understand more of the new texts they encounter, and that gives them more information for unfamiliar words that appear in these texts. Most vocabulary learning beyond basic conversational language takes place through inferring (and later verifying) the meanings of new words in the otherwise well-understood surrounding contexts. Interaction with others who understand the new words, such as the teacher, can play an important role, especially when the contexts are not well understood. Unfamiliar contexts are common when learning new material.

Second, knowing more grade-appropriate words enables students to feel rewarded rather than frustrated by the experience of reading, and that encourages them to read more.

Third, the more reading experience that children have, the more connections they will have to build words. As richer connections are developed, the meanings of words can be called up more readily when met in a new context. These rich connections also help students to make sense of the new context. For example, reading that a character is *lumbering* along may call up associations to other encounters with that word, such as describing the walk of an elephant. Such connections can help to create a full picture of the character and situation.

Fourth, building a vocabulary develops connections that enrich both known and new words: understanding *apology* connects to *forgive*; knowing the feelings that go with *win* and *lose* adds meaning to *victory* and *defeat*, as well as to *compete* and its partners *competitive* and *competition*; understanding what a *right triangle* is becomes more complete when *hypotenuse* is learned.

Fifth, knowing a variety of complex words from the Greco-Latin layer of English vocabulary offers a basis for students to recognize recurring patterns of form across meaning-related words: erode::erosion;

BUILDING VOCABULARY WITH ENGLISH LEARNERS

There are several ways to help English learners build vocabulary, drawing on best practice in vocabulary instruction for monolingual learners. For example, whenever possible, teachers can lead the instructional conversations described in Chapter 1, and they can create opportunities for second-language learners to interact with native English speakers.

Another approach entails exposing students to words through captioned videotapes. In a study reported by Neuman and Koskinen (1992), students who viewed captioned television generally outperformed students in the "just reading" groups. The results suggest that the visual representation of words is an important contribution to students' increased word knowledge. Another important finding is that students at the mastery level of linguistic competence and thus relatively fluent in English scored consistently higher than students who were limited English proficient.

Direct instruction of individual words is another method that helps students gain vocabulary. Studies reported by Biemiller and Boote (2006), Calderón et al. (2005), Carlo et al.

(2004), and August et al. (2006) involved teaching words in the context of narrative and expository text that was either read aloud by the teacher or read by the students. In some cases words were pretaught and in other cases they were taught in context. Moreover, across most of the studies, methods were used to reinforce word knowledge after the reading was completed. In many cases an effort was made to have students make semantic links to other words and concepts and thus attain a deeper and richer understanding of a word's meaning as well as learn many other words connected to the target word.

Another approach is to provide students with strategies they can use to learn words. Strategies include using context to figure out word meanings, using affixes, learning root words, using dictionaries or peers, and in the case of languages that share cognates with English, using cognate knowledge.

Finally, building word consciousness, which involves metacoginition about words, motivation to learn words, and interest in words (Graves, 2006), is also helpful for English learners.

corrode::corrosion; decide::decision; provide::provision; produce::production; deduce::deduction; receive::reception; deceive::deception; and so on.

Sixth and finally, word knowledge allows students to express more complex thoughts in more precise and sophisticated language in writing and speaking (Chall, Jacobs, & Baldwin, 1990; Hirsch, 2003; Stanovich, 1986). New knowledge in every subject builds, in part, with words: Without new words, there is little new knowledge.

Put simply, having a large vocabulary allows readers to expand their lexical resources at a faster pace. Inadequate or poorly developed vocabulary resources are, in fact, a major factor in the decline of students' ability to read and understand grade-level materials at this age. Students with inadequate vocabularies tend to read less than word-savvy students, and as a consequence, they have fewer opportunities to improve or expand their vocabulary knowledge.

Students' vocabularies should be growing rapidly and productively especially during fourth and fifth grades. Estimates vary, but successful students learn between 1,000 and 5,000 words a year (Miller, 1978) just to keep up academically. However, research suggests that only about 400 words can be taught through direct instruction every year. Therefore, students must learn many words on their own by reading or from classroom discussions if they are to develop the linguistic resources needed for academic learning (Beck, McKeown, & Kucan, 2002).

What Words Should Students Know?

While there are many sources of word lists that students should know, there is no one "right" list of the top 500 or 750 or 1,000 important words for fourth and fifth graders. The words that students encounter in grade-appropriate texts are the right ones to target for instructional attention in school.

Words vary greatly in familiarity and usefulness. It is important for students to learn words that add most productively to their vocabularies. Which words are most essential? There are several approaches to describing kinds of words. Beck, McKeown, and Kucan (2002), for example, describe an approach involving three categories of words:

1. Common (Tier 1) words are words that are known by most children by the time they enter school. These words have been variously labeled *everyday words* (because they are learned in everyday situations) and *high-frequency words*.

2. Literate (Tier 2) words are words that typify written language and academic talk. Students do not usually learn these words on their own but instead learn them at school or in other literate discourse. By comparison with Tier 1 words, Tier 2 words are more sophisticated, abstract, and useful for expressing complicated ideas. They are used to express nuance (*cautious* rather than *careful*), abstractions (*systems*), or aspects of reasoning (*analyze*). These words have broad use across subjects. They are sometimes called *academic words*.

3. Specialized (Tier 3) words are words that are used in specific domains of knowledge. These words encompass terms in a specific subject (*metabolize* in biology, *foul ball* in baseball, *integer* in mathematics). These words are sometimes labeled *low-frequency*, *technical*, or *topical words*.

Further discussion of each word category and its place in school follows.

COMMON OR TIER 1 WORDS

Common words (Tier 1 words) are learned in everyday ways: talk with friends and family about everyday things such as what happened to whom, where and when it happened, and what to make of it. These are words that are learned informally.

Children at grades 4 and 5 are learning many words, especially from peers. They acquire quite naturally and with considerable alacrity the current language forms of popular culture or of the peer group with which they are affiliated. These words serve to keep them socially connected and allow them to express their identification with family, community, or social group. Cultural, language, and social differences give rise to different everyday vocabularies. A student's everyday vocabulary will be the one that works in his or her world, and teachers should keep in mind that this world may not speak English.

These common high-frequency words are, however, not a productive category of word study for schools for the following reasons. First, most everyday words are familiar to students by the end the primary grades. Second, these words evolve from and refer to everyday situations. By their institutional nature, schools tend to exclude many of these situations or to formalize them. Hence, school situations provide an impoverished environment for employing these everyday words. Third, everyday life outside of school itself provides many opportunities to learn these words, so they need not be the focus of vocabulary instruction.

LITERATE OR TIER 2 WORDS

These words are essential for learning and success in school. School, for most students, may be the best (or the only) opportunity to learn these words. A vocabulary gap in Tier 2 words translates directly into an achievement gap. Closing the Tier 2 vocabulary gap is a necessary part of closing the achievement gap.

Literate words are words that students need to know in order to deal with literate language. These words are uncommon in oral language but characteristic of written text. They are encountered across many types of text, and in contrast to Tier 1 words, they are words that students are unlikely to learn on their own.

By way of exemplifying Tier 2 words, the following are some pairs of such words for the first five letters of the alphabet: *abandon, adamant; bargain, blunder; cautious, consider; deceptive, dedicate; elusive, encounter.* Notice that these words tend to be abstract rather than concrete. Notice, too, that in general, they do not represent new concepts but more sophisticated ways of expressing things that students already know about. For example, *cautious* is related to *careful, consider* to *think about.*

Another lens through which to view Tier 2 words involves seeing them as words that relate to reasoning. Many of the words in the Tier 2 category represent the academic language that students need in order to reason with the ideas met in text. Students use these words, for example, when they construct or analyze.

SPECIALIZED OR TIER 3 WORDS

Specialized vocabulary includes words used by people with a special interest in a topic, whether it's baseball, fashion, cars, music, politics, science, film, mathematics, computers, science, and so on. These words are learned in reading, talking, and writing within the community of people who share the interest. Specialized vocabulary is especially important in specific disciplines.

For example, when students learn about living cells, they learn many terms that refer to the structure and functions of the cell. Terms like *nucleus, cell membrane, mitochondria,* and *vacuoles* make sense only with reference to basic knowledge of the cell as a whole. These terms take important meaning from being labels on a diagram of the cell. In a sense, the words are outcroppings of an underlying concept.

Without knowledge of the concept, none of these words make sense. With knowledge, a batch of related words comes together.

In history, words like *treaty, negotiate, agreement, compromise, alliance, annul,* and *violate* belong together in a single conceptual scheme that makes sense as a whole. A reader's underlying schema for making sense of these words might be personal memories of the social transaction of making a deal or reaching an agreement. Such memories will be more than an external account; they will include the internal experience of motives and feelings and values. Without understanding of the conceptual scheme, the individual words make little sense. Many words crop out from each concept; one word does not equal one concept.

It is not only in the field of academics, however, that specialized words cohere around a single concept. In baseball, the word *inning* makes no sense without understanding what the words that make up the parts of an inning mean, such as *outs, hits, at bats,* and *runs.* Other words, such as *strike, ball, foul, home run, sinker, shortstop, double-play,* and so on, also contribute to the expanding meaning of *inning.* These specialized words don't have stand-alone meaning so much as they mark parts or configurations of some special knowledge. They share the knowledge with other words that mark other parts.

Reasoning With Words

When people communicate reasoning—for example, when they explain or argue—they weave ideas together into a web that makes sense logically (each idea is connected to the next in a valid way) and referentially (the reader can follow what the text refers to). The words needed to weave ideas together are used in all academic disciplines. They are words such as *justify, explain, analyze, conditions, enable, assumptions, system, distinction, responsibility, interpretation, realization, determination,* and *insufficient.*

Unlike the specialized words that are inside the knowledge they help represent, these "reasoning words" help people do things with knowledge. They help people reason with knowledge, explain it, connect it to other knowledge, revise it, dispute it, and so on. They are the thinking tools for standing outside our own knowledge and working with it. And they give us a way to communicate about this work.

Consider the following example:

> When you analyze the conditions at the time, it is understandable why so many concluded that the

Director was justified in dissolving the partnership. With hindsight, the disaster that ensued makes his decision seem pure folly.

It is almost impossible to understand this passage without understanding the words *analyze, conditions, understandable, concluded, justified, dissolving, ensued,* and *decision*. The core idea around which the others cohere is "Director's decision." Two judgments of the decision are referred to: "justified" and "pure folly." The "justified" judgment was what "many concluded" at the time (without hindsight). This judgment is itself judged "understandable" by virtue of analyzing conditions at the time (which did not include the disaster that ensued).

A further close reading of these not-so-simple lines would reveal the following:

> *When you* [the writer on the reader's behalf] *analyze the conditions* [examine systematically whatever might affect the decision the Director was about to make] *at the time* [what people then might know and consider], *it is understandable* [to the writer on behalf of the reader; understandable stops short of understanding and approving] *why so many* [people at the time] *concluded* [reasoning based on conditions at the time] *that the Director was justified* [his decision was reasonable based on conditions at the time] *in dissolving the partnership. With hindsight* [the writer's and reader's hindsight], *the disaster that ensued* [following his decision and the conditions at the time] *makes his decision* [the frame of reference for judging the decision has been transformed from conditions at the time to the ensuing consequences] *seem* [to the writer on behalf of the reader] *pure folly.*

Knowledge of the words propels successful connection of the ideas they represent and consequently supports development of comprehension. To make academic words a productive part of their vocabularies, students must encounter the words in a variety of contexts and engage with the words' meanings.

Certain kinds of Tier 2 words are especially important and useful for building knowledge in the subjects and reasoning with that knowledge:

- Words for categorizing superordinates, such as *artifact* and *grasslands,* and adjectives that identify class membership, such as *warm-blooded* and *monotheistic,* make it possible to talk in simple ways about diverse groups of items or phenomena. For example, *grasslands* make it possible to focus on what is common among prairie,

savanna, and steppe. Without the superordinate term, the writer or communicator constantly emphasizes the different members, not the common membership.

- Words for asserting relationships, such as *constellation, system, cycle,* and *triangle of trade,* are used to indicate that apparently separate entities or events are in fact related to one another and thus can be appropriately discussed as single items.

- Words that transform processes into entities provide a way of using language to make thinking easier. So, for example, words like *revolution, unemployment,* and *decline* are used to reify and make discussable entire narratives.

Knowledge Structures: Forms and Substance for Comprehension

What is knowledge? Knowledge is more than information. Knowledge has a form, a structure; it is organized. Information is like the substance that goes "in" the "form" or structure of knowledge. Knowledge, then, is both form and substance.

Vast domains of information share relatively few forms and structures that are used over and over again. These common structures enable connections and analogies across different knowledge. Texts produced within disciplines reflect common knowledge structures in terms of organization, syntax, and vocabulary.

Assume, for example, that students are studying the economies of New England and the South in the early 19th century. Information about these two economies could be organized by a compare–contrast structure that efficiently represents similarities and differences. (A Venn diagram could be used to show aspects of this structure.) However, this structure would not reveal the relationships between the two economies. The compare–contrast structure is blind to relationships; it focuses on same and different. The student would need a transaction structure to show relationships. The triangle of trade is such an organizing structure; it allows a student to show information about the two economies (and England's). The triangle represents the commercial relationships that connected the three economies. Upper elementary students need to command both structures (compare–contrast and triangle structure) and know which structure does what work. Knowledge of structures like this is part of the prior knowledge students need to bring to their reading.

There is no evidence to suggest that teaching abstract forms directly helps students learn them. Students need to work with, discuss, and write with the forms of knowledge that come up in the texts they are reading. And they need to read across enough different genres, topics, and disciplines to encounter the variety of forms.

Knowledge as Questions and Answers

A very common way to structure knowledge in school subjects is question and answer. Questions guide the reader's attention into the text. Questions are generated as a person reads, pulling the reader through the text. If the text is a story, such questions feel like suspense. If the text is a scientific explanation, curiosity often takes the shape of questions. Questions provide a framework for considering information from the text and incorporating it into the reader's own knowledge. In a way, questions reach out toward the text from knowledge the reader already has. Questions can be an opening in the reader's knowledge, a place for new knowledge, and a readiness to learn.

Questions show up as an important form in each academic subject. Students ask questions in discussions and when they are trying to understand something. The text asks and answers questions as an organizing device. Students read and are expected to answer questions on tests and other assignments.

The question–answer structure is familiar to students from past school experience and everyday life. However, academic question–answer structures often have a complexity of thought and therefore language that goes beyond the everyday language experience. Consider the following question:

> If there are 3 students for every computer in fifth grade at Chavez Elementary School, and there are 45 computers, how many students are in fifth grade?

A valid mental model of this question will capture the relationship between the number of computers and the number of students, which is given as a condition in the *if* clause. Perhaps a diagrammatic representation showing 3 student icons attached to 1 computer icon would prove to be helpful. A likely source of confusion is a textbase error that translates "3 students for every computer" into $3s = c$. This error comes from the bad habit students are encouraged to

form by well-meaning teachers and parents who go directly from the English language textbase to the mathematical language textbase. A good mathematics reader will comprehend the situation described in the problem first. The reader will build a mental model of the problem using the English textbase, and then formulate the mathematical textbase from the mental model. The phrase in the question leads to the diagram (from the mental model) showing 1 computer with 3 students. This formulates into the mathematical expression $3s/c$ or $c/3s$. These are mathematical phrases without verbs.

The question in the problem asks "how many students...?" This implies a piece of knowledge of the form, "The number of students equals...." This can be formulated as $s = ?$ The equal sign is the most important verb in mathematics. It means, in this case, that the number on the right will refer to the same quantity as s on the left: The number will be the number of students. It will not be the number of computers or the number of students for each computer. This is obvious from any valid mental model of the situation, including the question. The text gives one more piece of information that has to be in the model: "there are 45 computers." How do these conditions relate to each other? $s = (3s/c) \cdot 45c$ expresses the relationships in a single mathematical sentence. This sentence has the correct mathematical textbase that corresponds to the mental model.

If it is not obvious to a reader, the reader is stuck in the bad habit of trying to solve the problem without a mental model. Many of us were taught how to recognize a long list of characteristic problems from text features. We memorized methods for formulating calculations directly from textbase readings without building mental models. This actually works fine for simple problems as long as the list of problem types doesn't get too long or too strange. If we had learned techniques for building mental models of these same problem situations, and formulating the mathematics from mental models, we would have learned more mathematics as we went along. And we would have learned how to understand what we read as the mathematics became more advanced.

Knowledge as Explanation

A student was asked how he knows when he understands a scientific concept. He said, "When I can see it happen in my mind." He went on to use the example of how the tilt of the earth causes the seasons as first one and then the other hemisphere tilts away from the sun during the earth's annual rotation. As he spoke, he represented what "happens" by moving his hands around.

When a text explains a scientific concept like the seasons, the comprehension target is knowledge that has a "see it happen" structure like the one described above. This structure enables the reader to imagine objects in spatial relationship to each other changing in some patterned way over time.

In the case of the planet Earth's seasons, the reader "sees" representations of definite objects (the earth, the sun) moving. Often in science, however, the student must see indefinite, generic objects like light, energy, and warmth and generic behavior like rotation and revolution. What happens as described in the text takes place in generic time, not definite time—for example, "seeing" what happens in the exchanges of energy that lead to warming and cooling.

The "seeing it happen/spatial relations" structure is one of a few dozen distinct knowledge structures that cannot be reduced one to the other. Students need the full repertoire of these structures to understand academic (and probably world) knowledge. They also need the know-how to mix and coordinate these different structures.

Consider the two explanations for how a refrigerator works in the table below. They illustrate two different kinds of knowledge about the same thing. One explains how the refrigerator works, and the other explains why. One is useful for learning the mechanics a repairman might need to know; the other leads to a scientific understanding that connects to broad principles of science. One is practical; the other, academic.

Both explanations inform. But they inform different structures and connect to existing and developing knowledge in different ways. The scientific explanation contributes a deeper and broader understanding of scientific principles related to how energy transfers work in systems. This knowledge is extremely important in science. The refrigerator is used to explain science. In the practical explanation, science is used to explain the refrigerator. Notice how the practical explanation uses a narrative structure that tells what happens sequentially in time. The scientific

Practical	Scientific (Academic)
Electricity comes out of the wall to turn the compressor that compresses the refrigerant, a gas. Compression takes place outside the refrigerator box. This heats the gas because compressing gas raises its temperature. The radiator dissipates the heat into the outside room (why it is warm behind a fridge). The gas is pumped through tubes into the inside of the box where the diameter of the tubes gets larger. The gas decompresses in the coils of larger tubes and cools. Whenever a gas decompresses, it cools. The cold tubes cool the air inside the refrigerator. As they do, they warm up the gas, which is pumped back outside. In the outside coils the warmth is radiated into the room. This cycle continues until the air inside is the desired temperature.	A refrigerator is a system. It works by isolating air inside the box from air outside the box. Heat inside the box is transferred outside the box. The amount of heat lost inside the box equals the amount gained outside the box. Refrigerators warm the kitchen. Because the kitchen has so much more air in it than the inside of the box, its temperature goes up very slightly. Heat is transferred from coils of tubes inside the box to coils outside that radiate the heat into the room. The coils contain a gas, the refrigerant. The gas is compressed outside the box and decompressed inside the box. When a gas decompresses, it absorbs heat. In this case, it absorbs heat from the air inside the box, thus lowering its temperature. The absorbed heat is transferred outside the box as the gas moves to the coils outside. There, the absorbed heat is radiated into the room because room air is cooler than the warmed coils. To compress the gas requires energy. The energy comes from electricity that drives a compressor. This external source of energy must be added to the system to make it work. Compression also adds heat to the room. The energy from electricity enters the system and is converted to kinetic energy of the moving compressor and gas, and heat energy.

explanation tells how components of the system form the big picture (exchange of heat between inside and outside), how the exchange is accomplished through the principle of compression, and back to a big picture of conservation of energy. The practical explanation stays in a narrative sequence without developing scientific principles.

A student who read the scientific explanation with prior knowledge of what kind of structure a "system" is would use the system structure to make the information comprehensible. The facts presented would inform the system (a form). The reader would be looking for things that help make sense of any system: the exchanges (inputs and outputs) between inside and outside the system, the invariant relationships among variable parts, the states of the system, cycles, what varies and what stays the same. Such a reader would be formulating a system diagram that shows transfer of heat and energy. The curious might even want to know the quantitative values of the elements: How much electricity does it take to lower the temperature 10 degrees? How much heat is generated by a refrigerator?

A student without prior knowledge of a system would probably read the scientific explanation as though it were a poorly written narrative. If such a student tried hard, he or she could probably construct a mental model that would fit the practical explanation. In other words, the student would transform it into the practical version. This mental model would be perfectly functional and make good sense as an explanation of how a refrigerator works. But it would not add much to accumulating insights into science.

A program that settles for the practical explanations as a matter of course has low expectations for learning science. The practical explanation is fine; it should not be avoided. In fact it is helpful. But the scientific explanation is the goal and the basis for further learning of science.

A student in a science program focused mostly on practical explanations would have to learn hundreds of different explanations for refrigerators, homeostasis of warm-blooded organisms, climate, storms, why cars have radiators, and so on. Yet the same basic scientific concepts are central to understanding all these phenomena. Learn a few basic concepts and principles, learn how they apply across varied phenomena, and there is much less material to learn. A little form can organize a lot of substance.

Knowledge is organized at every level, from big-picture overviews to fine details. It is also richly cross-referenced within and across organized structures. Knowledge structures are reflected in text from sentence structures, midlevel organizers, genre structures, and even the relationships among texts (such as the trace of history across primary sources).

Many of these knowledge structures have mixes of several structures. For example, a more complete understanding of the seasons would include understanding how energy from the sun becomes warmth on earth. This requires some understanding of how energy is conserved and what heat is. These understandings are a mix of "seeing it happen" structures (radiation, like light, striking particles and causing acceleration of particles that amounts to an increase in temperature), more abstract relationships that are equations or the informal precursors of equations, and systems that maintain invariant relations among variable parts.

Knowledge and Text

A reader cannot comprehend a text without supplying much of the knowledge needed to build a textbase (knowledge of words, sentences, text, and genre) and a mental model. In the subjects studied in school, prior knowledge of the subject is fundamental for acquiring new knowledge. It is fundamental to comprehending texts. This prior knowledge of the subject includes far more than the facts. It includes the ways of thinking that lead to knowledge in that subject, and it includes the forms and structures used to organize knowledge, give it meaning, and connect it to other knowledge.

No one should pretend that reading alone will teach the reader content. To learn science, history, or mathematics requires a range of activities and experiences of which reading is one. Later, when a student is deeply into the subject, initiated into the language of its community, more can be learned from just reading.

Still, without reading, students stand little chance of learning as much as they need in any subject. Talk is ephemeral. An English language learner, a student struggling with the topic, a student daydreaming at the wrong time, will miss what is said and have no reference to find it again. Text stays where the reader can find it again and again, where she can reread, slow down, and speed up at will. Text can represent complexities that would be hard to capture in the ephemeral world of talk. There is no substitute for reading.

5

Effective Writing

*Composing consists of joining bits of information into relationships,
many of which have never existed until the composer utters them.
Simply by writing—that is, by composing information—you become
aware of the connections you make, and you thereby know more than
you knew before starting to write. In its broadest sense, knowledge
is an awareness of relationships among pieces of information. As you
compose, your new knowledge is your awareness of
those relationships.*

——ALBERT DOUGLASS VAN NOSTRAND, "Writing and the Generation of Knowledge"

In good literacy programs, writing is as important as reading. Although students learn and practice much of the knowledge and many skills related to effective writing in English language arts classes, fourth and fifth graders also should be writing in history, science, and mathematics (Guthrie et al., 2004; Halliday & Martin, 1993; Levstik & Barton, 2005; Whitin & Whitin, 2000).

A Perspective for Writing: Processes and Strategies

As with reading, there are a range of literary strategies and devices, as well as specific knowledge and habits, that are prime ingredients of an effective writing program. Our discussion of the knowledge and skills that students need to become effective writers reflects both research and classroom practice.

In this chapter, we discuss the individual habits and practices that make writing a dynamic collection of processes. And we show how fourth and fifth graders use writing strategies that add style to what they write as they help readers make sense of what they have written.

Setting the Stage: Context, Purpose, and Audience

All writing takes place within a *context* that influences what the writer says and how he says it. Context includes the writer, the audience (person or persons with whom the writer communicates), and the situation for the writing (Britton, 1997; Halliday & Hasan, 1989; Prior, 1998). Awareness of context benefits students' writing because it helps them consider who they want to communicate with, what information they want to convey, and how to communicate that information effectively.

The context for a research paper, for example, is shaped by the assignment: the number of references required, the topic to be addressed, the format of the report, and so on (Langer, 1986; McGinley, 1992; McGinley & Tierney, 1989; Newell, 1984; Prior, 1998, 2006). The context for a research paper assigned in history will include students' understanding about the quality of work expected by the history teacher; the knowledge structure of history as a discipline, including the importance of perspective and validity of sources; and the time constraints imposed by the teacher. The context for a research paper assigned in an English class, however, will differ. Students will consider the English teacher's expectations related to quality, the time constraints set by this teacher, the knowledge structure of literary criticism, and the teacher's stylistic preferences.

Writers write for many *purposes*. They write to persuade, to inform, to express, and to entertain. They write to plan and to learn. In school, students frequently write as a means of displaying an understanding of content, a facility with language, or an understanding of a literary form or genre (Britton, Burgess, Martin, McLeod, & Rosen, 1975; Kinneavy, 1980; Moffett, 1968).

Whatever their purpose, however, writers always take into account the *audience* for their text (Britton el al., 1975; Kinneavy, 1980; Moffett & Wagner,

1976). In school, the audience is often the teacher, but students benefit from the opportunity to write for audiences beyond the teacher. For instance, a fifth grader who wants to recommend a favorite book to readers might write a review of the book that will be published on the school or class website. In this case, she writes for her peers as well as for the larger audience of people who can access the website, including the school community, family members, and the public, which is likely an unknown audience. As she drafts and crafts her piece, she must keep in mind that her audience includes people who may not be familiar with her interests, her reasons for writing, the author, or the text. She will draw on her knowledge of the book review genre and her awareness of audience to help her shape her piece.

Writing Processes: Individual Habits and Practices

Writers actually develop several *processes* rather than a single fixed process for writing. The particular process they employ at any given time depends on the context for the piece they are working to produce (Atwell, 1987, 1998; Berkenkotter, Huckin, & Ackerman, 1988; Calkins, 1994; Graves & Kittle, 2005; Portalupi & Fletcher, 2001). Students develop their writing processes through their different experiences as writers. They may also learn about the processes of their favorite writers and use that knowledge to experiment. For example, they might mimic a writer who starts with a quick-write to get ideas down on paper and discover a perspective rather than with more typical planning activities. And they develop habits that support their writing, such as writing daily and using published pieces as models for their own work (Jenkins, 1999; Kamberelis & Bovino, 1999).

As writing assignments become more challenging in the upper elementary grades, students need to develop more sophisticated processes for meeting different academic demands. They must learn how to go from writing assignments in which they are asked to explore what they know to longer, summative assignments that require lengthier or more elaborate writing processes, such as research papers and on-demand writing.

In school, writing asks that students be competent using the standard process approach (planning, drafting, revising, editing), using an on-demand process, and using a set of processes to develop a research paper. All these approaches to writing vary widely among writers, and all three are most likely recursive in nature.

Process Writing: What's Involved

PLANNING: GETTING READY TO WRITE

Planning is crucial to producing an effective piece of writing (Flower & Hayes, 1981; Graves, 2003). During the planning stage, writers consider the context, purpose, audience, and genre for their piece, and they think hard about the subject of their writing. They consider whether they know enough about their topic to have something worthwhile to say. Often, the planning stage necessitates gathering information about the topic to find answers to questions such as these: Is my subject too broad? How can I expand or narrow my focus to make it manageable? How do I develop a big question that centers my writing?

DRAFTING: ROUGHING OUT IDEAS AND INFORMATION

Once they have a tentative plan for a piece, writers can begin to get ideas down on paper. They can rough out a draft that conforms to some genre expectations and contains the main chunks of information that they want to convey to readers. The process of putting an initial draft on paper gives writers the opportunity to see where they need to clarify their own thinking, perhaps by gathering more information about the topic or talking with others about the strengths and weaknesses of the piece as drafted (Atwell, 1987, 1998; Calkins, 1994; Gillet & Beverly, 2001; Graves, 2003; Graves & Kittle, 2005; Routman, 2005).

Writers' processes for drafting will vary depending on the subject area and genre. In science, for instance, the teacher might provide a table of contents for students to use as an organizing structure to present information they have learned. To write a position paper in English language arts, writers might plan the piece by developing a graphic organizer with the features of that genre. Or they might draw a timeline as a way to structure a fictional narrative. They then can refer to their organizer as they draft their pieces. (For more on writing in different academic subjects, Chapter 6.)

RESPONSE AND REVISING

Among the stages of the writing process, it is perhaps access to response from a reader that is most useful to a writer. The purpose of writing, after all, is the communication of ideas, emotions, and knowledge that the writer wants a reader to consider. As a result, writers are ever aware of their intended audience when they shape a piece, when they consider word choice, when they decide what to put in or leave out. Writing is intentional, and every decision counts if the author's message is to be well received and well understood by an audience.

Revising is a complex process. It is the writer's opportunity to reconsider everything about the writing so far, including topic choice and genre. Guided by responses from others, a writer may choose to reorganize a piece completely, to simply append a different ending, or to leave things as they are.

During the revision phase, writers should focus on big-picture issues, asking questions such as these (Atwell, 1987, 1998; Calkins, 1994; Calkins & Bleichman, 2003; Conner & Moulton, 2000; Graves & Kittle, 2005; Heard, 2002; Saddler, 2003; Scardamalia & Bereiter, 1986): Am I accomplishing my purpose for writing? Have I included enough information? Have I organized the piece effectively? Is the tone right? Do I need to clarify? Will people be able to understand my argument? Have I developed the characters enough? What about my lead?

EDITING

Good writers attend primarily to editing after they have addressed all the global revisions. When editing, writers review the piece for word choice and correctness of content and conventions. They check for ambiguous sentence structure, incorrect or missing words, spelling errors, and punctuation problems. Editing should be the final phase—otherwise, writers can become so concerned with correctness and language choices that they restrict what they write (Atwell, 1987, 1998; Calkins, 1994; Conner & Moulton, 2000; Gillet & Beverly, 2001; Graves, 2003; Graves & Kittle, 2005; Heard, 2002; Routman, 2005).

On-Demand Writing Processes

On-demand writing requires much planning, drafting, revising, and editing in a compressed and sometimes stressful amount of time. Students who have a good deal of experience as writers in less pressured, everyday circumstances have an advantage in on-demand writing tasks (Shelton & Fu, 2004; Wolf & Wolf, 2002; Wollman-Bonilla, 2004). Although few writers are comfortable expressing themselves in a first-draft-is-final mode, there are times when such writing is required. In school, most essay tests are first-draft-is-final events, as are state writing tests, though some states allow brief time and extra paper for planning. The process for a first-draft-is-final event is truncated, but there can be a process nonetheless.

PLANNING FOR ON-DEMAND WRITING

To plan an on-demand piece, students must pay particular attention to what they are being asked to do. This means understanding a prompt or essay question and reading it carefully to determine what, if any, requirements it imposes. Some prompts specify a particular genre; others do not. Some specify information to include, such as "Be sure to include *enough details* so that your reader can envision the sequence of steps," or "Trace the *political significance* of the work," or "*Relate this piece to the period* which fostered its central premise." Planning must take into consideration all the requirements (Downing, 1995; Flower & Hayes, 1981; Hillocks, 2002).

DRAFTING FOR ON-DEMAND WRITING

In most on-demand situations, the writing time is limited, so writers should go into the drafting stage with an organizational structure in mind. To the extent possible, they should try to get things right the first time. The most important consideration in drafting is attending to organizing the writing so that it follows a structure that readers can understand. (Here is where genre knowledge and understanding of midlevel structures can be extremely helpful.) Students also should focus on the task as specified, addressing the prompt and not diverging from the topic. Niceties of language are not the primary concern, but clarity, coherence, and exactness count a good deal on the first—and only—draft (Heard, 2002).

REVISING FOR ON-DEMAND WRITING

Revising an on-demand piece should be concerned first with the quality of the content. The writer should make certain that the piece addresses the prompt and that the information is valid. Beyond addressing content, the writer should try to read through the work a final time to assess its total quality, perhaps adding a thought here or there and checking to make sure nothing of importance has been omitted. The writer should consider the intended audience and check to see whether there is enough text to build background understanding, the stance is appropriate, the tone is appropriate, and the major sections fit together logically and coherently.

EDITING FOR ON-DEMAND WRITING

Students should pay attention to the correctness of sentence structure, spelling, and punctuation.

Writing Processes for Research Projects

In the upper elementary grades, students write research-driven and term research reports on topics that relate to their curricular learning. Such assignments require students to gather information about a topic and then synthesize this information in writing. Students might write to answer questions about their favorite authors, such as "How has Kate DiCamillo's life influenced her writing?" Or they might write about topics they are learning in science, such as "How has the reintroduction of wolves to Yellowstone Park affected the park's ecosystem?" Students need to be taught—and taken through—the steps involved in such a project (Derewianka, 1998; Kuhlthau, 1993; McMackin & Siegel, 2002; Nelson & Hayes, 1988).

PLANNING AND DEVELOPING QUESTIONS

Students must be taught to generate an open-ended research question or a controlling idea (thesis) that is general enough to be significant but narrow enough to be realistic. Nelson and Hayes (1988) make a distinction between *content-driven* and *issue-driven* reporting. Content-driven writing takes its shape from the content collected during the research process (based on a prompt such as "Write a report about the Battle at Lexington"). Issue-driven writing responds to a controlling idea or "big" research question ("Who fired the first shot at the Battle of Lexington? Why is it a debatable question?").

Students can learn how to develop open-ended questions by formulating questions relevant to their lives ("How can we recycle paper in school?") Then they can brainstorm about how they might gather information to answer these questions.

Students need a significant amount of background knowledge about a topic to come up with a big research question or a thesis statement for their research. Students should have time and support as they work through this part of the research process because this exploratory stage is vital to the success of the investigation.

Ideally, students should have some say about their topic to truly engage with the content (Chandler-Olcott & Mahar, 2001; Kent, 1997). Some choice—even within a specified unit of study—is important.

Conducting Research

Students need to articulate the main idea of their research before they begin collecting information. This doesn't mean they need to have preconceived notions of their conclusions, but rather that they know what they are trying to find out. If the topic isn't explicit, students often end up with a list of unrelated facts under predetermined categories, so they randomly include whatever facts they find in their research. When this happens, it's difficult for students to write cohesive and coherent reports. In addition, it's difficult for them to create a model of the research writing process that they can then transfer to other, similar situations.

According to Carol Kuhlthau (1993), researchers read in different ways at various points in this process. First, they read to get a general sense of the topic, to see if there is enough appropriate material available, and to generate a thesis or question. Once they have the research question or thesis, they revisit the texts with a focused goal in mind: to find answers or support for the thesis or question. Different skills are involved in each stage.

Drafting

Genre knowledge helps students in their planning and drafting because they can use their knowledge of the genre's structure to help them create an organizing framework for their pieces (Derewianka, 1998; Martin & Rothery, 1980, 1981).

If a student who is writing about Yellowstone Park knows that she wants to explain why reintroducing wolves to the park is important to conservationists, she can consider the claim–evidence–reasoning structure of explanation in the planning stages of her research before she even begins to collect information.

Knowing that she will use a claim–evidence–reasoning structure in her piece helps her draft her claim and guides her research. She knows what she's going to try to accomplish when she sets out to collect the information and how she might organize the information she finds to support her claim. As she finds information, she can begin to organize the ideas.

On the other hand, a student who knows before she begins to collect data that she will be comparing and contrasting conservationists' views and ranchers' views about wolves in Yellowstone Park will approach the task in a slightly different way. Students who haven't thought about text structure in the planning stages are often at a disadvantage when they begin to draft the report.

Revising

As students complete a first draft of a research paper, they should see where they need to gather more information and reorganize and revise their writing to match their developing understanding of the topic at hand. Students should receive suggestions for revision from their teacher and peers. The thesis or open-ended research question should remind students what they want to say and how to say it. Students' genre knowledge helps them mold the structure and incorporate the features of the genre when they revise their pieces. Global revision that focuses on structure and big ideas should be the priority.

Editing

After students address global issues, they can focus on grammar, punctuation, spelling, checking facts, and citing sources.

Citing Sources

Fourth and fifth graders need to understand why it's important to put information from sources in their own words and cite sources in a bibliography. Students do not know automatically how to put information from sources into their own words. Internet sources may be particularly seductive to young writers because it is so easy to cut and paste from an electronic file. Students must be taught to use information from sources to support *their* idea about the topic, and they must learn to paraphrase the information from sources and incorporate it into their pieces.

Writer Strategies:
Tools for Effective Writing

Fourth- and fifth-grade writers who have benefited from a strong K–3 writing program are, at the very least, familiar with several genres and can identify them by name. They understand the function of introductions and closings. They are aware that writing must be organized in such a way that readers can follow a story line or an argument structure or a compare–contrast format. They recognize the need for appropriate details, and they are mindful of sentence structure (Graves & Kittle, 2005; Heard, 2002; Pappas, Kiefer, & Levstik, 2006).

These writers likely have learned some writer strategies as well, although which strategies—and even the names for them—certainly will vary among writers and classrooms. There is no set list of "one size fits all" strategies for writing. Different strategies accomplish different purposes. Here we focus on a selection of strategies that writers use to make their writing clear and coherent for their potential audience; in other words, the strategies we describe are those that foster readers' understanding, that help them build a textbase and a rich mental model.

Writers typically employ genres and other predictable structures whose formats allow readers to follow a plot line or the development of ideas; they use cohesive devices to link sentences and paragraphs; they provide forecasting to give readers a roadmap of what is to follow; they create analogies to make the strange familiar; they employ precise word choice and details to create realistic people and situations or to help readers better understand information. All these strategies—and others routinely employed by writers—are characteristics of well-written prose. They keep us engaged and on track, and they are a hallmark of a writer who writes through a reader's eyes.

We are not suggesting that teachers label certain strategies as being important to help readers build a textbase and others as important to help readers construct a mental model. Many strategies serve both purposes. Teachers should simply build student awareness that making text intelligible is fundamental and that certain strategies are especially useful in accomplishing this purpose. The strategies that help readers build a textbase are those that make writing cohesive and coherent, make the writing flow, structure an argument, and follow a predictable format, genre, and midlevel structure. The strategies that help readers construct a mental model are those that make what is expressed resonate with readers (Halliday & Hasan, 1992) so that the text taps into readers' memories and knowledge base, allowing them to build a world (Kintsch, 1982).

The following samples of student work are illustrative of writing that is intentionally reader friendly. All come from students who have been part of a strong writing program for at least one year. They are in regular classes in schools with diverse student populations.

Writer Strategies That Help Readers Develop a Textbase

Some strategies used by writers to help readers link ideas appropriately include employing recognizable, familiar genres and midlevel structures; using signal words and cues to segment information, including paragraphing and punctuation; building a context for readers; addressing readers directly through forecasting; and creating cohesion among the sentences and coherence in the text as a whole. Even with all of these strategies, however, readers will need to make some inferences as they build a textbase, so simplicity and clarity of expression are essential. William Zinsser, author of the classic *On Writing Well* (1985), tells us, "The game is won or lost on hundreds of small details. Writing improves in direct ratio to the number of things we can keep out of it that shouldn't be there."

GENRES AND MIDLEVEL STRUCTURES

Writers use genres as a means of organizing their thoughts and communicating effectively with their audiences. Because genres are not rigid structures, writers have a good deal of latitude in how to employ them. For example, a narrative has sequence as its deep structure, but if the writer so chooses, he can "play" with time, using flashbacks and flash forwards; dividing the narrative into a series of vignettes, each devoted to a different character; or even embedding informational text in the story.

The example on page 61 is from a piece in which a fifth-grade writer contrasts a family trip to northern California with one to the Texas Gulf Coast. Notice how she makes the contrast through describing the similarity of events rather that through a more predictable

Then, my relatives came, just to miss the snow and cold weather back home. Their arrival was closely followed by long, peaceful walks on the the bluffs, accompanied by the waves' rythmical crashing on the silky, still untouched sand. None of us talked much, but when we did, it was just to say things like, "I remember when we would go on walks like these in the woods when we were little," or just to call the dog we were taking care of. When we came home, we were all muddy, dirty, cold, but happy.

Before I knew it, I was sitting on one of those itchy, uncomfortable airplane seats with my sister and my dad sitting next to me, going to Corpus Christi, Texas, to see my father's parents. Our suitcase was curiously packed, with nothing but sunglasses, shorts, funky old T-shirts, bathing suits, and baseball caps. Texas in wintertime is like summertime in Half Moon Bay. We spent the rest of our time jumping off sand dunes, swimming in the Golf, snorkling, surfing, and pushing eachother into the shallow warm ocean water. In the evening, we would come back home, sandy and wet yet happy, and play a good game of Croquet on my grandparents' perfectly-mowed lawn, get bitten by mosquitos, feasting on our sweet, California blood, and end the day itching like crazy, until we were back in the airport, back in the airplane on the itchy seats, and, after 4 long hours, back home, from where we started.

choice of elements, such as details about the weather or the physical characteristics of the two beaches.

The pictures this young writer creates set up a vivid contrast, although she never uses signal words (e.g., *by contrast*, *on the other hand*) typically used to set up the contrastive structure. Readers get a sense of quiet and calm associated with a northern California beach and of action and exuberance that comes with the warm Texas Gulf Coast beach. The similarity associated with the beaches is that both experiences are happy and family-oriented ones.

The following sentence is an example of a more traditional contrastive structure: "Charlie, on the other hand, wants a golden ticket." This signal is short and unambiguous, yet no less effective. It is not necessarily the subtlety of the structure or the length that is important. Rather, what is important is that readers can appropriately link the ideas.

USING SIGNAL WORDS TO LEAD READERS THROUGH A TEXT

Signal words lead readers through the text and allow them to link ideas. These are "signposts," as researcher Judith Langer (1984) refers to them: transition elements and other cohesive devices. These signposts provide a structure that, if not predictable, is at least logical. They produce "flow" at the sentence level and signal the logical progression of ideas throughout the text (Cox, Shanahan, & Sulzby, 1990; Fang & Cox, 1998; Halliday & Hasan, 1992; Meyer, 1975; Pappas et al., 2006).

Some signaling strategies are so obvious that even the youngest writers use them. Consider the need to signal sequence. As they mature as writers, kindergarten writers frequently move from "once" or "one day" to "and then...and then...and then" with no difficulty—or finesse—at all. The move from "and then" to simply "then" or "later" or "after that" or "the next day" may require some nudging but, still, this facility with "time cue" words—or transitions, the literal sign-posts—is well within the purview of young writers (Biber, 1988; Kamberelis, 1999). Most young writers know they have to tell readers that one action follows another so readers can "see" and follow the progression of action.

More proficient writers frequently omit signal words with the expectation that a logical organization of ideas coupled with readers' sophistication will carry an audience through the text. The "If your having a hard time..." excerpt here, from a piece written by a fourth grader, shows that the writer knows how to omit temporal signal words and yet leave no gaps in a reader's understanding.

Notice the repeated omission of the implied word *then*, in brackets here:

> If your having a hard time getting your foot in, [then] you can pour newt juice or dish soap into your binding to make it slippery. [Then] slip your feet in and [then] get in the water.
>
>   Once you have the handle in you hand, [then] sit in the water, [then] make sure you're facing the boat. Then, tuck your knees into your chest. Once the boat starts going, get up....

Notice also, in the second paragraph, the writer's use of a more sophisticated strategy for keeping readers on track: "Once you have the handle..." and "Once the boat starts going...."

COHESION

Some sentence-to-sentence progressions can be quite sophisticated. The repetition of "some" in the second writing sample here signals both contrastive and additive linkages.

This writer uses "some" to give contrastive information. Moreover, the repetition of "some" imparts a literary quality to this informational text. Perhaps this piece is original, perhaps the syntax is borrowed, and perhaps these three sentences are lifted whole cloth

If your having a hard time getting your foot in, you can pour newt juice or dish soap into your bindings to make it slippery Slip your feet in and get in the water.

Once you have the handle in your hand, sit in the water, make sure you're facing the boat. Then, tuck your knees into your chest. Once the boat starts going get up,

Introduction
ALL CRYSTALS
ARE DIFFERENT!
Some crystals grow from lava and some grow from sea salt. Some are circular and some are triangular. Some crystals are colorful and some are not, AND THAT'S WHAT MAKES THEM SO WONDERFUL!

Writing and the English Language Learner

Findings from the research on writing for second-language learners indicate that students benefit from explicit teacher attention to form and the opportunity to make revisions based on this attention. For example, in a study by Gómez, Parker, Lara-Alecio, and Gómez (1996), in one condition, teachers responded to student's writing through written comments about the content but did not correct students' errors. In the second condition, teachers corrected errors, focusing on those deemed most important, and students were instructed to focus on ensuring these errors did not appear in the next segment of their work. In the latter condition, students demonstrated superior growth in five of the nine areas assessed rather than in only one area, as was the case in the first condition.

In a second study (Prater & Bermudez, 1993), second-language learners were placed in peer-response groups with monolingual English speakers. Group members made topic suggestions, responded to first drafts, and cooperatively edited the papers, with group members taking on different editorial responsibilities. The result was that students wrote more, but their writing did not necessarily improve. As the authors noted, "it may be necessary for the teacher to provide more direct instruction in specific aspects of the writing that were assessed by the scoring rubric" (p. 108). They also suggested more modeling of appropriate responses and explanation of group general procedures.

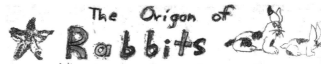

The Origon of Rabbits

You are on the egde of the woods standing alone, then you hear a loud thumping as loud as a heard of wild buffalo. The noise echoes trough the grassy plains. Then you hear the noise again it is coming closer toword you. Then you hear the noise louder than ever. You look behind you, it is a wild rabbit pounding his hind legs and looking out onto the plains. He starts to stare into your eye. As soon as you blink he is gone in a flash, zig zagging away 25 miles per hour.

from a reference book. However, though it is not all included here, the remaining text from which this excerpt has been taken features syntax that is equally sophisticated.

Leading Readers Into a Text by Building Context

Very young writers often begin their informational text in one of two ways. Either they announce up front the topic of their writing ("I'm going to tell you all about whales") or they expect the title of their piece to provide the context for readers, so they dive right into the substance of their writing (Chapman, 1995; Donovan, 2001; Kamberelis, 1999; Newkirk, 1989; Sowers, 1985). As students mature as writers, their opening strategies become more sophisticated, as shown here in "The Origon of Rabbits."

This is a very nice lead-in for a piece of informational text about rabbits. However, using a direct opening, known as forecasting, can be an effective strategy as well. The sample opening with "Intro" on the next page illustrates this.

In another interesting opening, the writer speaks directly to readers to introduce the topic and explain the context for the piece:

The first time I really got interested in guide dogs was when I was at school. I was watching a play and one of the characters had a guide dog. I realized that without the dog the person would not be able to go places. So two years later I decided to do my report on guide dogs because I was interesting in them. I started by looking on the internet. I wanted to know how guide dogs are trained from beginning to end.

"The Author and his Literature" on the next page shows another introduction that forecasts the writer's intent to discuss the similarities (setting and characters) in Roald Dahl's books.

Intro:

Before you buy a finch you first need to know what it needs and how to take care of it to keep it happy and healthy. This pamphlet will tell you the basics.

What to Buy

step 1: Buy a cage big enough for your finch to fly around in with perches to rest on.

step 2: Than fold some newspaper and fit it on the bottom of the cage.

step 3: If your cage doesn't already have a food dish or water dish you can buy one at any pet shop but make sure it's not too big for your small finch.

step 4: After you buy the water dish and food dish buy a nesting box with cut up string or special nesting hair in it and hang it in your cage for your finch to rest in.

#22

The Author and his Literature
By ▬▬▬

All the books Roald Dahl has written are very similar. They have the same setting, England and the plots involve a poor or orphaned child trying to do some good, paired up with a horrible adult. For example in Matilda, She is a 5 year old girl who gets treated like dirt from her rotten parents and the abominable trunchbull at school.

The charectars all have different personalities. Some can be rude, obnoxious and so scary they'll make your blood turn to ice, while others are so nice and sweet that you can't believe that they're in a story about filthy witches or giants named bonecruncher or bloodbottler. Like I said their total opposites. The bad guys always get punished and the good guys always win.

Roald Dahl paints pictures in my mind. He makes up words that make the story fun, such as whizzpoping from the BFG. He is such a cool author. Heres a example from the witches:

Helping Readers Segment Text With Punctuation and Paragraphs

Writers use punctuation and paragraphs to help their readers chunk information appropriately, create pacing, and make text intelligible (Schuster, 2003; Smith & Wilhelm, 2006; Weaver, 1996).

Punctuation.   In the sample below, the writer uses a strategy known as "exploding the moment"—a way to slow readers down through a series of short sentences (Lane, 1993):

INTRO

Today's your big day. You stare out at the bright-green baseball feild. You step into the dug-out, the place where you wait to bat. You wait on-deck while your best friend, Tony, is at bat. He hits the ball and makes it 20 second base. Now it's your turn. Nervously, you step up to homeplate.

The sentences, which are marked by periods and at times commas, cause readers to pause at each punctuation mark and so "build up" to the big moment (Berger, 2003; Fletcher, 1992). This writer also helps readers construct a mental model of the situation by providing details on the series of events preceding the narrator's big moment.

The next example of the effective use of punctuation, this time ellipses, should resonate with anyone who has heard the almost mandatory pause announcers make before naming a winner. The young writer of "Suddenly, she heard the announcer say" (opposite) wants the dialog to be authentic and uses punctuation toward this end.

"Surfing on some Fun" offers another example of a writer using ellipses, this time for a different effect. The ellipses signal the end of one thing and the start of something else, something more significant for the writer—the final school bell before Christmas break. Ellipses do not seem to intimidate young writers. In fact, they seem to use them correctly in most cases and, sometimes, with aplomb: As one young writer

Suddenly, she heared the announcer say, "Holy cow! We have a winner! The winner is..... Patricia ▓▓▓ from ▓▓▓ Junior High!" Patricia lifted herself out of the water and yelled, "I did it! I did it! Wahoo!" Somebody handed her a shiny trophy. The crowd went wild, cheering her name, "Patricia! Patricia!" they screamed. "Thank you!" she shouted back. She had never been so proud.

Surfing on some Fun

01/04/02

It all started with a "Yippee!" and a "Harray!" from my fellow classmates when the relieving sound of the 3:00 bell rang in the classrooms with an echoe following close behind. We all rushed out the door, pushing and shoving eachother playfully without even bothering to push in our chairs. It was the end of quizes, pencil-sharpeners, and squeaky desks opening and closing... and the beginning of a long, relaxing Christmas break, and the beginning of "Mommy, Mommy, I ate too much turkey and gravy!"
"Well, tough luck!"
My backpack felt as light as though I were carrying a butterfly on my shoulder.

wrote, "Ellipses are...you know...a way of slowing a reader down...making him pause."

All three of these examples, because they lead readers through the text and because they create a sense of authenticity, illustrate how strategies can be useful for creating both a textbase and a mental model.

Paragraphing   Strunk and White (1999) describe the paragraph as "a convenient unit." Hence, a writer who uses paragraphs correctly helps readers chunk units of meaning relating to a single topic. Students who produce expository text also frequently use paragraphs to signal the move from one major topic to another. Paragraphs have no explicitly prescribed length; they are generally long enough to develop a single idea or to create a linkage or transition between ideas. (For examples from student writing, see Chapter 7.)

ENGAGING READERS WITH WORDS

Word choice is significant on a number of levels (Beck, McKeown, & Kucan, 2002; National Writing Project

Chocolate Blackberry Truffliets

I am a truffle sort of person. I love See's candy and I beg my dad to make homemade ones. So since he still almost never makes them, and I knew my parents wouldn't spend a bunch of money on candy, a couple of weeks ago I decided to try to invent some of my own. And I ended up with what I dubbed Chocolate Blackberry Truffliets.(I came up with the word "truffliet" after thinking that they were "a little variation on truffles." Since adding "et" to the end of a word usually means it is a little version of that word, I thought if I added an "i" to that ending it would be a "variation on little." So if you think about it backwards enough it literally means (sort of) "little variation on truffles."

So since I had a recipe (and a name for it), I could make delicious candy whenever I wanted too.And now so can you!!!

北 Ai 季 爱 ought to be my name but my mother and father calls me Bǎo Bāo (that means baby in Chinese.) I was living in China, and my family only knew a little bit of English. One day while I was playing on the slide, I glanced at my parents. They were sitting on a wooden bench. Their faces were urgent and it looked as if they were having a serious convorsation. Two weeks later, my mommy said our family would be going to America soon.

& Nagin, 2006; Smith, 1996; Williams & Hufnagel, 2005). Word choice makes meaning explicit, paints pictures in readers' minds, and establishes a writer's credentials. We discuss each of these in turn.

Consider the introduction to a piece of functional writing entitled "Chocolate Blackberry Truffliets" (above), in which the writer explains the meaning of "truffliets" and uses the stem of that word to give readers insight into her personality.

All word choice is not so deliberate, of course, but careful word choice is of fundamental importance in painting an exact picture. In "Ji Ai ought to be my name…," the writer helps readers understand that what she's describing is more than just a typical adult conversation. The word *urgent* cues readers that the conversation is indeed serious, and it is exactly the right word to help readers imagine the expressions on the parents' faces.

The appropriate use of specialized vocabulary demonstrates students' understanding of concepts and validates their expertise. An integrated science program known as CORI (Concept-Oriented Reading Instruction) requires students to use science vocabulary in their writing (Guthrie & Cox, 1998; Guthrie et al., 2004; Swan, 2003). CORI specifies the reading that students do to gather information. Students use planning sheets to scaffold their understanding of sci-

ence concepts. Then students must list certain scientific terms and define them in their own words. These words become part of the classroom conversation, which students are expected to weave into a cumulative writing assignment. "Different Interactions in the Grasslands" is a sample of student writing from the CORI program.

Different Interactions in the Grasslands

There are many other interactions in the grasslands. Along with other interactions, there are other interaction types.

One type of interaction is **predation**. **Predation** is when one animal gets a benefit and the other one dies. The lion and the rabbit are an example of **predation**. The lion hunts and eats the rabbits that live there.

Another type of interaction type is **parasitism**. **Parasitism** means that one animal gets a benefit and the other gets a negative. An example of a **parasitism** relationship is the impala and ticks. The ticks come and suck the impala's blood. The impala doesn't die but it looses some blood.

In "The first days at the school...," the writer uses the word *dog* to build cohesion and move readers through the sentences. Notice also the substitution *its* for *dog* in the second sentence.

> The first days at the school may be hard for the young dog. Within a few days the dog trainer becomes it's new best friend. Dogs really do get attached to people fast. The two are together most of the time, at the kennel, and sometimes at the trainer's house. Soon the dog is having a fine time playing "training games". Training is always made fun. I wonder what training games are? A guide dog has to like it's work. During training the dog gets used to wearing a harness. With the harness around the dog's body the dog is taught to pull forward while walking on the left side and ahead of the trainer. It usually takes a guide dog several days to learn to stop at each curb and wait for a command, to go forward or to turn. Training a guide dog is a lot more complicated than I thought.

SENTENCE STRUCTURE

Notice the syntactic variety of "The Author and His Literature," a fifth-grade writer's piece. He is comparing books he read for an author study. Much of what he says reflects scaffolded learning. The sentence structure, however, with all its richness and variety, is entirely his own. One sentence flows from another; the logic of the text and the structure of the sentences and fragments support the meaning.

> The Author and His Literature
> By ▬▬▬▬▬
>
> Have you ever read one of Roald Dahl's books? The Witches? Charlie and the Chocolate Factory? Matilda? Well, in case you haven't, I'll tell you a little bit about them. For one thing, all of the main characters are kids. Charlie, Matilda, or the grandson. But these aren't just any ordinary kids. These kids are geniuses, orphans, even witchophiles. And now you're probably thinking, what in the world is a witchophile? Well, a witchophile is a real expert on witches. They know how to identify a witch, what to do when you see one, and other important facts. In this case, the witchophile is the grandson in The Witches. His grandmother filled him in on all the important witch things you need to know. In Matilda, the genius in the story is Matilda. Charlie is not necessarily an orphan, but he is extremely poor in Charlie and the Chocolate Factory.

Writer Strategies That Help Readers Build a Mental Model

Helping readers build a mental model requires writers to decide how much and what kind of detail will make text come alive for readers and enable them to relate to at least some part of it (Kintsch & van Dijk, 1978). Consider the Harry Potter series that captured the imaginations of readers both young and old. Most readers can describe Harry's school (Hogwarts), his guardians (the Dursleys), and his friend Hagrid, all with great consistency and little or no effort. To bring this fantasy world to life, to make it intelligible and real, author J.K. Rowling had to select just the right details—including details readers would relate to—and decide what could be left unsaid. Rowling used enough detail to create a realistic imaginary world for her audience. She used a school as her primary setting to "ground" her readers, most of whom were of school age. She counted on her readers' familiarity with teachers, good and bad, and classmates (again, good and bad) to help readers enter her fantasy world and imagine other details. So, though the action is fantasy, readers can "buy into" the story because there's enough real-world knowledge they can bring to bear.

As we described in Chapter 2, readers work to comprehend text by simultaneously developing a textbase and building a mental model. The textbase is developed from the words, phrases, and sentences on the page—that is, from the actual text. The mental model, however, draws as well from the richness of readers' knowledge and experiences. Thus, writer strategies that help readers connect their own knowledge and experience (including texts they have read on the same or a related topic) with the ideas, characters, or events in the text are most helpful in enabling them to build a mental model. Among these strategies are providing sufficient and adequate detail; creating a context or background readers can relate to; incorporating analogies, similes, metaphors, and visuals; and, to some degree, building in sufficiency and predictability.

USING DETAILS TO ESTABLISH A CONTEXT OR BACKGROUND

Writers must decide how much background knowledge they need to provide in order to help readers understand or relate to a topic, a point of view, or a narrative sequence, for example. "The Potato War" has an opening that leads readers into a series of events by establishing a detailed setting and hinting at the story

The Potato War

In the summer when I came to my grandma's house, it was time to harvest the potatoes in her back yard that she grew. The yard was huge and colorful with many green plants. Beautiful flowers grew on the bushes. But the potato garden stuck out the most. It was a big dirt field, only speckled with some green. And there was a big white wall that seperated her yard from her neighbors.

My dad and the other adults harvested the good potatoes and left the bruised or young potatoes behind. After the adults were gone, as I looked at the remaining potatoes on the dirt, I felt an opportunity coming on. Even though my mother warned me to not play on the field, my big brother Micheal, my cousin Sandrew, and I decided to ignore my mother's warning.

to come. Notice how the writer paints a picture of the setting for readers and at the same time deftly insinuates the action to follow and the persona of the narrator: "I felt an opportunity coming on."

USING DETAILS TO BRING A CHARACTER TO LIFE

In "My Grandpa," the writer introduces his grandpa as "cool." He goes on to provide the details that for him comprise the definition of cool. This young writer clearly knows his grandfather well. He selects one word to characterize him for his readers and then paints a picture of this individual made up not of physical characteristics but of actions that exemplify "cool." *Cool* is a familiar concept that will resonate with most readers.

My Grandpa

My grandpa was the coolest grandpa in the world. He was in good shape, he had a motorcycle, and he was the best video game player ever! I went to his house all the time and played video games, ate bar-b-que wings, and played catch.

Player   By
His hoves pound against the ground thump, thump, thump. They sound like a person knocking on a door. His mighty body moves aggressively. He breaths with a mighty snort. His tail whips in the misty air. He is as black as the empty midnight sky. The spot above his tail is the color of a doves wing.

In "Player," the writer describes his horse in such a way that readers can understand not just the horse's appearance but also his character. This is a powerful horse. He's aggressive and awe inspiring. The writer's inclusion of details helps readers form a strong image. Several verb choices suggest power as well: *pound, break, whip*. And the writer uses a simile, *as black as the empty midnight sky*, to paint an explicit picture in the reader's mind.

USING DETAILS TO SCAFFOLD AND SUPPORT READERS' UNDERSTANDING

"Grownup Dingoes are 5 feet tall…" shows a writer using details to help readers understand precisely the size of a dingo both by providing measurement and by referencing a more familiar animal (the German Shepherd) to make the image explicit.

Grownup Dingoes are 5 feet tall, and their tail is 14 inches, and they mostly weight 45 pounds. If you measured one of it's shoulder, it is smaller than a German Shepherd. Their food is mostly awake at night so they hunt at night. A Dingo's diet is farm animals, rabbits, Kangaroos, and small marsupials. They hunt in packs like horses

There are four kinds of tornadoes: weak tornadoes, strong tornadoes, violent tornadoes, and waterspouts. A weak tornado is a tornado that has winds 112 miles per hour or less. Weak tornadoes are the most common. Strong tornadoes have winds travelling from 113 to 206 mph. Only about 1/4 of the tornadoes reported in the United States each year are strong. Violent tornadoes have winds travelling from 207 to 300 mph. Only about 1 out of 50 tornadoes in the United States are classified as violent. Waterspouts are tornadoes that form over water, or move from land to sea. If they start in the ocean, and come onto land, they can send down showers of salty rain.

The details in "There are four kinds of tornadoes" are also very specific and communicate to readers a wealth of information, some of which should strike a familiar chord. In a second tornado piece, the writer describes what the approach of a tornado might look like. While this lacks the technical data of the previous piece, the quality of the description make readers feel as though the writer is actually there, observing the tornado's approach. Hence, the writer helps create a mental model by using details in a different way.

> It's late in the afternoon on a hot day. The air is thick and moist. Tall, fluffy clouds appear in the sky, and as they move toward you you can see the dark undersides. As they day goes on, the air cools and the sky turns into a weird, yellowish glow. A wind starts to blow getting stronger every minute. Soon enough, the wind starts whipping your hair against your cheeks. A piece of paper goes sailing through the air. Tree branches bend, leaves and weeds fly through the air. A tunnelish shape comes down from the clouds and touches down. It starts tearing apart everything in it's path, and flinging things in the air. It's time you took shelter, because a tornado is heading your way.

It's difficult to believe this text is wholly original. We can't be certain, but in this case, the writer's teacher says it is fairly typical of the young writer who turned it in.

Most of the time, we are less skeptical about authorship because students at grades 4 and 5 are novice writers. "The One, the Only, Great America" is one young writer's description of an amusement park. Even though

The One, the Only, Great America
by ████████

I get out of the humongous parking lot and then I walk into the 100 acre Great America and it is heavenly. The sun beams down on me, I smell fried food, I see the giant pond in front of me. There are bright flowers next to the pond to greet me. There's a slight breeze in my face. The fast rides zoom in front of me click-clacking and whooshing past the giant, chattering crowd.

we're not certain this piece is wholly original either, we question it less because the topic and tone are typical of upper elementary students. The details this writer chose to include will resonate with other students his age.

USING DIALOGUE TO DEVELOP CHARACTERS

In a fictional exchange involving "a girl named Amanda," a student writer uses dialogue to illustrate character (see next page). Notice how the writer provides additional clues to Amanda's character through further description of her interactions with the writer: "She glared at me...and then she sniggered."

A girl named Amanda (a 5ᵗʰ grader) said, "Were watching this? I've watched this before and I have the movie at home." "And," she continued, "it's not really good for young children like you." She glared at me, and I shivered, and then she sniggered. She is one of my worst enemies. I told the teacher and he told me to ignore her. I was just about to ask what ignore meant, but I did not want him to think I was unintelligent. One of the stories I remember from the movie was about a witch.

Food

Fact: Dolphins two main emenys are the shark and killer whale.

If you see a dolphin and it zooms right by you it might be looking for food. Bottle Nose Dolphins mostly eat fish and squid. Dolphins can catch up to 10 to 20 pounds of food each day. A dolphin might be swimming and see a flock of hunting birds, then it would know were the fish are.

The Body

Using Visuals to Amplify Text

Visuals present readers with specific information that expands or clarifies or recasts the information in connected text. As such, they aid readers in constructing a mental model. Students in fourth and fifth grades frequently see visuals in the printed and online texts that they read. Most of these students are comfortable inserting visuals in their own writing (Kress & Van Leeuwen, 2006; Paillotet et al., 2000).

In the "Food" example, the writer uses both a visual and a formatting technique to provide detail for her readers. The drawing is minimally labeled; the interesting additional information is boxed to draw attention to it. "The Body," which accompanies a writer's prose on rabbits, gives readers additional information through the labeling provided. Notice that this drawing is less anthropomorphized (it has been given fewer human qualities) than the preceding drawing of the smiling squid and fish. "A Prairie Food Web" (facing page) is the most technical of the three. Here, the writer displays the relationships among various creatures.

A Prairie Food Web

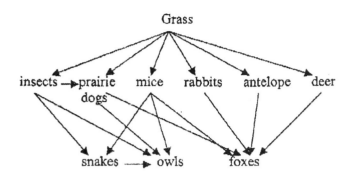

MAKING USE OF WRITER STRATEGIES

The strategies illustrated in the preceding pages are at least "pretty good" examples from typical students. However, they are snippets from papers whose overall quality is not uniform; that is, the whole of these texts is not necessarily equally accomplished.

It is important to recognize that for fourth and fifth graders, strategies may be well done, done too rarely, or, as in "Hope," overdone. In this case, the use of detail, with its repeating scenarios of dire situations, overwhelms readers. But at least the writer has made an attempt to use a strategy (repetition), and that is one of the first steps in becoming an accomplished writer.

Finally, consider this reflection by a fourth-grade writer at the end of the year:

> In my writing I use tension, some transition words, colorful language, and some strong words and I make pictures in peoples minds.

Here is a writer who clearly understands the needs of her audience.

Hope

My cat, Hope, has been missing for three weeks. We were going to put up flyers, but we didn't have any pictures of her. Each day I hoped that Hope would come back. I keep on wondering; has she been run over by a car and lying on the ground flatend with her blood and other body parts lying around her? Has Hope been eaten by a dog and barely alive with about only two more hours to live, sitting in a bush, curled up and hiding in fear?

Is Hope hiding in a field living off mice and snakes crouching down with her razor sharp claws out ready to pounce on a fat mouse only a few feet away waiting for it to get a little bit closer so she can kill it for her meal? Is she so hungry that she doesn't have the energy to find her way home, and so skinny that she has her ribs showing like they are trying to pop out?

Has Hope been beaten with rocks and sticks and lying there with an eye poked out, bones broken, and bleeding? Is she so badly hurt that she can barely move and has to recover before she comes back home?

Is she hiding somewhere with newly born kittens and preparing to attack any sort of danger lurking in the dark waiting for her to leave her kittens for one minute and steal one to eat it for its supper?

Hope had been gone for 3 weeks. My mind was full of terrible possibilities.

6

Reading and Writing With Understanding in School

[G]uiding one's learning in a particular subject area requires awareness of the disciplinary standards for knowing. To illustrate, asking the question "What is the evidence for this claim?" is relevant whether one is studying history, science, or mathematics. However, what counts as evidence often differs. In mathematics, for example, formal proof is very important. In science, formal proofs are used when possible, but empirical observations and experimental data also play a major role. In history, multiple sources of evidence are sought and attention to the perspective from which an author writes and to the purpose of the writing is particularly important. Overall, knowledge of the discipline one is studying affects people's abilities to monitor their own understanding and evaluate others' claims effectively.

——M. Suzanne Donovan and John D. Bransford, *How Students Learn: History, Mathematics, and Science in the Classroom*

Why do we read and write? These are the questions we started with. We come back to them now and approach them from a fresh angle.

Yes, we read for comic relief or solace or thrills. We read for information, knowledge, and understanding. And each of these grand purposes leads to another reason we read: to think deeply about ideas that emerge when we dig our minds into texts. This is different from figuring out what the text contains and what it means. This is taking the essence of comprehension into the realm of interpretation and exploration.

Likewise, we write to express ourselves, to communicate, and to demonstrate what we know. We try to write within a framework, or genre, that conveys understanding of our audience, purpose, and topic. We also write to interpret and explore the connections among the facts and information we accumulate as we learn and to think critically about how this new knowledge illuminates our conceptual understanding.

This is the kind of thinking that fourth and fifth graders should be challenged to take on. Success in school requires intellectual flexibility and critical judgment. Interpreting and exploring texts—their content as well as their form—are good ways for students to develop this prowess.

RICH POSSIBILITIES, NOT A CHECKLIST

This chapter is rich with possibilities for reading and writing in fourth and fifth grades. We cover a lot of ground. However, this is not a checklist. We do not expect every student to be able to read or write texts in every genre, in every academic subject, every year.

Not only would this be overwhelming, if not impossible, it would run counter to a central tenet of this book: that students must learn to read with deep comprehension and write clearly and effectively. This takes time. In some cases, it makes sense to linger on and revisit new, unfamiliar genres—genres that matter tremendously in school—so students have a chance to gain mastery in them.

Still, it is reasonable to expect that over the course of these two years, fourth and fifth graders will explore many genres in their academic subjects. States and school districts differ in their requirements for students. The ideas in this chapter can be used to enrich teaching and learning of these requirements.

We realize that some of the reading and writing we describe in this chapter will be new ways of learning for fourth and fifth graders. Indeed, the learning we describe is more frequently associated with upper grades. We believe fourth and fifth graders are ready to begin learning in these ways, but we expect novice levels of performance, given students' age and maturity.

Literacy and Learning in Each Academic Subject

By fourth and fifth grades, reading and writing in school are almost always connected to *learning* in academic subjects. Yet most literacy programs do not pay much attention to the differences between reading a novel in English language arts and a textbook in science. Nor do they consider the differences between writing a report in history and a report in science. Even reasonably good students struggle in fourth and fifth grades because they don't understand that the point of reading and writing, and the kinds of texts and the topics of inquiry, vary considerably from subject to subject. But interpretation and exploration hinge on these differences. As Hirsch (2006) points out, "While it is true that proficient reading and critical thinking are all-purpose activities, they are not content-independent formal skills at all but are based on concrete, relevant knowledge and cannot be exercised apart from what psychologists call domain-specific knowledge."

Strong readers and writers approach texts through the lens of academic subjects, using their knowledge of literature, history, science, or mathematics to shape their understanding of new ideas and information. They carry in their minds the big ideas, questions, and issues that arise in these subjects. For savvy readers and writers, these points of view shape comprehension, written expression, conceptual understanding, and knowledge acquisition. Further, these points of view enable students to interpret and explore texts *in the context of what matters in different academic subjects*.

APPROACHING TEXTS ACROSS DISCIPLINES

Heller and Greenleaf (2007) list discipline-specific ways of approaching texts:

1. Translating real-world things and events into mathematical symbols
2. Focusing on the historical circumstances in which the text was written
3. Maintaining an objective voice in science description
4. Studying the relationship between form and content in literature

Most fourth and fifth graders are novices at reading and writing with this mindset. After all, they are only beginning to experience school life that is organized around different academic teachers, subjects, and texts. But now is the time for them to begin to learn.

This mindset is not entirely new. Many schools offer special programs in which students are taught to think like a historian, see life like a scientist, become a mathematician or a writer. These programs are valuable and should be part of everyday classroom learning for all students.

Reading and writing are not the only ways that students will learn academic content, of course. Students should be engaged in *doing* history, science,

and mathematics—engaging in discussion, doing science experiments and projects, for example. But fourth and fifth graders need to begin learning to comprehend grade-level, subject matter texts, and that means cracking the *knowledge codes* that characterize their academic subjects.

Reading and Writing in English Language Arts

Why do we read literature?

● For the "story": the setting, plot, characters, conflict, theme, suspense, resolution

UNDERSTANDING HOW STUDENTS LEARN

In the influential report *How People Learn: Bridging Research and Practice*, Donovan, Bransford, and Pellegrino (1999) highlighted three fundamental and well-established principles of learning, which are highly relevant to reading and writing:

1. Students come to the classroom with **preconceptions** about how the world works. If their initial understanding is not engaged, they may fail to grasp new concepts and information, or they may learn these new materials for purposes of a test but then revert to their preconceptions outside the classroom.
2. To develop competence in an area of inquiry, students must (a) have a deep foundation of **factual knowledge**, (b) understand facts and ideas in the context of a **conceptual framework**, and (c) **organize knowledge** in ways that facilitate retrieval and application.
3. A **"metacognitive" approach** to instruction can help students learn to take control of their own learning by defining learning goals and monitoring their progress in achieving them.

In 2005, the National Research Council released a follow-up report, *How Students Learn: History, Mathematics, and Science in the Classroom* (Donovan & Bransford, 2005), which stresses "disciplinary standards of knowing" as crucial factors in learning.

Learning is a lifelong process of transforming limited, random, and personal understanding of the world into formal or scientific bodies of knowledge within socially recognized fields of study. These bodies of knowledge are known as *disciplines* and *domains*—in other words, subject matter or

content knowledge. Disciplines typically refer to broad subjects, such as literature, history, science, and mathematics. Domains are branches of knowledge within disciplines, such as biology within science, which also include specific fields of study, such as microbiology or genetics.

Researcher Patricia Alexander (1998) describes the learning process like this:

As a young child, I understood that the bright, round object in the sky is what those around me called the sun. Not only was my conceptual knowledge of the sun limited at this age, but it was also very unscientific and unexamined. Later, I learned more about this heavenly sphere as part of my education both in and out of school. Simultaneously, I learned more about my own planet and about other bodies and forces that exist in the universe. Likewise, I began to sense the relationship between and among these concepts. As this process transpired, my conceptual knowledge of sun, in effect, became part of an emerging body of knowledge in the domain of astrophysics.

For most people, acquiring domain knowledge requires not just everyday experience but also systematic instruction that addresses students' misconceptions, builds factual and conceptual understanding, and gives students discipline-specific strategies for monitoring their understanding. In this way, students can connect their concrete experiences to mental representations of these experiences and eventually to abstract concepts.

SCAFFOLDING STUDENTS' LEARNING

Scaffolding, which refers to the kinds of assistance teachers provide to help students learn, is a useful instructional model for teaching students to read and write in the content areas. Scaffolding is a practical way to take advantage of what scholar Lev Vygotsky (1986) termed the "zone of proximal development," or the instructional space that is just beyond—but not too far beyond—what students know and can do. The idea is for teachers to adjust their instructional approaches, classroom routines, and supports to challenge and assist, but not frustrate, students. Scaffolding encourages students to strive for goals they may not be able to reach entirely on their own.

Scaffolding suggests instruction "to produce appropriate understanding of a particular problem for a learner at a particular level of ability" (Rogoff & Gardner, 1990). Teachers start out teaching a new topic or skill by providing students with exemplary models, structured guidance, and supported opportunities to practice. Scaffolds are flexible but temporary supports. As students become more proficient, teachers gradually reduce their extra assistance (Wood, Bruner, & Ross, 1976). Eventually, students take more ownership of their new knowledge and skills.

As Pearson and his colleagues characterize it, thoughtful scaffolding by teachers allows students to use a process "before they fully understand it while they gradually gain control of it" (Pearson, Roehler, Dole, & Duffy, 1992).

- For insight into ourselves, our feelings, and our experiences
- For insight about humanity and the world
- For the language
- For the form
- For pleasure

What literary genres should we expect fourth and fifth graders to write?

- Literary narratives, such as fiction and nonfiction stories and personal accounts
- Arguments, such as literary essays and position papers
- Poetry

Interpreting and Exploring Literary Narratives

We read literature to understand the text. Unlike reading in any other academic subject, literature demands close attention not just to content, but to language—word choice, turns of phrase, and style, for example. The way writers tell their stories and bring readers to think about the world is as important as the story itself.

In fourth and fifth grades, students should be reading and writing literary narratives, both fiction and nonfiction, in their English language arts classes. Literary narratives typically explore the human condition in the world—characters' interactions, goals, motivations, and conflicts, and the ways in which these play out for characters in different settings and situations. Stories mix the real with the imaginary, the plain with the fantastic. They also reflect various settings, time periods, and styles of writing.

Literary narratives are rich with interpretive possibilities. This is true even at the elementary grades. Good children's literature is real literature. It deals with the great themes and exhibits finely wrought elements of craft. This genre is familiar to students. They have listened to and read literary narratives for several years. They have worked to comprehend these kinds of texts, both enjoying them and appreciating their quality. And, with the assistance of their teacher, they have explored the literary themes and elements that distinguish children's literature.

Consider *Hatchet*. To comprehend the story, students must understand that most of Brian's adventures take place in the harsh Canadian wilderness. To interpret the story, students might focus intently on this setting. With their teacher's guidance, they might explore such questions as What role does the setting play in this story? Why did the author pick this place for Brian to be stranded? How does Brian react, respond, and adapt to this setting as the story advances?

Guided by their teacher, students also might wonder what the author is trying to accomplish in *Hatchet*, exploring such questions as What is this book really trying to say about Brian? What insights about him and his adventures does the author want us to come away with? Is "the secret" important? Is this a man-against-nature story or a coming-of-age story—or both?

Students might attend to the language of *Hatchet*, exploring such questions as Are there words, sentences, or passages that are pivotal or memorable in this book? Is the author's style effective?

And students might want to broaden their exploration of *Hatchet* by taking its measure against other stories as part of author or genre studies: How does *Hatchet* compare with other books by Gary Paulsen? How do different authors handle man-against-nature or coming-of-age stories?

Note that all of these questions are open ended and none have simple answers. Matters of interpretation in literature, by their nature, imply multiple, different, individual, and nuanced points of view. Yet interpretation still must be based on the text, and students need to use evidence from the text to support their assertions.

Writing Effective Literary Narratives

Fourth and fifth graders should write both fiction and nonfiction narratives and personal accounts as they explore literature and become fluent in the literary narrative genre. (For examples of well-done narratives by children at these grade levels, see Chapter 7.)

Writing literary narratives enables students to use story as a means of transforming their personal experiences into useful, conceptual knowledge about literature and literary narratives. They can explore narrative structures and use literary language to shape their own insights into themselves, other people, and the larger world. These are the "big ideas" of literature that students can make their own in English language arts assignments.

STORIES AND PERSONAL ACCOUNTS: DEVELOPING A SENSE OF NARRATIVE

Fiction stories, nonfiction stories, and personal accounts give students the opportunity to try their hand at creating the narrative. Literary writing is different from writing in many other genres in that it requires students to use narrative elements and literary language designed to evoke particular responses in readers. The language, in fact, is paramount in literature. This is what sets literature apart from other disciplines, where the emphasis is typically on the information rather than on the expression of that information.

HELPING STUDENTS READ LITERATURE IN ENGLISH LANGUAGE ARTS

Addressing misconceptions. Many fourth and fifth graders believe that the point of reading literature is simply to get through the text and then slot the text into a known category as they build an understanding of the plot and identify characters as protagonists or antagonists. Instead, they need to learn that literature is often timeless; the writer expects the reader to understand that the characters are generally typical of people everywhere, that *this* will always happen as a result of *that*, and so on.

Building a conceptual understanding. Fourth and fifth graders should learn to question the structure and the language for what is said—and what is left unsaid—in literary narratives and poetry. Are there important lessons about how people should live their lives? What does the author have to say about common literary themes, such as good and evil, fate and human choices, survival, or coming of age? How do the characters change—or resist

change—as they struggle through life? Are the characters believable? What other books have similar characters or themes?

Using metacognitive strategies. Fourth and fifth graders need to learn to read, and sometimes reread, the text carefully, examining the accumulated evidence of story or poetic structure and language to discover deeper meanings that are explicit or implied. Students need to go beyond an understanding of the textbase and even the mental model, probing the text and their own minds with a sense of discovery. They might learn to ask themselves such questions as What can I take away from this text? What does the author want me to think about? Why does this character make this choice? How would I react in this situation? What does the author mean with these words? Can I find evidence in the text to support my understanding of what the author wants to convey?

Although as readers they are more familiar with this genre than others, many elementary students struggle to write stories. Stories are hard to craft—and harder to perfect. Writing fiction that creates a believable imaginary world for readers, characters who seem lifelike while they are grappling with conflict, an ending that emerges logically from the story line—this is difficult for professional writers, much less fourth and fifth graders, to bring off. With nonfiction stories, organizing a collection of events and focusing only on those that have significance is challenging. Saying it all just right while attending to literary elements that fourth and fifth graders are still learning to control makes writing hard work. These challenges often require students to revisit and revise their stories again and again to make them worth reading.

On the other hand, most students can use their imaginations and experiences, their familiarity with genre structure, and the writing strategies of their favorite authors to shape their stories. By reading widely and using familiar stories as models, students can develop ideas for their own writing.

Because fictional stories can be difficult for students to write, teachers frequently ask students to draw from their own experiences as the basis for their writing. When students use what they know best—their own experience—as their subject matter, they are free to focus on structure and craft to develop conceptual knowledge of this literary genre.

Personal accounts are similar to stories in that they have a narrative structure and employ the stylistic elements of narratives. But personal accounts are not necessarily built around the conflict–resolution structure that is fundamental to stories. Students often choose to write about events that stand out in their minds as important, such as getting a shot at the doctor's office, starting in a new school, or learning a new skill. These events don't necessarily involve conflict.

Students who write exceptional stories or personal accounts are often avid readers who draw on their knowledge of literature and narratives to create effective pieces that reflect their own style and point of view.

Understanding the Narrative Genre and Narrative Elements

The conceptual knowledge that students need to write fiction stories, nonfiction stories, and personal accounts is an understanding of the narrative genre, and they need agility in using a range of narrative elements effectively.

Stories and personal accounts push students to structure their pieces with clear beginnings, middles, and ends. Fourth and fifth graders typically omit irrelevant incidents that do not contribute to the narrative. Instead, they organize their pieces around a focal event, establish a context for the piece, and develop a story line or plot.

Within this narrative framework, students can create dramatic openings or leads that set the stage for the text that follows. They can take a decided point of view, provide evocative descriptions and details to develop plots and characters, and provide a sense of closure to end their stories, using such literary techniques as a short, telling sentence, a reflection, or a surprise.

Students who read widely or who have been provided with explicit instruction also can use a range of literary strategies to develop their narratives, including foreshadowing, flashbacks, monologue, dialogue, dialect, pacing, and literary language.

Putting Concepts Into Practice: Writing Processes for Literary Narratives

The quality of thinking, validity of content, and clarity of expression are important in every academic subject. However, in the English language arts classroom, there is a further, significant consideration: the felicity of expression. Unlike writing in any other academic discipline, writing processes in English language arts should reflect this demand. Let's consider how students can tailor their writing processes to write a literary narrative.

Planning.   Students who are familiar with the characteristics of narrative writing might begin planning a fiction narrative by thinking through the pivotal event or problem and the series of episodes that will make up the story and then sketching them out on a timeline. They also should think through their characters and have an idea of the nature of the people they want to create. They should make decisions about whether the setting is important and, if so, think through what that real or imaginary place or time period is like. They should identify the narrator (or narrators) and decide the perspective from which they tell their story.

Students may find it helpful to talk through their ideas with their teacher or peers. Making notes may or may not be an important part of planning, but identifying a starting point and ending for the piece will keep fourth and fifth graders from taking on too much or having a hard time closing the story.

Drafting.   With a plan sketched out on paper or in their minds, students will have idiosyncratic ways of drafting their stories. Some students will write the story "in order," with an initiating event, then events that follow, developing their characters as they move through their text. Some students will write the climactic action first because that is the event they have clearest in their minds, then work backward to craft an opening and subsequent events that build the plot.

At this stage, students should feel free to let their ideas flow, experiment with different ways of developing characters and plots, and incorporate language that feels right to them. There may be several rounds of drafting as students refine their story structures, plots, and characters. Students' knowledge of the narrative genre will help them draft their pieces—they should know in general how a story progresses.

Revising. To revise, students should work to refine the story line where necessary, providing details that will help a reader imagine the world created in the story and envision the characters and events. They should pay attention to whether their dialogue rings true and is effective in revealing character or in moving the story forward. They should work at this stage to craft the story by lifting the level of language with imagery, pacing, varied syntactic patterns, and so on—the kinds of literary strategies that will elevate their pieces and set them apart to meet the expectations of writing in English language arts. In short, they should make the quality of their writing as polished as possible.

Editing. The editing that students should do for a literary narrative includes attention to correctness: use of conventions, punctuation, and capitalization. Special attention should also go to the traditional problems that accompany paragraphing and the use of dialogue.

Exploring Poetry: Its Structure and Literary Elements

Poetry, like fiction, concerns itself with expressing many different aspects of experience. The language, however, is more condensed and figurative than the language of fiction. Moreover, both the structure and language of poetry are vital parts of its message.

Poetic structure is not as neatly defined as comparable text structures for narrative or informational texts. In fact, some poems, such as epics or descriptive poems, share features with narratives and informational texts. Nevertheless, three structural features typically occur in poetic language: line structure, stanza structure, and rhythm or meter (Friedrich, 1986; Friedrich & Dil, 1979; Tannen, 1989). At a minimum, fourth and fifth graders can learn to recognize these structures as a cue that they are reading a poetic text.

LINE STRUCTURE

The line (rather than the sentence) is the fundamental organizational unit of poems. Sentences within poems often are broken up into two or more lines to achieve particular rhetoric and aesthetic effects. In Gary Snyder's poem "April" from *Left Out in the Rain,* for example, one sentence is organized into three short lines:

> I lay on my back
> Watching the sun through the
> Net glitter of your gold hair.

This line structure has the effect of encouraging readers to process three distinct images rather than a single scene.

STANZA STRUCTURE

Lines in poetry typically are organized into stanzas rather than paragraphs. Much like lines, stanzas tend to mark the content within them as both distinct from and related to that of adjacent stanzas. In another poem by Gary Snyder, "This Poem Is for Bear" from *Myths and Texts,* two boys experience the same event—the arrival of a bear—in different ways:

> Kai was alone by the pond in the dusk. He heard
> a grunt and felt, he said, his hair tingle.
> He jumped on a bike and high-tailed it down
> the trail, to some friends.
> Scott stood alone in the dark by the window. Clicked
> on his flashlight and there out the window, six
> inches away, were the eyes of a bear.

The images, sensations, suspense, and surprise conjured up by this poem depend to a large extent on the line and stanza organization.

RHYTHM OR METER

Rhythm or meter refer to the pattern of continually repeating sound units in poems. Metric patterns can be very complex, but even fourth and fifth graders can get a sense of meter from a poem like William Blake's famous "Tyger! Tyger!" Here's a stanza from this poem:

> Tyger! Tyger! burning bright
> in the forest of the night,
> What immortal hand or eye
> Dare frame thy fearful symmetry?

The meter in this stanza consists of one long, accented syllable followed by one short, unstressed syllable, a style that establishes a definite "beat" for readers.

Figurative or poetic language is rooted in natural language, but it differs from everyday oral language in degree, in that poets use forms that are a bit different than natural language patterns, and in intent, in that poets attend carefully to the effects and richness of meaning of their words. Three basic linguistic processes characterize figurative language: intensification of form, imagery, and analogy.

INTENSIFICATION OF FORM

Poets often use repetition and parallelism or meaning and structure to create poetic language. This poem by Walter de la Mare exemplifies how natural language is transformed to poetic language through intensification of form:

SOME ONE
Someone came knocking
At my wee, small door;
Some one came knocking,
I'm sure—sure—sure;
I listened, I opened,
I looked to left and right,
But nought there was a-stirring
In the still dark night;
Only the busy beetle
Tap-tapping in the wall,
Only from the forest
The screech-owl's call,
Only the cricket whistling
While the dew drops fall,
So I know not who came knocking,
At all, at all, at all.

The repetition of sounds within the lines (*sure—sure—sure*; *At all, at all, at all*) and the rhyming stanzas redouble this poem's effect.

IMAGERY

Imagery is another of the primary features of poetic language. Poets use detail and figurative language to convey meaning, as this poem by Lilian Moore demonstrates:

IN THE FOG
Stand still.
The fog wraps you up
and no one can find you.

Walk.
The fog opens up
to let you through
and closes behind you.

(From *I Feel the Same Way* by Lilian Moore. Copyright © 1967 by Lilian Moore. Used by permission of Marian Reiner.)

Here, the fog is a figurative coat or blanket in the first stanza and a figurative door in the second. These images encourage readers and listeners to use their knowledge of common objects to imagine the fog.

ANALOGY

Poets invite comparisons by using figures of speech such as similes, metaphors, and metonymy—that is, they use words for one thing to associate it with another. Here's a poem by Paul Fleischman, "Fireflies," meant to be read with two voices:

Light	Light
	is the ink we use
Night	Night
is our parchment	
	We're
	fireflies
fireflies	flickering
flitting	
	flashing
fireflies	
glimmering	fireflies
	gleaming
glowing	
Insect calligraphers	Insect calligraphers
practicing penmanship	
	copying sentences
Six-legged scribblers	Six-legged scribblers
of vanishing messages,	
	fleeting graffiti
Fine artists in flight	Fine artists in flight
adding dabs of light	
	bright brush strokes
Signing the June nights	Signing the June nights
as if they were paintings	as if they were paintings
	We're
flickering	fireflies
fireflies	flickering
fireflies.	fireflies.

(Text copyright © 1988 by Paul Fleischman. Used by permission of HarperCollins publishers.)

In this poem, fireflies are associated with writers and artists who create words and images in the night sky.

Together, poetic structure and language overlap in their effects, firing the imagination of readers and listeners as they respond to both the message and the language of the text.

With conceptual knowledge of the structure and literary elements of poetry, students can think about what the poem says and how the poet says it: What stands out in this poem as truthful, memorable, or surprising? What does this metaphor, symbol, or image stand for? What is the tone of the poem? (Serious? Humorous? Ironic?) Is there more than one way to read or understand this poem? How do the sounds of the poem help convey meaning? How does the form or structure of the poem contribute to its meaning? In what way does the craft of a poem support its meaning?

Writing Arguments: Using Evidence to Support Claims

Students put their disciplinary knowledge of literature to the test when they write arguments in the form of literary essays. The literary essay is one form of the argument genre that requires students to organize their writing with a claim–evidence–reasoning (warrant) structure. Literary essays, of course, are based on texts. Another form of argument frequently assigned in English language arts class is the position paper, which does not rely on texts—although it does follow the claim–evidence–reasoning pattern.

LITERARY ESSAYS: INTERPRETING AND EVALUATING TEXTS

Built on their class discussions about texts, literary essays (often called response to literature) require students to examine a text (or texts) thoughtfully, make interpretive or evaluative claims about some literary aspect of the work, and use evidence from the text and their knowledge of literature to support their claims. Effective papers in this genre demonstrate a comprehensive understanding of the work—often by providing a summary to orient readers, for example—and persuade readers to accept an interpretation or evaluation by referring to the text. The writing is evaluated on the quality of the thinking in the piece as well as by the text's clarity, coherence, and logic. Because they are writing for their English language arts classes, students may focus on the literary themes, techniques, elements, and language of the text and use literary language in their own pieces as well. When students write literary essays, they deepen their conceptual understanding of texts, authors, and genres.

PUTTING CONCEPTS INTO PRACTICE: WRITING PROCESSES FOR LITERARY ESSAYS

The writing processes for constructing an argument in the form of a literary essay in an English language arts class differ decidedly from the processes for writing a narrative. What counts most is the strength of the argument, not the literary language—although students may use literary language to make their points and assume a knowledgeable stance.

Planning. Planning a literary essay requires students to make a quality judgment, or an interpretive claim, about a text or an author: *"The BFG* is Roald Dahl's best

RESPONDING TO LITERATURE

The literary essay is a fundamental part of the curriculum, and it is assessed in many school districts and states throughout the United States. But it is important to note that it is only one of several ways that readers and writers respond to literature and only one of several encouraged by teachers in school. Responding to literature can take many different forms. For example, sometimes students are asked to develop a topic by replicating a genre form. The point is to determine if students understand the form.

Our expectations for literary essays center on the formal, written genre that follows the argument structure. In the world outside of school, this genre is realized in published reviews of books, poetry, short stories, or other texts. Reviews are judged for the writer's ability to craft thoughtful, effective, and defensible commentary—a coherent analysis that is supported by evidence.

An example of a well-done fifth-grade response to literature appears in Chapter 7.

book," for example, or "The theme of *Soda Jerk* is...." The writer takes a stand and makes a judgment.

To do that, of course, students first have to understand the literary work or author they are judging. Students must decide what they think about the text or author and must have some criteria for their evaluation. For example, if they assert that a book is "the best this author produced," they must consider What is their basis for this judgment? The plot? The interesting characters? Suspense?

Students have to zero in on a particular point they want to assert and find evidence in the text or develop evidence through research on their own that supports their claim. They may want to anticipate what kinds of evidence will be convincing to their audience.

Drafting. To draft a literary essay, students should focus on using their genre knowledge of argument, the claim–evidence–reasoning structure, to persuade their audience. They should also establish a context by making a general statement about the literary work or providing a brief summary. Their evidence should come from text citations, which are vital in a literary essay, and the evidence should be linked back to the claim. This linkage is called a *warrant*.

Students should make the structure of their argument transparent and provide readers with sufficient detail. Their stance should be knowledgeable.

Revising. To revise, students should focus on the logic of their claim and the strength of their evidence and reasoning. Is the argument structure transparent? Does it provide sufficient background information? Is the summary of the text sufficient to demonstrate understanding? Does the piece present a knowledgeable stance? How will the audience react? Does the argument anticipate and respond to counterclaims?

Editing. To edit, students should make sure their writing is clear, unambiguous, coherent, and powerful. They should read for spelling, punctuation, and conventions. Their citations should be properly punctuated and accurately worded.

Position Papers: Supporting Claims With Facts and Evidence

Students are frequently required to write a subgenre called the position paper (sometimes called a persuasive paper) for their state tests. Teaching this form of writing typically falls to the English teacher.

In position papers, writers state a position about a topic or issue and provide evidence to support their position. They can be called upon to address topics from any academic subject or topics from outside the curriculum. For example, students may be asked to argue whether global warming is destroying the environment or whether schools should extend the school year.

Whatever their topic, fourth and fifth graders can learn to state claims about issues and support their claims with evidence: examples, personal anecdotes, quotes from authorities, and so on. They can learn to write an introduction that includes a claim and some discussion of the importance of the topic; the body of the text, made up of evidence to support the claim; warrants that link the evidence logically to the claim; and a conclusion. Teachers can scaffold this learning for students.

Students must have a clear understanding of the issue to make solid claims and support them with specific evidence. Students who write effective position papers use facts and reason to influence readers. They are aware of their intended audience and attempt to anticipate and address readers' concerns.

Topics for on-demand position papers typically are very general, so not much background knowledge is required to produce them. Student writers do not have access to sources that would provide them back-

Helping Students Write Arguments in English Language Arts

Addressing misconceptions. Many fourth and fifth graders are still novices at writing arguments. A list of unelaborated reasons does not count as evidence, as many young writers think.

Building a conceptual understanding. Students need to learn how to structure an argument by making a claim, supporting it with relevant evidence from texts or from facts, and making reasonable connections (warrants) between the evidence and the claim.

Using metacognitive strategies. Students should learn to put their arguments to the test, asking themselves such questions as Have I made my claim clear? Do I have enough relevant, specific evidence—from the text or from the world—to support my claim? Does my reasoning make sense? Is this a convincing argument?

ground knowledge because the position paper is most frequently an on-demand assignment. (For more on the on-demand process, see pages 57–58.)

An important point: What counts as evidence in a position paper for English language arts differs from what counts as evidence in other subjects. For example, in English language arts, a student could cite the melting of polar ice caps as an example of global warming, using that example as acceptable evidence. In science, though, examples do not count as evidence. For more on arguments in science, see pages 86–89.

Reading and Writing in History

Why do we read history?

- To find out about the past
- To understand the world in the context of history
- To learn how historians interpret the past

What genres should we expect fourth and fifth graders to write in history?

- Arguments, such as explanations
- Historical narratives

The chronicle of time is the domain of historians. Historical knowledge encompasses historical events, themes, cultures, ideas, and people and their movements. Historians explore, analyze, and interpret the past using various sources of information.

Historians spend much of their time in close, critical reading of documents and other evidence to find out how things happened and why. Because historical evidence is often patchy and open to question, historians must make judgments about their sources. They probe texts for clues about writers' trustworthiness, motives, and perspectives; they read from multiple sources before drawing conclusions; and they maintain a healthy skepticism about claims in texts (Donovan et al., 2005; VanSledright, 2002).

With this robust approach to examining evidence, historians create stories about the past that can build a sense of community about the shared experiences of a nation or a people. They write explanations about what may have happened and why. Historical authority comes from a combination of good judgment and compelling explanations about historical evidence.

Interpreting and Exploring Historical Texts

As they read history, fourth- and fifth-grade students should approach texts in the manner of historians. In reality, most students this age and even much older tend to think that any printed, online, or authentic-looking text is true, factual, and correct. Instead, they need to learn to question who wrote the text and why. And they need to learn that no matter how much or how well they read, they might never find out the "truth" about what happened in history—although they can develop reasonable historical narratives, advance plausible explanations, and make effective arguments.

Students also need to learn to question the difference between original or copied documents and between primary and secondary sources of information. They should learn that sources are not all neutral, equal, or even credible.

Students routinely should read more than one source of information about a topic or event, which will push them to probe discrepancies, weigh credibility, examine perspectives, and make judgments about historical accounts. At times, they should engage in sustained inquiry into multiple primary and secondary sources about a topic to learn that history is the synthesis of many—often conflicting, incomplete, or biased—pieces of evidence (Donovan et al., 2005; Van Sledright, 2002).

With this mindset, students can begin to interpret and explore historical narratives and explanations. Consider a history unit on state history, which is common in fourth grade. When reading an explanation about pivotal events in their state history, students can reflect on questions such as Who wrote this and why? Is the source believable? Why? Is this a primary or secondary source? How can I tell?

These questions may be hard for fourth and fifth graders to answer. There may be no clear right answers. But simply mulling over the questions gets students reading and thinking critically—like historians.

When reading additional texts, for example, a biographical account of a famous state hero or heroine, students can question the historical record further: What happened at this point in time? What events did this historical figure put into play? How did this change history? What did different groups of people think about this person?

Reading in history feeds discussion and writing, which in turn motivate more reading. Reading cannot

---

HELPING STUDENTS READ HISTORICAL NARRATIVES AND INFORMATIONAL TEXTS

Addressing misconceptions. Many fourth and fifth graders have a naive understanding of ideas that are central to understanding history. Their sense of time focuses on their own daily or weekly schedules, not on historical dates, chronological events, or lengthy periods of time. They tend to think that historical changes occur in single, explosive events, not as a result of longer, progressive shifts that may have no grand event. They have a hard time understanding that the ideas, beliefs, and values of people and periods in history may differ from their own. They believe people cause things to happen; they don't understand that there may be an assortment of conditions—social, environmental, or industrial—that may affect history as well. And they believe that history is an accumulation of known facts rather than interpretations and explanations based on qualified evidence. Students must learn to question their assumptions about what they think they know about the past.

Building a conceptual understanding. Students must learn how historians approach history—how they develop historical narratives and explanations through careful scrutiny and judgment of many pieces of evidence. And they must learn about substantive concepts in history, such as economic, political, social, and cultural human activity. These concepts may include such ideas as *trade*, *nation*, *migration*, *treaty*, or *president*, which occur as students learn about particular topics in history.

Using metacognitive strategies. Students must learn to examine many pieces of historical evidence critically, as historians do, with questions such as Is this an eyewitness account or a secondhand account? What is this source's connection to this event? What was this source trying to accomplish? What side was this source on? Should I believe this account? Students need to learn that history is not one fixed story but many stories that may change over time as new evidence becomes available—and as our own perspectives change (Donovan et al., 2005).

---

stand alone as the source of knowledge of history, nor can history be learned without reading.

Writing Arguments: Using Evidence to Explain Historical Topics

Students write a form of argument in history known as explanation. As in all argument genres, students make claims, use evidence, and link the evidence to the claim. In history, the process of writing an explanation begins with an examination of the sources to form a judgment that is best supported by the evidence. The structure of the explanation, then, is the judgment (or claim), the evidence (from multiple sources) in support of the claim, and the link (or warrant) that explains how the evidence gives validity to the claim.

These kinds of pieces can be challenging for students, who must have an in-depth understanding of the subject matter to be able to write well about it. They must understand each piece of evidence, select evidence that is relevant to the writing prompt, and then use the evidence effectively to construct an argument that makes sense. Students need a lot of scaffolding and support to write explanations. (For examples of well-written history papers by fourth and fifth graders, see Chapter 7.)

Writing in history helps students comprehend and remember the concepts and facts they are learning through their reading and class discussions.

EXPLANATION: DEVELOPING A PERSPECTIVE AND PROVIDING EVIDENCE

For explanations in history, students provide evidence that comes from primary and secondary sources (such as textbooks, websites, videos, firsthand accounts of events, paintings, advertisements, and so on) to support their claim. Students also must learn how to explain the reasoning that connects the claim with the evidence.

In these pieces, students consider such topics as how a region's geography shapes the life of its inhabitants or perspectives on a historical event. Just as students need to have a comprehensive understanding of a chapter book to write a strong literary essay, so too must they understand a particular topic in history to write an explanation.

They also must be able to make judgments about the relevance and strength of their evidence, something that is difficult for students. They need to weigh everything they know to select the evidence that supports their claim.

To support students in this writing task, which is commonly new to fourth graders, teachers may scaffold students' understanding by providing them with the claim and helping them learn to include evidence to support the claim. Eventually, students should learn to do this work on their own.

PUTTING CONCEPTS INTO PRACTICE: WRITING PROCESSES FOR EXPLANATIONS

Planning. The planning processes for writing arguments in history amount to *learning* about history. Students must do a good bit of reading before they take on this assignment. They should study multiple sources, considering the perspectives and examining the credibility of the authors. They must understand the historical context and significance of the topic. They should examine the corroborative evidence, if any, that exists for their claim. Acquiring a deep understanding is the prerequisite for explaining or interpreting an event or change or motive in history. Based on this accumulated knowledge, students can make a claim and organize evidence to support their claim in planning to write.

Drafting. To draft an explanation, students should use the claim–evidence–reasoning structure, stating their claim clearly and making a logical, coherent argument. They should demonstrate their understanding of the topic by citing its significance and situating it in its historical context. They should cite their evidence, with direct references to sources and documents to support their claim. They should compare and contrast different perspectives from different texts, showing that they understand that history is based on judgments of evidence that may not tell a single story. They should make it clear why they believe one source, or one version, of history and not another by evaluating the sources' credentials. They should use conditional language because perspectives differ. And finally, they should justify their explanations or positions with sound reasoning (VanSledright, 2002).

HELPING STUDENTS WRITE IN HISTORY

Bruce VanSledright (2002) lists the following criteria for judging an exemplary interpretative essay in history:

Cites directly from the documentary evidence (e.g., refers to specific documents and/or points of view represented). Shows evidence of intertextually corroborating sources. Works with assessing status of sources (e.g., perspective of authors, presence of bias) in forming a coherent, historically situated interpretation that indicates or suggests historical significance of the incident. Repeatedly uses couched, conditional language because evidence conflicts and partisan perspectives prevail in sources.

While students at grades 4 and 5 may need a good deal of scaffolding before they meet these standards, these criteria should nonetheless guide their writing instruction along the way.

Revising and Editing. When they revisit their explanations, students should focus on what matters in history: the evidence from multiple sources, the significance of the events, the credibility of the sources cited, and the logic of the argument. The writing should, of course, also be checked for spelling, conventions, and punctuation.

Writing Narratives in History

Unlike the literary narratives students write for English language arts, historical narratives privilege accuracy of content that has historical significance. Every stage of the writing process should reflect this priority.

In history, students write narrative text most often to recount a series of historical events. They are in a sense retelling a story about an individual or a sequence of events of historical import. They construct an "event model" of what happened, selecting from their sources the most relevant information to convey their stories (Leinhardt, 1997).

This is a difficult task. Students need to consider everything they've learned about a topic and then recognize what is significant and what is trivial. They need to piece together bits of information from various sources into a coherent whole (Wineburg, 1994).

PUTTING CONCEPTS INTO PRACTICE:
WRITING PROCESSES FOR NARRATIVES

Planning. What matters in planning for the historical narrative is considering the assignment or task and then focusing the narrative only on the events that have historical import.

For example, students who are asked to tell about the life of Ben Franklin should build the narrative around the events Franklin shaped as a scientist, inventor, writer, or patriot. Although Franklin might have had an interesting perspective on house design or planting a vegetable garden, this information is not fundamental to the persona of Ben Franklin, American statesman, scientist, writer, and inventor. If anything, these are interesting asides, bits of information that may be true about the man but not representative of the historical figure. These asides should be considered extraneous.

As another example, if students were to write about the American Civil War, they would be expected to focus only on the events that led up to the war, that were part of the war itself—famous battles—or that were the effects of the war. They should not address the weather of this time period, the economy, or health problems—unless these were in some way war-related topics. This scanning of memory and then retrieving only the relevant information is fundamental to writing a strong historical narrative.

The planning stage should be used, then, at least in part, to sort through all that students know about the topic and focus on only the most relevant information.

Drafting. When students draft a narrative in history, their goal is to present relevant information clearly, coherently, and correctly. Drafting, then, is more an exercise in which the writer draws down from a storehouse of knowledge and checks for completeness than sketches out an imaginary series of events or an embellished recount.

Revision. Revising narratives for history assignments focuses on the quality, completeness, and organization of the information. Students can ask for review from response groups or partners. In all circumstances, they should ask, Have I got this right? Does it make sense? Do you see anything I've left out or any mistakes I've made?

Editing. Spelling, conventions, and punctuation should be the focus of the editing stage. When possible, students should check sources of information to make corrections.

Reading and Writing in Science

Why do we read science texts?

- To find out or explain how the natural world works
- To answer questions that arise in science learning
- To learn about the scientific method for studying the world

What genres should we expect fourth and fifth graders to write in science?

- Informational texts
- Scientific explanations of natural phenomena
- Narratives with scientific themes

Scientists are interested in how the natural world works. Science begins with questions. Questions lead to investigations. Investigations generate evidence. Evidence is organized into theories that explain how the world works—why it is the way it is. There are strict principles for what counts as evidence and what counts as an explanation based on evidence. Theories have to be testable through observation.

Understanding and Exploring Science Texts

Science is not a solitary enterprise. Scientists will accept only evidence observed using methods that could be repeated by other scientists to verify the observations. Scientific knowledge is created by a community of scientists committed to common principles. Written documentation and communication are fundamental to the development of scientific knowledge. But so are hands-on investigations, field observations, and experiments. Science cannot be learned without reading, but neither can it be learned by reading alone.

Strong readers of scientific texts come to their reading with questions about the natural world—or they come looking for questions early in the text. Curious readers of an informational text about the digestive system may ask

- How does the digestive system work?
- What are the parts of the digestive system, and how do they work together?
- What function does the digestive system serve in the life of the organism?

- What does the digestive system look like? What is its form and structure?
- What happens when I swallow?
- What happens to food as it goes through the digestive system? How is it changed?

Scientific explanations answer questions about the natural world. Scientific knowledge is framed by common themes that many science teachers may recognize from the National Research Council. These themes, in their grade-appropriate versions, can serve as signposts that point to the scientific content of texts.

HELPING STUDENTS READ SCIENCE TEXTS

Addressing misconceptions. Fourth and fifth graders are naturally curious about the world and the way thing work. They enjoy exploring and experimenting and discovering. Yet they are not natural scientists, willing to suspend conclusions and to reason in disciplined ways from scientific evidence. Students need to learn to examine the world—and the texts they read about the world—for insights that may go against their understandings from everyday observations.

Building a conceptual understanding. Researcher John Guthrie and his colleagues (2004) have observed that for third, fourth, and fifth graders, comprehension of science texts develops from lower to higher levels of conceptual understanding. In their study, students read multiple texts on a variety of animals and how they live in various biomes (for example, lions live as predators in the grassland), with these distinctions in comprehension.

- **Level 1. Facts and associations: Simple**. Students present a very few simple characteristics of either biomes or organisms. Their statements exclude ecological concepts or definitions.
- **Level 2. Facts and associations: Extended**. Students correctly present several relevant facts, appearing in the form of a list. In ecology, they may have classified several organisms.
- **Level 3. Concepts and evidence: Simple**. Well-formed, fully elaborated definitions of one or two important concepts are given with minimal supporting information in the text. In ecology, definitions of several biomes are often accompanied by a substantial number of organisms accurately classified. The student states a concept such as predation or competition necessary to survival, with some minimal support.
- **Level 4. Concepts and evidence: Extended**. Students present multiple concepts central to the text with support and exemplification of each. In ecology,

students display conceptual understanding of organisms and their survival mechanisms in one or more biomes. They present specific organisms and the physical characteristics or the behavioral patterns that facilitate these organisms' survival. Students may include higher-level principles, such as food webs or interactions among ecological concepts, with limited supporting information.

- **Level 5. Patterns of relationships: Simple**. Students present multiple concepts explicitly linked together, with at least minimal evidence. In ecology, students show command of the ecological concepts with highly detailed descriptions or relationships among different organisms and the biomes they inhabit. Interactions are central to the statement.
- **Level 6. Patterns of relationships: Extended**. Students present many concepts, elaborately interrelated, with detailed examples and supporting information. In ecology, students describe complex relationships among multiple organisms and their habitats. The concepts and principles presented are thoroughly supported by statements directly relating them to specific organisms' behaviors or physical adaptations.

Using metacognitive strategies. Students must learn that understanding science texts requires more than picking out the facts, making a list of what the text contains, or defining terms. They need to understand that the facts and definitions describe important scientific concepts and that many concepts, taken together, can explain the natural world and the way things work. They need to connect the facts and concepts into patterns of relationships. This deep comprehension of scientific texts is, clearly, dependent on scientific knowledge.

Students can learn to ask themselves questions when they read scientific texts, such as That's an interesting fact. I wonder why that is?

They serve as framing ideas for building mental models from science texts.

- **Systems, order, and organization.** The digestive system, the solar system, and a local ecosystem are common systems. Knowledge of a system explains the relationships and interactions among parts that make up a whole. An informational text about the digestive system would explain how all the organs work together to digest food.

- **Evidence, models, and explanation.** Models represent phenomena well enough to fit the data and explain new evidence. Simplified models make the structure of the phenomena comprehensible to readers. An informational text about the digestive system may include a graphic illustration of the organs that make up the digestive system.

- **Change, constancy, and measurement.** Scientists observe what varies and what stays the same and measure change. An informational text about the digestive system may explain that the esophagus tightens during swallowing and that the stomach may expand.

- **Evolution and equilibrium.** Systems settle into equilibrium. When disturbed, a new equilibrium settles in and the system evolves over time. Many explanations have this kind of structure. An informational text about the digestive system may explain the stages of the digestive process.

- **Form and function.** Scientists are never satisfied just knowing what something looks like—its shape and form. Scientists also want to know what it does and what function it performs. An informational text about the digestive system may explain the unique attributes and functions of the organs of the digestive system.

Fourth and fifth graders are not likely to know about these common themes, of course. But their teachers can guide them in asking and answering questions about these big ideas of science—if they don't come up with these questions on their own.

Reading with curiosity and questions about how the world works will help students interpret and explore science texts for answers to these questions. The big ideas help students organize knowledge so they can remember it.

Writing Informational Texts

In school, science students are most frequently asked to produce reports. Text structures for report writing vary, but one common structure is the statement (or definition/classification) and explanatory details (facts or steps). Reports contain specialized language; specific and accurate facts or information; and, frequently, charts, graphs, and other visuals. Before doing any writing of informational texts, students must understand fully the content to be addressed in the writing. (For examples of strong science papers by fourth and fifth graders, see Chapter 7.)

We recognize that students in good science programs also produce lab notebooks. However, because they do not conform to a standard genre format, they are not discussed in this book.

PUTTING CONCEPTS INTO PRACTICE: WRITING INFORMATIONAL TEXTS IN SCIENCE

Planning.   Like writing in history, writing in science requires students to know a great deal about their topic. *Learning* about science is the most important step in planning to write an informational report.

The model program CORI, discussed on page 66, gives students time for extended, engaged reading so they can acquire knowledge about science topics. The goal in science learning is for students to understand concepts and their relationships rather than simply to memorize facts. CORI also provides scaffolding to help students manage and organize their knowledge. The planning process, then, enables students to learn deeply about science topics and to chunk information appropriately. Students can use these chunks of information to structure the sections and subsections of a report.

Drafting.   With scaffolding from their teacher, students can draft a short science report without too much difficulty. Scaffolding is highly recommended for fourth and fifth graders. Sometimes a sample outline or table of contents for a longer report is all they need to get going and produce a draft from their own information, as long as enough time is spent in reading and learning the content of the assignment. Students likely also need to see models of effective uses of charts and graphs. As they write, students will need time to sift through notes and resources. Organization of material, accuracy, and sufficiency of information drive the process.

Revising. When they revisit their pieces, students should pay attention to the accuracy and sufficiency of their information. They should consider whether they have shown extensive knowledge of facts and associations, concepts and evidence, and patterns of relationships. They should make sure they use technical language to demonstrate knowledge of their topic and the layout of their final reports.

Editing. The final question students should address is, Is this good science? Without an affirmation answer, the entire text should be re-examined.

Writing Explanations

There is no single agreed-upon definition for what counts as a scientific explanation. Some researchers use the term *explanation*, while others use *argument*. We use *explanation* to be consistent with the American Association for the Advancement of Science Standards and The National Research Council Standards.

According to McNeill, Lizotte, and Krajcik (2004), a scientific explanation is an adaptation of Toulmin's (2003) model of argumentation. It has three components—a claim, evidence, and reasoning:

> The claim is an assertion or conclusion that answers the original question. The evidence is scientific data that supports the claim. These data can come from an investigation or from another source, such as observations, reading material, or archived data. The data need to be both appropriate and sufficient to support the claim. The reasoning (called a warrant) is a justification that links the claim and evidence and shows why the data count as evidence to support the claim by using the appropriate scientific principles. (McNeill et al., 2004)

Putting Concepts Into Practice: Writing Explanations in Science

Planning. If students do not understand the content, they will not be able to write an accurate explanation, even if they understand how an explanation is constructed. Having something to say depends on knowing deeply about the subject to be communicated. Therefore, reading, investigation, observation, lab experience, collecting data, and analyzing the results to answer the question all are part of the planning process.

Drafting. When writers produce an explanation, they follow the claim–evidence–reasoning structure. For young writers (upper elementary and middle school students), scaffolding is almost always required. Ideally, the scaffold should direct writers first to produce a claim: one sentence that is the thesis for the text. The claim should be followed by at least two pieces of evidence: data that support the claim. The evidence is followed by reasoning: a statement that connects the evidence to the claim using the appropriate scientific principles.

Revising. Revising a scientific explanation involves checking the data and making certain what is in the text constitutes good science.

Editing. During the editing process, writers should focus on correctness of punctuation, spelling, and usage.

Reading and Writing in Mathematics

Why do we read mathematics texts?

- To learn about mathematical concepts
- To learn how to carry out mathematical procedures
- To understand and solve problems

  What genre of texts do students read in mathematics?

- Explanations of concepts
- Explanations of procedures
- Word problems

Interpreting and Exploring Mathematics Texts

We don't usually think of how students learn to comprehend mathematics texts, but it's time to change that. Here's why.

In mathematics, the reading challenge can be great enough to block mathematics learning. Readers have to deploy their knowledge of mathematical terms and notation embedded in a peculiar dialect of academic English to make sense of text at the most basic level. Often, diagrams in the text help students to comprehend. The logical consistency of mathematics can make comprehension easier, even while the logical complexity makes it harder.

There are three genres of text frequently encountered in school mathematics: explanations of procedures, explanations of concepts, and word problems. Each is concise and dense. The procedural explanations are frequent and easy to follow but hard to remember. The conceptual explanations can be as dense and abstract as they are important. Making sense of word problems requires knowledge of genre conventions for one of the most peculiar genres ever devised.

Readers, used to stories, follow the references to characters and events. The text uses pronouns, phrases, and clauses to make these references. In word problems, the important references are to quantities instead of people and to the relationships among quantities instead of the relationships among people. Readers must sort out what quantities are being referred to and how they are related to develop a text-base. In multistep word problems, students must infer the existence of a quantity not explicitly referred to in the text. They must infer it from their mental model of the situation described by the problem. Without a mental model, they probably will fail to solve the problem.

Students need to learn how to build mental models for this peculiar genre. Many students cannot deploy and practice the mathematics they know because they cannot comprehend word problems. Prior knowledge of mathematics is crucial. So is knowledge of the way language, including mathematical language, is used in each genre.

Comprehending Explanations of Mathematical Concepts

The role of reading in learning mathematics is, as in science, ancillary to what students do, talk about, and think. Yet it is an essential role. Talking, thinking, and doing are ephemeral except for what students keep in the privacy of their minds. Text endures. Text is available for return visits and shared visits. And text can be a source of expertise that goes beyond the resources of the classroom. Text is also what students write.

Explanations of mathematical concepts in texts are written with the assumption that readers will be engaged in work on related problems, classroom discussions, and activities designed to build concrete intuitions that can support understanding of the concept. In this sense, reading comprehension is embedded in a social context designed for learning. Hence, students will build mental models of the concepts explained in the text from a combination of concurrent experience, prior learning of mathematics, and the text.

Mathematical explanations typically depend on previously learned concepts in detailed and precise ways. If students bring misconceptions about mathematics to their reading, these can interfere with comprehension. A student cannot distinguish prior knowledge from misconceptions. Sometimes prior knowledge can interfere with comprehension. Comprehension may entail revising prior knowledge. Many so-called "stubborn" misconceptions that plague mathematics comprehension are really correctly learned bits of mathematics that are being misapplied where they do not apply.

Definitions play a special role in mathematics. Definitions are used to justify steps in an argument (they justify claims that lead to other claims). They

LEARNING CONTENT, LEARNING ENGLISH

To help second-language learners develop content knowledge *and* English-language proficiency, educators have employed sheltered instruction or specially designed academic instruction. These approaches attempt to make grade-level academic content comprehensible for second-language learners by incorporating specialized techniques.

One model of sheltered instruction that has been validated by research is called the Sheltered Instruction Observation Protocol (SIOP). The protocol forms the framework for a comprehensive model of professional development. The teaching components that SIOP addresses include preparation, building background, comprehensible input, strategies, interaction, practice/application, lesson delivery, and review/assessment. A study by Echevarría and Short (2006) implemented and tested this approach with teachers of adolescent English-language learners and found improvements in students' academic literacy measured though an expository writing assessment. One important characteristic of SIOP instruction is "explicit language instruction targeted to and slightly beyond students' level of English proficiency, presented in every lesson" (p. 207) with concurrent development of content knowledge.

are more precise than in other fields in a way that can challenge a fourth or fifth grader. Mathematical definitions eliminate ambiguity by using a genre convention that says, "The definition means only exactly what it says; it does not mean anything else." Mathematical definitions mean much less than we, as readers, are used to. In fourth and fifth grades, the definitions are often couched in less formal language, but their abstraction and sparseness of meaning is still a challenge. For example, a widely used fifth-grade math textbook has this definition:

IDENTITY PROPERTY

When 0 is added to any number, the sum is that number.

Of course, the definition is accompanied by examples that make its meaning concrete. Yet students need to understand the definition as a justification they can use to support their own reasoning and writing. This aspect of understanding is difficult to grasp from seeing examples.

Mathematical explanations typically use diagrams and specialized notation and symbols. The diagrams often depict a concrete situation used to make the mathematics less abstract. From the concrete grasp of the idea, the explanation has to explain how the idea applies to other situations and where it does not apply. In other words, a particular concrete concept is generalized to a more abstract concept. Good text will use varied examples and analogies to assist the generalization. Often, the more general form of a concept can be most elegantly expressed symbolically. A reader who cannot make good use of the symbolic expressions faces added difficulty in building a mental model of the concept.

EXPLANATIONS OF PROCEDURES

We all remember the step-by-step example problem worked out as a model. Our homework was then to follow the example with a set of similar problems. It was a little like learning a new dance each day, rehearsing each night, and then performing on the end-of-chapter test several weeks later. For many, that is mathematics.

But mathematics is not merely a chain of procedures. A strong mathematics student should be able to solve unrehearsed problems that draw on conceptual knowledge and strategic proficiencies as well as procedural competence. Indeed, most uses of mathematics

that matter, from state tests to real-life applications, involve unrehearsed problems.

If the reader approaches procedural text as a tool for getting the homework done and, later, for rehearsing for a chapter test, then that reader is unlikely to comprehend the aspects of the text that would contribute to proficiencies with unrehearsed problems. In other words, the mental model of the procedure (if there is one) does not connect to other knowledge in usable ways.

Often, readers of a complicated procedure will say, "I'm lost." They sense that they have lost track of where they have been and where they are going. Feeling lost is a metacognitive signal that comprehension has broken down. The procedure being read frequently refers to subprocedures "learned" earlier. Here is a typical example for adding fractions (from a popular text):

1. Find the least common denominator.
2. Write equivalent fractions using the least common denominator.
3. Add. Simplify the sum, if possible.

An easy procedure, if the reader has prior knowledge of what a least common denominator is (52 pages earlier), how to find one (50 pages earlier), what equivalent fractions are and how to write them (44 pages ago), how to add fractions with common denominators (10 pages earlier), and what *simplify* means (42 pages ago) and how to do it. That is a pretty intricate web of procedural detail scattered over more than 50 pages of text, interrupted by many other topics. Five hundred pages of procedures per year in fourth and fifth grades are probably too many for anyone. Unless the student is consolidating the mental models in some way, unless she is building connections, the text will eventually become dense with obscure references. Students need to learn how to read for conceptual coherence across many pages of text, not just to engage in procedural rehearsal.

Comprehending Word Problems

A word problem describes a situation. To comprehend the problem, students must understand the situation described—that is, they must build a mental model of the situation. The students' prior knowledge of mathematics and of the problem setting play a major role in how they build their mental model. Mathematical representations can be important parts of the mental model.

Readers must imagine the situation described in the problem, just like readers imagine the situation when they read a story. In a story, readers naturally focus on the characters, their motives, and their actions and reactions. This would not be a productive focus for mathematics word problems. What students learn about reading stories does not transfer without additional instruction to reading word problems. The action in a word problem is not between characters or about the scenery.

Consider this problem from a popular text:

> The upper Angel Falls, the highest waterfall on Earth, are 750 m higher than Niagara Falls. If each of the falls were 7 m lower, the upper Angel Falls would be 16 times as high as Niagara Falls. How high is each waterfall?

A well-meaning teacher might "activate prior knowledge" by asking who has seen a waterfall. Such a mis-reading of the word problem genre leads to diagrams that look like this:

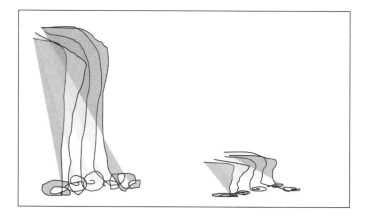

Such diagrams and the mental models on which they are based are not focused on the relevant "meaning" of the word problem. If waterfalls were replaced by hills or helicopters, the mathematical meaning of the word problem would not change one bit. This problem is not about waterfalls; it is about *height*. The relevant prior knowledge is about height, specifically, comparing two heights. A more relevant question for a teacher to ask is "When have you compared two heights? Yours to your friends?" A useful (valid) mental model would focus on height and lead to a diagram that shows vertical lines representing height, as on the right of the figure at the bottom of the page.

To learn to read word problems, students need to acquire genre knowledge specific to word problems. A key element of this genre knowledge is knowing how to focus on quantities rather than on people or waterfalls. Comprehension involves mentally modeling the quantities in ways that support reasoning about the relationships among the quantities. The action in word problems is between *quantities*.

To understand a story, readers have to recognize which characters and events are being referred to—by name, pronoun, phrase, clause, or implication. To manage these references is easy if—and only if—readers have imagined the situation in which the characters act. Likewise, readers of a word problem have to recognize and keep track of what quantities are being referred to—by name, phrase, clause, or implication. Further, readers have to track what is being said about the relationships among the quantities.

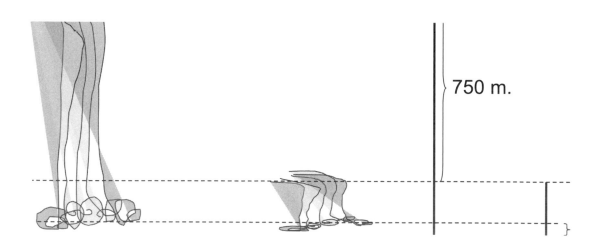

750 m.

Look at the situation described in this problem:

> Joe has set up 60 chairs for a show in the yard. He set up 12 rows. How many chairs are in each row?

Three quantities are referred to in this problem: the number of rows, the number of chairs, and the number of chairs in each row. Two quantities are known, and the reader is asked to find the third. What is the relationship among these quantities?

Without imagining the situation, a reader can use generic knowledge of word problems to guess what to do from the words and numbers: "Let's see, you add, subtract, multiply, or divide the numbers." Many programs encourage students to look for cues in the words rather than understand the situation. Even with problems this easy, that is a mistake. A reader might correctly guess that the text has no "more," "less," "difference," or "total" words. So it will not be adding or subtracting. But should you multiply or divide? And if you should divide, then divide what by what? This deliberately meaningless approach to word problems avoids asking the students to comprehend the text, and, as a byproduct, it avoids asking students to learn mathematics from solving the problem.

For anyone who takes the time to comprehend the situation in the text, it is an easy problem. A diagram showing 12 rows and indicating the unknown number of chairs in each row might help a reader imagine the situation. In fact, attempting to draw the diagram would lead the reader to realize that he does not know how many chairs to draw in each row. This is an example of how questions are embedded in mental models. In word problems, situating the question—the unknown—in a mental model makes the problem comprehensible.

Working out a mental model that shows the relationships among all the quantities will provide students with a scaffold for solving the problem. More important, the mental model of the relationships *is* the mathematical content of the problem-solving activity. Learning how to make such models is the mathematical objective of doing such problems.

By taking the time to comprehend the situation first, readers can understand any question asked about the situation. Comprehending the situation requires a reader to represent the situation to him- or herself in a way that makes sense. Representing problem situations demands skills that can be taught and learned.

Putting Knowledge Into Practice: Writing Mathematical Arguments

The most common writing challenge in fourth- and fifth-grade mathematics is prompted by the words *explain* or *justify*. With these words, students are being asked to write a well-reasoned argument within the world of mathematics. That means something different from a good argument in other fields and contexts. Ultimately, by the secondary grades, students will be asked to formalize their arguments into proofs. But in the upper elementary grades, that formalization and abstraction are not appropriate.

The following are some desired qualities of good writing in mathematics.

- Less is more: Concise statements bring the logic into the foreground.

- Examples, by themselves, are not valid evidence, but they can be used to illustrate how something works.

- Counterexamples are a valid way to show that a statement is not true.

- The logic that strings claims together is the focus of the writing.

- The justification for each statement can come from a limited set of sources: definitions, rules, already justified claims, counterexamples, properties of numbers and equality.

- *Equals* is the verb of most mathematical sentences (claims). The most common move in a mathematical argument is to change one claim into the next one in the string by applying a rule that preserves equality. Stating the rule is the justification.

- Definitions play a special role in mathematical reasoning. They limit meaning to precise specifications. It is easier to rely on unambiguous definitions in reasoning. They don't mean too much.

- Specification of the domain of numbers being discussed, such as the number of chairs or the height in meters, is explicit. This can involve the use of quantifiers like *all* or *there exists a number...* or *for all even numbers....*

Fourth and fifth graders will use concrete examples and objects to reason much more than older students. They explain their insights into how the mathematics works by using illustrative examples. The challenge for them is carrying the argument beyond the examples and explaining why a statement is always true, or true under certain conditions, or never true.

In other words, students have to generalize validly from examples. For students who regularly do this in talk, the writing will follow. If they rarely do it in talk and writing, they will have a very difficult time. They will not know what is wanted. They will not know the genre "mathematical justification."

An important component of writing in mathematics is abstracting relevant aspects of a situation and representing them in a diagram. A diagram has two purposes: communication and as a tool for reasoning about the situation diagrammed. Students can learn to draw diagrams. The diagram of a situation should show and label the relevant quantities. Students should try to show all the quantities, but sometimes this is not practical. Labels help.

Graphing and tables are essential tools for representing situations. A graph shows the relationship between two quantities. Graphs are fundamental representations for functions and equations. Making sense of graphs builds on solid understanding of the number line.

In fourth- and fifth-grade mathematics, writing serves three main purposes:

- **Helping students think about complex and abstract situations.** Writing is a thinking tool. It is possible to think $219.0125 \times .0067$ through to an answer when you write each step; it is impossible for most people to think it through in their heads alone. Writing adds capacity to thinking in mathematics. Students are the audience for their own writing, although writing can be used to "explain your thinking" in discussions.

- **Showing what students know.** This includes "show your work" and "justify your results." The teacher is the main audience for this writing, although other students can serve as an extension of the teacher.

- **Recording work and thinking for future reference.** The student is the main audience for this kind of writing, often in the form of notebooks, journals, and folders of saved work.

Given these purposes, most writing in mathematics is brief and piecemeal. It is an outgrowth of mathematical work and learning. Planning, drafting, revising, and editing do not emerge as distinct processes because the process is driven by the mathematical learning activity. The writing is more of a byproduct, albeit an essential one.

7

Reading and Writing Performances

The intent of this chapter is to put a human face on the elements of reading comprehension and writing that have been presented in this book. The students whose work is showcased are all fourth and fifth graders who are performing at—or almost at—grade level. They all attend public schools, most with low socioeconomic student populations. None is enrolled in a gifted curriculum.

Reading

The reading comprehension section of this chapter contains

- Description of a fiction and a nonfiction text whose levels of difficulty are appropriate for fourth- and fifth-grade readers
- Excerpts from transcripts of students responding to prompts about these texts
- An analysis of student responses to the texts

The prompts are designed to illustrate readers' thinking as they build a textbase and a mental model. The textbase prompts focus on issues around linking ideas (coherence), processing words and attaching meaning to them, and inferring omitted connectives. The prompts designed to demonstrate building a mental model ask students to make inferences that go beyond the text and connect ideas in the text to their relevant background knowledge.

The first example is from Doug (not his real name), who has just finished a silent reading of "A Bad Road for Cats" by Cynthia Rylant. This short story is an appropriate selection for strong fourth-grade readers, though particularly at fourth grade, readers would likely benefit from focused questions to clear up ambiguities and resolve misconceptions. This example shows how scaffolding questions can support a reader's comprehension.

Doug is very methodical, whether reading silently or aloud. While reading to himself, he can be heard reading the words aloud in order to move through the passage. In spite of these decoding struggles, he

Cynthia Rylant's "A Bad Road for Cats": Summary

This story, written in the third person, tells how a woman changes as she searches for her lost cat. It is basically a character study. The story opens on Route 6, where the woman, Magda, originally found her cat, Louis, and where the cat now, four years later, has presumably gone missing. Route 6 is an extremely oppressive and dangerous highway: trucks roar down the road, honking their horns and spewing smoke and dirt. As she searches, Magda grows increasingly concerned about Louis, fearing that he is dead. Magda is very attached to Louis; she lives a solitary life, and he is her only companion.

Eventually, Magda sees a sign advertising "4 Sal. CAT." She goes to the house where Louis is being offered for sale and encounters a very strange boy who clearly does not want to give the cat up. Louis is in very bad condition: malnourished, dirty, and close to death. Magda tells the boy that the cat is her cat, but the boy will not give Louis up until Magda pays him $20.

Magda is enraged by this situation, but she pays the boy, grabs her cat, and takes Louis home.

She nurses Louis back to health, and in time her feelings toward the boy change. She realizes that in his own way, the boy was attached to Louis; to give him up, he must have needed the money badly. She also realizes that the boy must have had no sense of how to care for an animal; he himself looked ill cared for. As a result of this awareness, Magda makes the boy a toy cat that resembles Louis.

There is one flashback in the story that explains the circumstances under which Magda originally found Louis.

demonstrates notably solid comprehension skills in contrast to his fluency.

Doug worked hard to create a cohesive textbase. For example, he initially believed that there were two cats in the story and that the reference to a "kitten" in the flashback must have been a reference to another cat. However, Doug later realized that Louis was the kitten, and then he was able to understand the flashback. During the course of the interview, it became apparent that he required a considerable amount of time to read through the text. Clearly, the structure of the questions assisted him in building a comprehension model.

Doug would benefit from a guided reading of the story. Although Doug is a candidate for retention who exhibited poor academic performance in the classroom, in the following interview, he makes a heroic attempt to make sense of what was, for him, a very challenging story.

Doug reads the story silently before the interview begins.

Interviewer: Why don't we start with you telling me in your own words what this story was about?

Doug: It was about this cat named Louis and this lady named something, I forgot her name, her name was—darn it, darn it—it said her name a whole bunch of times in here, Magda, Magda, her name was Magda, and she lost her cat on Route 6 or something like that. She called it a dirty road because it was like dirty bars and, and stuff, but then she had to walk down it someday, um, she walked down it one day to look for her cat, uh Louis, yeah, Louis. And she went to a, um, diner, no she went to a gas station and then, uh, and then she found a little cat that was orange and white just like Louis, and, but it had its tail cut off 'cause of a door and then she, um, walked

Doug's summary of the text is flawed because he misses the flashback and so misreads the sequence of events at that part of the text. Overall, however, he is able to link appropriately the event series to construct a textbase that is relatively accurate.

down the Route 6 and she went to a diner—I mean a bar, or whatever, and then she got a coffee and then she drank it. And then she seen a sign that said a missing cat that they found and then she went to the house and this, like, crazy kid was there. Not really crazy, but he smiled and he, like, had weird, he had missing and, and, uh, rotten teeth and then he sai—she said, I know what the cat looks like, and then she said orange and white, and then the kid shut the door on him and then, and then it was, um, and she knocked a whole bunch of times and he didn't answer, and then she knocked and she—she had to pay twenty three dollars to get the cat back, and then she got the cat back, and cleaned it all up. And it was just like that. But then she fattened it up, and she cleaned it. So it's about this lady and she's lookin' for her cat.

Interviewer:	So what happened to the other cat?
Doug:	The other cat? I don't really know what happened to it. I think it like, um, I forgot, it was like right, I think, yeah, right here. (*starts looking back through the text and reading it under his breath*) Oh, that's not it....
Interviewer:	Oh, that's okay. I was just wondering if you had an idea in your mind what happened to that cat in the story.
Doug:	I don't know. I think she might have took it, oh no, I think she, like, took it to an animal shelter or something. I forgot. I don't know.

Drawing on background knowledge about what people sometimes do with unwanted pets, Doug struggled to correct his mental model. The struggle reveals that when questioned, he monitors his comprehension.

(*The interviewer asks Doug to read the story again, this time aloud. She explains that she will stop him occasionally to ask questions.*)

Interviewer:	So can you tell me just so far in this part of the story what's going on?
Doug:	The lady lost her cat, and she's walking down Route 6, and she's calling out for the cat, and it's been two weeks.
Interviewer:	So, what would you say is the setting of the story?
Doug:	Route 6, this part, yeah, Route 6.
Interviewer:	Who are the characters?
Doug:	In that just little part?
Interviewer:	(*encouraging*) Mmm-hmm.
Doug:	The lady, it didn't say her name yet, it says the woman, and the cat.
Interviewer:	So, Doug, can you tell me what's going on in this part of the story?
Doug:	Okay (*looks back*), hmmm, well, this tells, tells about who Magda is, yeah, pretty much it, and then it tells,

and it tells that she's in a uh, gas st—it tells who Magda is and what she looks sorta like, mmm-hmm, and then it says, yeah, and what she does, she works at a, she works at uh—yeah, uh, and right here it says, it says that a truck pulled in, a tank truck.

Interviewer: Can you tell me what you think this sentence means, on this page when it says on this page, "The woman's eyes pinched his"? And let me show you where it is, right here. What do you think that might mean?

Doug: It means like he—she gave him a nasty glare.

> Here Doug makes an inference about the meaning of the metaphor: "The woman's eyes pinched his."

Interviewer: So what did we learn about Magda? What kind of person is she?

Doug: She's—she's not old but she calls herself like a old strong woman, she has black hair like an Indian, but she's not Indian. She comes fro—ommmm here (*looks back in text*), she comes from France and she works as a, I forget what it's called, she works at a, I forget what it's called, she works at a—she's a (*clears throat*) thing, she's um, she's a um, she's a thing, she does something with her sheep.

> Here Doug clearly struggles with the concept of a loom.

> With the exception of his substitution of "calls" for "carried," Doug demonstrates his construction of a fairly accurate fragment of the text-base. The relevant text from the story is "Magda was not old, but she carried herself as a very old person might."

Interviewer: What does she do with her sheep?

Doug: She uses her loom.

Interviewer: She uses the loom? So how does Magda feel about the cat?

> Although he doesn't understand what a loom is, he knows that it is related to the sheep and their wool.

Doug: I think she loves her. She loves the cat because she doesn't have anybody. She doesn't have her husband or her kids. She's all alone, but her cat—she has her cat. (*reads aloud, pausing to speak in the first sentence*) Ohhhh, so Louis was the little cat. This is like a flashback sorta, when she felt Louis in the gas station, he had his tail chopped off and, yeah, he...yeah, this is about when she (felt? found?) Louis.

> Here Doug infers that she loves the cat because without the cat, she would have nobody. His inference demonstrates that he can infuse relevant background knowledge (his understanding of human nature) with his textbase to create a valid mental model.

> Doug corrects his mental model, explaining the flashback. He uses setting and character details to support the fact that it is a flashback, accounting for a new, readjusted mental model and timeline.

Interviewer: On this page you see a conversation between Magda and a gas station attendant. So when did this happen, this conversation?

Doug: It happened— (*coughs hard*) Oh, my God.

Interviewer: Are you okay?

Doug: My throat feels scratchy. Um, it happened when Mag— (*clears throat*) when Magda first, um, found, uh, Louis.

Interviewer: Okay, so how long ago was that when she first found Louis? Could you just throw out a time?

Doug: I don't really know. Uh....

Interviewer:	Okay, so you mentioned it was a flashback. How did you know it was a flashback?
Doug:	Because in the beginning it says that she was walking down Route 6. And in this it says she decided to walk down Route 6. And this, she lost him in this one, and she found him in this one. But he was a kitten in this one, and he wasn't a kitten in that one, and stuff like that.

{ Doug further demonstrates his understanding.

(*Doug takes a break for recess. When he comes back, he reads aloud the next section.*)

Interviewer:	So, Doug, can you tell me, what's going on in this part of the story you just read?
Doug:	Um, Magda, she went to uh, uh, a dairy, dairy bar, and she ordered coffee and she wanted to be away from the pe—from the loud horns and dirt and stuff, and she thought about the time when Lou—Louis jumped from the balcony and broke his leg.
Interviewer:	So, what's a dairy bar—you said she went to a dairy bar. What kind of place do you think that is?
Doug:	It's probably like a café.
Interviewer:	Can you tell me, what do you think it means on page 60, when it says, "but the trucks were making her misery worse"? (*Doug looks intently at page*) Why is that?

{ Here Doug uses information provided in the text about Magda wanting coffee and the description of the dairy bar, and he draws on his own experience with cafés to infer that the bar is a café.

Doug:	Ohhh—I would think that maybe 'cause she might think that the cat got hit by a truck or something.
Interviewer:	Mmmm, why do you think she might think that?
Doug:	'Cause she got lost on Route 6 and there's a lot of trucks there, and she might've been crossing the road and she, she had a accident before with her tail.

{ Here Doug uses information from the text ("The trucks were making her misery worse") and his own knowledge to infer that Magda was worried that the cat may have been hit by a truck.

Interviewer:	What did we learn about Louis?
Doug:	Louis, the cat? What we learned about him? Hmmm, through just this passage, uh, he's sort of wild 'cause he jumped off a balcony and, yeah.

{ Here Doug uses his understanding of the textbase (the description of Louis's behavior) and his own knowledge to make an inference about Louis's character.

(*The interviewer instructs Doug to read aloud the last section of the story.*)

Interviewer:	So, Doug, can you tell me, why did the boy slam the door in the woman's face?
Doug:	Because, 'cause he know, he knew it was her cat and he didn't want her to just take it. He wanted money.

{ Doug infers the boy is afraid he won't get any money for the cat because the cat belongs to Magda and she has a right to take it.

Interviewer:	How do you think Magda feels about the boy, and why?	
Doug:	I think she thinks he's sort of weird and cruel because he didn't give her the cat for free, and it was her cat and he probably knows that. Now she feels sorry for him though, because, 'cause, because he's, like, didn't have the cat anymore. And he—she's seen the tears in his eyes.	Here Doug links ideas from the textbase (not having the cat and crying because the cat is gone) to infer that the boy misses the cat.
Interviewer:	Could you describe the boy? What kind of person do you think he is?	
Doug:	A weird person, 'cause he like, he like, he like had the cat, the cat was all dirty when he was taking care of it. And his teeth were all, were all messed up, but that doesn't make him weird 'cause his teeth, but he had the cat dirty and he didn't, he probably didn't take care of it, and she said he was missing for probably like two weeks, and he didn't clean him, clean him, for like two weeks.	Doug infers the boy is strange because he had the cat for two weeks and didn't clean him.
Interviewer:	What do you think had happened to the cat?	
Doug:	Huh, I don't really know. Hmmm, I think like he mighta, might've, she might've took it when, when, uh, they were grocery shopping and she might've, and it might've run away. 'Cause while she, maybe while she was driving home, it might've jumped out or something.	Using the information from the textbase, Doug attempts to construct a mental model that would account for the cat being lost.
Interviewer:	Why do you think the boy didn't wash the cat for two weeks?	
Doug:	I don't know, because he, maybe, hmmm. Why didn't he wash the cat? (*laughing*) 'Cause he's weird.	
Interviewer:	Do you think this is a realistic story?	
Doug:	Realistic?	
Interviewer:	Like it could happen.	
Doug:	Yeah, yeah, it could happen.	

WHAT WE CAN LEARN FROM THIS EXCERPT

This example shows how scaffolding questions can support a reader's comprehension. The interviewer asks questions that invite the student to reflect on what he has learned from the text and to look back at the text and think more about it. For example, the interviewer asks Doug, "So what happened to the other cat?" when it was clear that Doug thought there were two cats instead of only one. She doesn't correct him. Instead, she guides him to reflect on an important part of the text and to reason things through for himself.

Some of the interviewer's questions invite inferences: "Can you tell me, what do you think it means on page 60, when it says, 'but the trucks were making her misery worse'? Why is that?" The interviewer also asks open-ended questions that highlight important elements in the story: "So what did we learn about Magda? What kind of person is she?" Other questions invite Doug to build a textbase by making links between events and correctly sequenceing them: "Okay, so you mentioned it was a flashback. How do you know it was a flashback?" Still other questions prompt Doug to think about the meaning of particular words, such as *dairy bar*: "So what's a dairy bar—You said she went to a dairy bar. What kind of place do you think that is?" The questions scaffold Doug's comprehension.

Doug's initial response—his retelling of a lengthy summary of the story—shows that he is able to link events and so form a relatively accurate textbase. Although he struggles to understand both *loom* and *dairy bar*, he makes inferences about these words that are not off the mark and do not detract from the meaning of the text.

Doug's background knowledge allows him to build a mental model that fosters a variety of inferences: about what some people do with unwanted pets, about the importance of pets for lonely people, about Louis's character, and so on. He is also able to adjust his mental model to incorporate new information about Louis once he understands the flashback.

The second excerpt also comes from an interview focused on "A Bad Road for Cats." This time, however, the reader, Sherrell (not her real name) is a fifth-grade student, so the text does not provide quite the level of challenge that it did for Doug, the fourth grader. For example, Sherrell has no problem at all

identifying the flashback and handling the resulting changes in tense.

As in the previous interview, the reader has read the story silently and is asked to provide a summary before reading the text again, aloud this time, and answering questions related to particular sections.

Sherrell builds a mental model that provides a rich and full account of the main character, Magda—her fundamental character traits, her emotional state, her motivations, and her actions. Although Sherrell describes key events, she does so in the service of unpacking aspects of character, such as tracing the evolution of Magda's feelings about the cat and the boy. Sherrell focuses on character from the outset and maintains that focus throughout the conversation.

One might expect that a reader, in building a textbase, would include an explicit description of events in the multiple settings of the story. Sherrell, however, omits most of the details about the story's settings (e.g., Magda's house, the gas station, the dairy bar, the boy's house). When Sherrell provides descriptive detail, it is more about the characters than the actual events. She provides a strong, empathetic, character-driven reading that subordinates plot to character.

Interviewer:	What is the story about?
Sherrell:	The story is about a lady named Magda. And she, she has long black hair. She looks like if she's a Cherokee Indian, but she's really French.
Interviewer:	(*encouraging*) Uh-huh.
Sherrell:	And, um, she lost her cat on a Route 66 and at the end, where the...she finds out that this boy is selling her cat. And he slams the door in her face, and she keeps knocking and knocking. And finally, he comes back with the orange and white cat covered in oil. And so she kept pulling a dollar saying, "Enough, is this enough?" And finally she pulls out a twenty. The boy snatches the money and gives her the cat. She takes him home and gives him a bath. But she's still mad at the boy for selling her her cat when it's almost dead. And, um, after that, eventually her cat's better and starts being its old self again. And she remembers the boy was crying when he gave it away. And, um, she forgave the boy. And once she was on her way to the grocery store, she made this cat out of orange and white wool and gave it a little pink tongue and wrapped it up in a paper bag and dropped it at his door.
Interviewer:	What's going on here? (*points to a particular section of text*)

> Sherrell summarizes the story, including details about the character's physical characteristics and actions, linking ideas in the textbase that she has constructed to give a relatively accurate summary of the plot.

> In her summary, Sherrell demonstrates her understanding of the change in Magda's emotions, as described in the text: "For many days she was in a rage at the strange boy.... Her rage grew smaller and smaller until finally she could forgive the strange boy.... She came to feel sympathy for him."

Sherrell: Um, she had lost...[inaudible] she had lost her cat. And she had been waiting and waiting and looking and looking, but it had been two weeks and her cat, she still hadn't found it. So she started going out and looking in the road and, um, looking for her cat.

Interviewer: What is the setting of the story?

Sherrell: Um, really noisy place, lots of, like, roads and oily and dirty and loud, lots of smoke. It had these little coffee shops and rest stops. Lots of trucks and highways.

> Building an accurate textbase, Sherrell describes the setting much as the author describes it.

Interviewer: Okay, thanks. Who are the characters?

Sherrell: The characters are Magda, her cat, Louis, the little boy, um, and the little long-haired girl who told her about the cats.

Interviewer: Can you describe Magda?

The accuracy of Sherrell's mental model is revealed here through her inferences about Magda's personality.

Sherrell: Magda. She's...she's kind of a strong-willed person who has a drive to do what she wants and get what she wants. Um, judging from the story, she, um, she's not really that old. She's really pretty. She has long hair kind of like an Indian. And she's French.

> The textbase she constructs includes adequate details to support her inferences. For example, the inference about Magda being pretty is reasonable: The text says she has "shiny black hair," is "skinny," and is "of French blood, not Indian."

Interviewer: Okay. How about the boy? Can you describe him?

Sherrell: I think the boy, in my opinion...

Interviewer: (*encouraging*) Uh-huh.

Sherrell: I think he'd be a little greedy. Because, I mean, it was her cat and she's giving a lot. And then, suddenly, she pulls out a twenty dollar bill and he forgets about the cat. He just takes the money.

> Sherrell infers that the boy is greedy, although he still wants the cat.

Interviewer: (*encouraging*) Uh-huh.

Sherrell: And he kind of cries like he still wants the cat. But I still think he's greedy.

Interviewer: So you think from the story, he's pretty...

Sherrell: Greedy.

Interviewer: ...he seems like he's greedy. Interesting. Okay. Alright. You can keep reading.

(*Sherrell reads aloud another section.*)

Interviewer: What did we learn about Magda in this part?

Sherrell: We learned that Magda is not French, I mean not Indian.

Interviewer: Right.

Sherrell: She's French. Um, she is a widow. Her husband died. She lost her cat, obviously. And she has no children.

Interviewer: What kind of person is she?

Sherrell: She's kind of grumpy, strong-willed, tall, and skinny.

Interviewer:	I'm curious that you said she was grumpy and strong-willed. Can you say more about that?
Sherrell:	Well, it's like when she went into the gas station and she asked the man about her cat. She kinda, like, you know, kinda got an attitude when he said you started talking about her dog when she asked about her cat. But you know, well, he saw a dog, he didn't see a cat.
Interviewer:	Right.
Sherrell:	There's really no reason for that. And then it kind of told you, you know, she was really a strong woman, so it kind of makes you think that she's strong-willed.
Interviewer:	So, what's going on in this part of the story?
Sherrell:	Um, she was at the gas station getting a fill-up. And, um, she walked in thinking she was buying cigarettes. So she was dropping a quarter in the cigarette machine, and all of a sudden this cat comes in. And she picks the cat up, considering whether or not she should take it. And then she sees the tail. She starts asking the gas station attendant questions about the cat, like whose is it and what happened to it.
Interviewer:	(*encouraging*) Uh-huh.
Sherrell:	And after that, she took it to [the] veterinarian and got its tail fixed and kind of adopted it.
Interviewer:	(*encouraging*) Uh-huh.
Sherrell:	Right. So she adopted the cat and named it Louis after her grandpa.
Interviewer:	So what's going on in this part of the story?
Sherrell:	She's having flashbacks.
Interviewer:	(*encouraging*) Uh-huh.
Sherrell:	She's at a gas station, drinking her coffee. She finally gets a little peace and quiet away from the trucks. She's resting from looking for a kitten, and then she starts having flashbacks about when Louis was a kitten and how he'd play with the yarn and leave tall grass around in the living room.
Interviewer:	(*encouraging*) Uh-huh.
Sherrell:	And how he, um, broke his leg and what she did to cheer him up is she would draw funny faces on the cast. So....
Interviewer:	Uh-huh. Okay, thanks.
Sherrell:	Basically, she just had flashbacks.
Interviewer:	Uh-huh. Can you say more about what you mean by that?
Sherrell:	What, flashbacks?
Interviewer:	(*encouraging*) Uh-huh.

Sherrell explains Magda's personality with details from the story. She also explains how she inferred that Magda was strong-willed.

Again, Sherrell provides an accurate rendition of events in the plot, illustrating her ability to link the series of events in order to build a valid textbase.

Sherrell realizes that there is a time change in the story, as evident in Magda's memories.

Sherrell:	Um, she's like, she's having memories.
Interviewer:	(*encouraging*) Uh-huh.
Sherrell:	I guess. Memories about her kitten. Well, not a kitten, a cat now.
Interviewer:	Right.
Sherrell:	When it was a kitten.
Interviewer:	Right. Okay, on page 60, it says, that the trucks were making her misery worse. Do you see that?
Sherrell:	Uh-huh.
Interviewer:	Okay. Why is that?
Sherrell:	Well, it's kind of like she feels bad because her cat's gone. She can't find it. And then it's like the trucks; they're kind of invading her space. She doesn't like the noise or the smoke.
Interviewer:	(*encouraging*) Uh-huh.
Sherrell:	It's like spitting out dirt and stuff at her. It's just…it was kind of like, I think it makes her even more mad and more upset, you know? She's trying to deal with the loss of her cat that she can't find. And then here comes all these trucks with all the noise and the smoke and the smells and everything. So I think that's kind of why.
Interviewer:	Why do you think the boy slammed the door in the woman's face?
Sherrell:	I think it's because he knew that, when she asked whether it was yellow and white, he knew it was her cat, and then he didn't want to give it away, so he kind of slammed the door, but then he went to get the cat, like, "Man, I don't want to give her the cat, but I have to." So he kinda slammed the door in her face and then went to get the pet cat after she knocked two more times, and then, then, when she was [inaudible].
Interviewer:	Uh-huh. How does Magda feel about the boy?
Sherrell:	Well, at first, when she gets her cat back, she's kind of mad at him 'cause of the way he—the way she got the cat. He's in a bad condition. And, um, but later she remembered he was crying and that he actually wanted the cat, I think, and after that, she kind of felt kind of sorry for him, so she gave him a play cat.
Interviewer:	You just started, but can you describe the boy a little more?
Sherrell:	Um, well, I think that once again the boy is creepy, you know, he wanted her money, took twenty-two dollars, but, um, then again, kinda, I think that he kind of

> Sherrell demonstrates her understanding of the technique called flashback. She accurately defines it as, in the case of this story, "having memories."

> There are two reasonable inferences a reader could make at this point about the trucks and Magda's misery: (1) that the trucks pose a danger to her cat and (2) that the trucks and their noise and the smell of their diesel fuel affect her adversely ("making her feel sick inside, stealing some of her strength"). Sherrell focuses on the latter.

> Drawing on her own knowledge of human nature to construct her mental model, Sherrell provides a reasonable interpretation of the boy's actions as described in the text. Her mental model allows her to make inferences about the boy's feelings.

> Sherrell provides an accurate summary of what the text has to say about the change in Magda's feelings about the boy: "She came to feel sympathy for him, remembering his tears."

wanted the animal, like he loved the animal, like he took it in and was [ready to] sell it, but if he would've kept the cat, I think he probably would've done the same thing Magda did. He probably would've cleaned it up and tried to help it get better or something like that. So I think not just that he was creepy but that he kind of loves animals, I guess.

> Here Sherrell reasons through the boy's situation: He seemingly loves the animal but wants the money, so he will part with the cat. Sherrell makes a prediction about the boy's future actions had he kept the cat based on her mental model of the boy.

Interviewer: So, what kind of person is he, would you say?

Sherrell: Well, judging that he slammed the door in her face, kinda rude, but then, you know, kind of sympathetic towards cats and animals, maybe all kinds of animals, you never really know. And, um, I don't know anything else to describe him with.

WHAT WE CAN LEARN FROM THIS EXCERPT

In this example, Sherrell's reading performance illustrates the importance of background knowledge. Sherrell is able to use her knowledge of people's motivation to flesh out her textbase and create a rich mental model. Sherrell, for example, can understand, maybe even empathize with, the actions of the boy in the story: "I think the boy...he'd be a little greedy. Because, I mean, it was her cat and she's giving a lot. And then, suddenly, she pulls out a twenty-dollar bill and he forgets about the cat. He just takes the money.... And he kind of cries like he still wants the cat. But I still think he's greedy." It is this understanding of character and motivation that enriches Sherrell's mental model.

The third excerpt is again from Sherrell, but this time the text is informational rather than narrative. In her reading of an Internet text about the water cycle posted by the Missouri Botanical Gardens, Sherrell again demonstrates competence. The model of meaning she builds for the text is grounded in the knowledge she brings to the task (see Sherrell's prereading response), and she is able to reconcile challenges to that knowledge through careful reasoning. She reveals a lot about processing, showing that she has been taught effective reading strategies and that she has strong metacognitive awareness and a disposition for establishing a high degree of coherence in both the textbase and the mental model she builds. Sherrell is able to articulate in great and explicit detail the kind of strategies and the range of internal resources she uses when reading the text.

Interviewer: (*prior to Sherrell reading*) Tell me what you know [about the water cycle].

Sherrell: Um, I know that evaporation happens when heat changes water from a liquid state to a gas state. And then it goes up to condensation, and warm air meets cold air, and it forms a cloud. And after that, when the cloud gets too heavy with tiny droplets, it rains. And then it keeps going on and on and on. So technically, we kind of have the same water from thousands of years ago.

> Sherrell's comment shows that she recognizes and is able to explain the nature of the water cycle. She sees the relationships among the various processes in the water cycle.

(*Sherrell reads the text.*)

Interviewer: So what do you think the author wants you to learn from reading this page?

Sherrell: I think he wants [us] to learn that, like, um, the statistics, like the numbers and the percents, of how much water is on Earth and how much water humans and plants and animals are able to use. And, like, where

> Although she does not mention specific details, such as percentages, or technical terms, such as *precipitation* and *evaporation*, Sherrell's summary of the concepts introduced in the first section of the text illustrate that she has understood the information provided and has constructed a fairly complete textbase.

most of our water can be found. And also, like, basically what the water cycle is. What the different names to the [inaudible] of water cycle, I guess.

Interviewer: If you had to summarize what's important, for example, what would you say would be the most important things?

Sherrell: Well, I'd basically say that there's lots of numbers to water. I'm just kidding.

Interviewer: (*laughs*)

Sherrell: I'd say that the water cycle is kind of a tricky kind of situation. I mean, uh, it's like...okay, the weatherman says all the water evaporated this time, but it ends up evaporating this time. And then the water evaporates too quick and your plants die. So it's kind of like a hard kind of...it's like a complex cycle. They oughtta called it a complex cycle, not a water cycle. Uh, so yeah, it's kind of complex with a lot of numbers and percents to how much water we can use.

> Here, Sherrell illustrates the mental model she has formed from fusing the textbase with knowledge from her own experience about what happens to plants when water evaporates "too quick" and the plants don't have enough water.

Interviewer: Okay. So the water cycle is complex?

Sherrell: Exactly.

Interviewer: Sounds good to me. Okay, um, in the second sentence in paragraph one, it says that, "The water cycle is a complex process." What does it mean to say it's complex?

(The interviewer indicates where the phrase is located in the text.)

Sherrell: (*reading from text*) "They're all part of the water cycle. A complex process that not only gives us water to drink but fish to eat and also weather patterns that help grow our crops."

Interviewer: Yeah, that's right.

Sherrell: Um, I think...complex. *Complex* means like, you know, it's kind of hard, tricky, or requires a lot of thinking, sort of. It depends on, like, how you use it. Like, if you're using, like, saying a math problem is complex, that means it requires a lot of thinking. But in this case, it's like the water cycle is kind of a tricky kind of situation. It's, like, hard. But it's water, so you don't have to really think about it.

> Sherrell applies her background knowledge to clarify a vocabulary word. Her definition of *complex* does not quite fit the context, but it is good enough to keep her moving through the text.

Interviewer: Right. What do you mean...? You mentioned that it's tricky. Can you tell me a little more, explain a little more about what you mean by that?

Sherrell: It's like you don't know.... Like, say you water your plants in the afternoon. Then a few hours later, you come back to check on them, and some of them are dying. You don't know why. But then you watered them in the afternoon. Well, I watered them, so why are they dying? Well, it's kind of like evaporation. It's like the water evaporates, which means it leaves the plants and the plants die. So if you didn't know that, then it'd kind of be a little tricky. You'd have to think about it a lot. Why are my plants dying when I just watered them?

Interviewer: Okay, so in the second paragraph...that's where it says, "Water is an integral part of this planet." Do you see that?

Sherrell: Uh-huh.

Interviewer: What does that mean?

Sherrell: Um, water is an *important* part of our planet? I think so. I've never seen that word before. I'm just using context clues.

When Sherrell encounters an unfamiliar vocabulary word, she identifies and uses a strategy.

Interviewer: Okay. So, um, so given the context clues, you think *integral* means important?

Sherrell: Uh-huh.

Interviewer: Okay. Is that, um... What's another way that you could... is that usually how you figure out words you haven't seen or...?

Sherrell: Uh-huh. I figure out words I haven't seen and then...I kind of...like when I ask my...like I'm reading [inaudible]. Right? And I ask my mom, "Mom, what does this mean?" She's like, "What's the sentence?" And I read her the sentence, and then she'll tell me, "Well, how is it used?" Like, uh, and I tell her how it's used. And then, so that's what it means. So I just start...I kind of like read the sentence and use the words around it to figure out what that particular word means. And sometimes if I'm really stuck and, you know, I'm home by myself and can't ask Mom, I'll just go to the dictionary. And if that word isn't in the dictionary, then I'm stuck. Because I have a children's dictionary and it doesn't have all the words in it.

Sherrell's comments show that she is metacognitively aware of her reading strategies (i.e., her use of context clues and of the dictionary to figure out unfamiliar words).

(*Sherrell reads the next section.*)

Interviewer: Okay, how does evaporation work?

Sherrell: Evaporation works when heat touches a liquid and then it warms it up, and if you were to use water, when the heat touches the water, then it'll make steam. That's kind of like a visual evaporation kind of thing. Um, so it turns from a liquid to a gas because of heat basically.

Linking information gained from different sentences of the text, Sherrell builds a textbase to explain the concept of evaporation and the role that heat plays in it.

Interviewer: Okay, so how does condensation work?

Sherrell: Condensation happens when something cold, like when warm air meets cold air, and then it forms tiny droplets, which form a cloud, I guess. That's

Sherrell explains the concept of condensation and the role of temperature (or, as she says, "cold air") in the process, using several of the actual words of the text (e.g., *droplets, form,* and *cloud*). She uses her own background knowledge of what happens when warm air meets cold air and forms "tiny droplets."

the quickest way I can sum it up. So basically precipitation...

Interviewer: Yeah?

Sherrell: ...is rain. When the water drops.... The bigger they get, then the quicker they fall. And once they get really big, the cloud gets heavy, and all the water pours out in little droplets, sometimes bigger droplets, frozen ones too.

Interviewer: What is surface runoff?

Sherrell's theory of precipitation is that when water droplets get "really big," they become too heavy for the cloud to hold. Using her own knowledge, she attempts to explain the facts provided in the text: "the small droplets of water in clouds form larger droplets and precipitation occurs. The raindrops fall to earth."

Sherrell: Surface runoff is when it rains and all the water hits the surface, the surface, wow.... When the water hits the surface and basically it runs off. It doesn't run off. Just kind of flows off. It flows off into rivers and streams and lakes. And then all those rivers, streams, and lakes [inaudible] the water, it flows downhill and into the ocean. And then it gets evaporation again and again and again.

Interviewer: Right. Why is it so...why is...why is the... Sorry. Why is surface runoff so important?

Sherrell: Surface runoff is important because when it goes back to the...That's where most of the evaporation happens.

Interviewer: (*encouraging*) Uh-huh.

Sherrell: It happens right over the ocean. So the more water you have, the more water will evaporate, and the more water you get back. So the more, the better, in this case.

Again, Sherrell demonstrates her understanding of the nature of the water cycle. Taking a cue from the text, "much of the water returns again to the oceans, where a great deal of evaporation occurs," her theory of the cycle highlights the importance of water getting back to the ocean because that is where much of the evaporation happens.

Interviewer: How does infiltration work?

Sherrell: Infiltration works... Uh, I have never learned about infiltration. Oh, okay, I think I got it. Infiltration, it kind of works...when the ground is permeable, the water flows underground, and then the ground, like the soil and the rocks, they basically filter the water. And it's clean underground. That's why it's fresh. I think that's how it works.

(*The interviewer affirms Sherrell's answer and asks further about infiltration.*)

Sherrell demonstrates that she can easily accommodate new information. Although she notes that she has "never learned about infiltration," after reading the text, she is able to describe the filtering effect of the water's passage through the soil. To this description she adds a claim all her own: that it is "clean underground."

Sherrell: Um, well, that infiltration filters our water, which makes it clean and drinkable. Because, I mean, the warm water that you have is not drinkable; the less water that you have for us to use.

Interviewer: Right.

Sherrell: Which means that highers our rate of dying.

Here Sherrell integrates her newly acquired knowledge of the infiltration process that makes water clean and drinkable with her background knowledge of what can happen when there is not enough clean water to drink.

WHAT WE CAN LEARN FROM THIS EXCERPT

This excerpt of Sherrell's performance reading an informational text illustrates her metacognitive awareness and intentional use of reading strategies.

Interviewer: "Water is an integral part of this planet."…What does that mean?

Sherrell: Um, water is an *important* part of our planet? I think so. I've never seen that word before. I'm just using context clues.

As in her reading of "A Bad Road for Cats," Sherrell relies heavily on her background knowledge to construct a mental model that enriches her understanding of the text. She demonstrates she is able to retrieve relevant knowledge to aid her interpretation. She knows what she does and doesn't know, and she uses her knowledge to figure things out:

Sherrell: Infiltration works… Uh, I have never learned about infiltration. Oh, okay, I think I got it. Infiltration, it kind of works…when the ground is permeable, the water flows underground, and then the ground, like the soil and the rocks, they basically filter the water. And it's clean underground. That's why it's fresh. I think that's how it works.

Again, the interviewer's questions scaffold comprehension. The interviewer asks about big ideas in the text: What do you think the author wants you to learn from reading this page? How does evaporation work? How does condensation work? Follow-up questions probe deeper understanding: What is surface runoff? Why is surface runoff so important? These kinds of questions support Sherrell's comprehension.

Summary

What have we learned by looking at these three reading performances?

1. Readers' comprehension depends heavily on their having at least some background knowledge and knowing when and why to apply it. (Prior knowledge is necessary for constructing a mental model.)

2. Readers who are consciously aware of the strategies available to them can bring them to bear in making sense of texts.

3. Readers can benefit from a close reading and questioning process to resolve problems and link ideas and events appropriately, which facilitates building a textbase.

4. Teachers can scaffold and enhance comprehension by asking questions that get at the big ideas in texts and that invite readers to return to and reread the text for information to clarify their interpretations and for evidence to support their assertions.

Now, let's consider writing.

Writing

The writing section of this chapter contains examples of student work from English language arts, history, and science and includes commentaries. Rather than simply overlaying English language arts values on other content areas, the commentaries use criteria that reflect each particular domain's values. For example, one criterion for writing in history is the authenticity of sources, and one criterion for science writing is the scientific validity of the writer's conceptual framework. These criteria are uncommon in English language arts classrooms regardless of the content area; however, all commentaries are respectful of clarity of expression, coherence of ideas, and correctness.

All but one of the writing performances come from regular classrooms in public schools, most of which enroll a majority of students of lower socioeconomic status. None of the student work comes from a gifted curriculum. All of the student samples come from students who received writing instruction on a regular basis and who had sufficient time to understand and address their topics. The performances that exhibit the most proficiency grew out of a long-term effort such as topic study, an author study, or a portfolio project. In addition, when writing in science and history, students had spent time learning how to write appropriately for their content area and had sufficient time to develop an understanding of the subject they addressed and the kinds of knowledge that the discipline values.

The samples that follow illustrate student writing from grades 4 and 5. There are two examples of narrative discourse; two responses to literature; two examples of science writing; and two pieces from social studies.

Discipline- and genre-specific features are italicized in the introductory commentaries.

The Swimming Competition
Fourth Grade, Narrative/Blended Genre

Carol enriches a narrative story line with elements of procedural writing. The piece opens with the introduction of the story's *major character* and then moves quickly into *the plot*. Carol's *focal point* is a race in which the story's main character must perform various swimming strokes, each of which Carol *details* and *illustrates with accompanying drawings*.

The drawings are all illustrative of how it looks when a swimmer performs a particular stroke. There are no irrelevant events or details provided in the text, and the story *flows smoothly*, though the pacing is a bit forced when Carol tries to provide a buildup to the start of the race. The *conclusion* is nicely wrought although somewhat predictable.

The excerpted portions that follow are representative of the text as a whole.

Carol orients and engages the reader by introducing her central character and explaining why she is remarkable.

Out of all the people in ▮▮▮▮ Junior High, Patricia ▮▮▮▮ the best swimmer. She swam the fastest, she won all the swim trophies, and when a new semester came, she always tried out for the swim team and made it.

One day, Patricia's swim coach, Ms. ▮▮ said, "Patricia, you are the best student swimmer I've ever seen. Would you like to be entered into the County Swim Competition?" "Ohmigosh! You don't mean it, Ms. ▮▮, do you?" "I mean it." said Ms. ▮▮. "You are the best student I've seen in all my years of teaching ("Which is probably a million." muttered a jealous student), and we have to enter in somebody, so I'm choosing you."

Carol sets the plot in motion. Patricia will be the school's entry in the county swim competition. At the same time, she injects some humor into the narrative through the jealous student's remark and through the coach's remark about having to enter somebody.

Carol provides detail to pace her story and at the same time enable the reader to envision the pool.

Patricia strode out of the locker room. She passed the 25-yard-long pool with 5 lanes and aqua-blue water.

In a few minutes there was a gunshot that could be heard for miles around. The starter's gun! Patricia lunged into the water. When she hit the water, she started to do the front crawl (The front crawl is a bit like crawling. Your legs kick one after the other, and your arms move in circles, but they shouldn't be at the same place at the same time. You breath every other arm).

Carol embeds information about how to do the front crawl.

The information about how to do the front crawl is presented again with a picture to illustrate a swimmer's movement.

The ellipsis is used here to indicate a pause/hesitation on the part of the announcer, a very common way of announcing a winner.

Suddenly, she heared the announcer say, "Holy cow! We have a winner! The winner is..... Patricia ██████ from ████████ Junior High!" Patricia lifted herself out of the water and yelled, "I did it! I did it! Wahoo!" Somebody handed her a shiny trophy. The crowd went wild, cheering her name. "Patricia! Patricia!" they screamed. "Thank you!" she shouted back. She had never been so proud.

Blood, Steers, and Drowning Fears

Fifth Grade, Narrative

Ben moves the story line of *Blood, Steers, and Drowning Fears* smoothly from event to event. *Character development* is accomplished both through Ben's *choice of language* and the actions of the three boys. The range of *syntactic structures* in this text is remarkable for a fifth-grade writer, as is the *coherence* of the piece. Even the *title* works to reinforce the story line. The *persona of the narrator* is developed through the narrator's reaction to and participation in the story's events. Ben provides *details* selectively: they *describe actions*, *create images*, *develop characters*, and *contribute to the development of the narrator's persona*. Ben's piece exhibits a remarkable *control of conventions*. It is clear that the sentence fragments are used intentionally and effectively.

Blood, Steers, and Drowning Fears

The car pulled in the driveway like a topper dropping sail just kiting. Jack and George, both of them short, blond, and freckly, hopped out of the car and ran around the yard as if they'd been burned. Shouting Hello to a wall and then rushing back for hugs, these boys were bent on making their visit a lively one.

This year's prank was tucked away in a small, flat box. The label on it said Special FX. Taking a wild guess at what was contained inside this parcel, I tapped Jack on the shoulder and indicated that we should go to my room. Clambering up the spiral staircase two at a time, we paused for a minute on the landing to catch our breath, then pushed the door open and flopped down on the floor. Jack waited until I had locked the door, then he opened the box.

Various types of wax, makeup pencils, and powder were revealed as we lifted the lid. When I didn't seem to be cottoning on, Jack explained. He stuck out his arm and rolled up his sleeve. A huge, gaping, scabby dark wound had decorated his arm with trails of blood. Suddenly the makeup made sense. The FX could make people gasp, faint, scream, or puke, whichever the applicator preferred. You could cover yourself in false bruises, mock scars, and pretend cuts, and not even pick a fight or touch a knife. All I could do was gape.

There is something immensely satisfying about having people flinch when you walk by, so Jack, George, and I spent the afternoon experimenting with FX. I found that by adding water to the "wound" you could get trails of blood. George discovered that putting a purple tint on the white scar makeup made it more convincing. Jack realized that by adding a spot of

---

Ben uses a simile to create an image.

Ben incorporates special vocabulary to develop the personality of the narrator.

Ben opens the piece by introducing two of the three central characters and describing their actions to engage the reader and at the same time hint at the personalities of these two boys.

Ben's use of sentence structures is sophisticated.

Ben provides descriptive details so the reader can clearly envision the character and his actions.

Ben uses both short sentences and a sentence fragment for effect.

Ben ties the title of his piece to the three kinds of bloody injuries his characters fabricate.

The ending of this piece continues the humorous tone and neatly brings the action to a close.

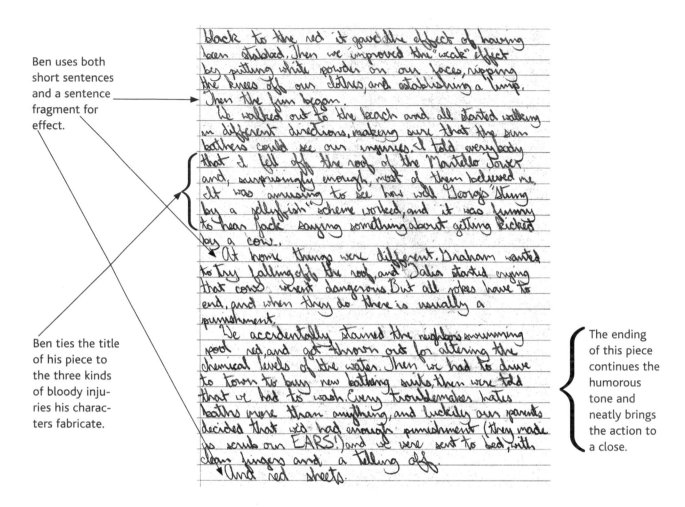

black to the red it gave the effect of having been stabbed. Then we improved the "weak" effect by putting white powder on our faces, ripping the knees off our clothes, and establishing a limp. Then the fun began.

We walked out to the beach and all started walking in different directions, making sure that the sun bathers could see our injuries. I told everybody that I fell off the roof of the Martello Tower and, surprisingly enough, most of them believed me. It was amusing to see how well George's "stung by a jellyfish" scheme worked, and it was funny to hear Jack saying something about getting kicked by a cow.

At home things were different. Graham wanted to try falling off the roof, and Julia started crying that cows weren't dangerous. But all jokes have to end, and when they do there is usually a punishment.

We accidentally stained the neighbor's swimming pool red, and got thrown out for altering the chemical levels of the water. Then we had to drive to town to buy new bathing suits, then were told that we had to wash. Every troublemaker hates baths more than anything, and luckily our parents decided that we'd had enough punishment (they made us scrub our EARS!) and we were sent to bed, with clean fingers and a telling off.

And red sheets.

What We Can Learn From These Samples

Both of these writers clearly have had instruction that addresses genre elements: They provide an orientation for their readers, organize the series of events coherently, develop their characters, and provide closure. While Ben uses narrative strategies to make his story come alive, Carol embeds elements of procedural writing to add interest to her text. They provide sufficient details and use dialogue appropriately. Finally, their writing is unusual in that Carol and Ben attempt—and bring off—humor. Ben's use of vocabulary and sentence structure is both purposeful and effective. His piece is particularly distinguished by his choice of language ("cottoning on") and the link between the title and the prank.

All of these things need to be taught. They do not come to young writers naturally but are the result of a well-planned curriculum, targeted instruction, and ongoing feedback.

Fight for Life

Fourth Grade, Response to Literature

When Madeleine wrote *Fight for Life*, she was a fourth-grade student. Her piece is fairly typical of students at this grade level if they have not been taught how to *weave evidence for their claims* about books throughout their responses. Madeleine *summarizes the events* of the book accurately and at length but reserves her *interpretive comments* until the very end of the piece, when she offers some *evidence from the book to support her claim* that Anderson's message is "If you do good things, you'll get good things." She explains that Maggie is allowed to go to her grandmother's Wild At Heart Animal Clinic when she improves her grades.

Madeleine would benefit from instruction in *paragraphing* and *punctuation*.

Madeleine introduces the topic of her piece by naming the book, the author, and the central character.

She demonstrates a comprehensive understanding of the plot through her detailed summary.

Madeleine makes an assertion about the book's quality: "it was really good but it was sad, too."

Fight for Life

Laurie Halse Anderson

Fight For Life, by Laurie Halse Anderson, is about a girl named Maggie who lives with her grandma. Maggie's grandma ownss the Wild At Heart Animal Clinc, Maggie likes to help her grandma with the clinic and the animals. When Maggie's grades go down her grandma bannes her from the clinic until they go back up. So Many sick or abused puppies have been going to their clinic. The weird thing is all of the sick or abused puppies came from the same puppy mill. Maggie is very mad because she found out the owner of that puppy mill abuses and doesn't take care of his dogs. So Maggie reported him to the police for animal cruelty and dog abuse. When the police got to the puppy mill they arrested the owner, and Maggies grandma was proudd of Maggie. At the end Maggie's grades go back up and she is allowed at the clinic again. This book was really good but it was sad too, because some of the puppies died. I like this book because I love dogs and when I grow up I want to be a vererinarian. I think what

Madeleine presents an interpretation of the book's theme/message and provides evidence in support of the interpretation by referencing events in the text.

> Laurie Halse Anderson is trying to say in this book is if you do good things you'll get good things. I think this because when Maggie's grades go down she is banned from the clinic but when they got back up she is allowed in the clinic again. If you like dogs or want to be a veterinarian I recommend this book to you, and even if you don't you should still read Fight For Life by Laurie Halse Anderson.

Madeleine provides adequate closure by appealing directly to her audience.

Author Response: Roald Dahl

Fifth Grade, Response to Literature

Giovanni, a fifth-grade writer, discusses several books by the same author in *Author Response: Roald Dahl*. He *notes similarities* among the texts, focusing on *global elements* that the books have in common. When he compares elements in the text, he provides evidence to justify his claims. For instance, Giovanni justifies his claim that *The Witches* and *The BFG* "are alike" and that the characters have "the same problem" by explaining how the central action in each book includes people stopping others from doing evil. It is obvious from this piece of writing that Giovanni *understand the texts* he discusses. Although Giovanni would benefit from some instruction in *sentence structure* and *paragraphing* to make his work more intelligible to readers, his effort to *support his claims by citing from Dahl's books* is noteworthy.

Author Response: Roald Dahl
By:

Roald Dahl is a very interesting author to me. That's because he knows what a kid wants to hear. He has a "kid's mind". He is the only author that I know that makes up interesting words like Inkland, fizz wizard, and gobble funking. All his stories are the same type. I don't mean the same story written again and again. What I mean is that they all have imagination, made up words, and disgusting thoughts. Some of his stories that have those things are <u>Charlie and the Chocolate Factory</u>, <u>Matilda</u>, <u>The Witches</u> and <u>Danny the Champion of the World</u>. <u>The Witches</u> is the book that I am reading right now, and it is like <u>The BFG</u>, another book that is by Roald Dahl. They are alike because in <u>The BFG</u>, Sophie and the BFG, (the big friendly giant), are trying to stop other giants from eating human beings. <u>The Witches</u> has the same problem. The Boy, (he has no name), is trying to stop the witches from turning children into small

Giovanni engages readers and develops reader interest by explaining why Roald Dahl is an interesting writer. The opening lines also make assertions about the quality of Dahl's works.

Giovanni establishes a context and conveys a knowledgeable stance by summarizing some of the literary elements in Dahl's books and by including a list of the Dahl books he has read.

His comparisons of global elements and the details he provides as evidence to support them indicate that he understands the basic stories in the two books he compares (*The Witches* and *The BFG*). Giovanni identifies global elements, such as plot.

(*continued*)

Giovanni uses literary terms in the piece ("Dahl uses lots of similes").

mice, and then killing the mice by stepping on them. Both stories have to stop evil people from doing something horrible. Roald Dahl uses a lot of similes. Some similes that he used that I like are: Up he shot again like a bullet in the barrel of a gun. And my favorite is: They were like a chorus of dentists' drills all grinding away together. In all of Roald Dahl's books, I have noticed that the plot or the main problem of the story is either someone killing someone else, or a kid having a bad life. But it is always about something terrible. All the characters that Roald Dahl ever made were probably fake characters. A few things that the main characters have in common are that they all are poor. None of them are rich. Another thing that they all have in common is that they either have to save the world, someone else, or themselves.

Giovanni does not provide a summary sentence to close the piece. Instead, he closes by describing a point of comparison between the texts.

What We Can Learn From These Samples

The quality of these two pieces is obviously uneven. Madeleine's piece illustrates a novice understanding of the elements expected in a traditional response to literature in that most of the piece is concentrated on her detailed summary of the book. While the summary demonstrates her understanding of the text, its length detracts from what should be a more even development of the genre. There is scant mention of the book's big idea, "If you do good things, you'll get good things," and only one piece of evidence given in support of this assertion. All the elements expected in a response to literature are present, unevenly developed though they may be: There is an introduction that names the book and its author, a plot summary, an evaluation of the book's quality, an interpretative assertion with evidence in support of the assertion, and closure.

Giovanni's rendering of the response-to-literature genre is more complex. His opening is unusual. He names the author (Roald Dahl) and provides an evaluation of him as a writer ("interesting") with evidence to support his evaluation: "he knows what a kid wants to hear...." Giovanni compares several works by the same author, discussing how the plots are similar, how Dahl uses some of the same elements in his books ("imagination, made up words, and disgusting thoughts"), and how the central characters share certain qualities ("they are all poor" and "they either have to save the world, someone else, or themselves"). Because of his comparison structure, Giovanni presents only global summaries of the plots, but he demonstrates a comprehensive understanding of the books through his assertions about points of comparison and the specificity of evidence he presents from the texts. Giovanni, furthermore, quotes from the text both interesting words, "fizz wizard," and similes, "they were like a chorus of dentists' drills all grinding away together." Closure is provided through his use of a final point of comparison between the books.

All Crystals Are Different

Fourth Grade, Informational—Science

The following excerpt, written by Samantha, a fourth-grade writer, is part of a lengthy report on crystals formatted as a picture book. The proficiency exhibited in this excerpt is typical of the text as a whole. The writing is almost completely free of error. The *illustrations represent the concepts* being described. The evidence is strong that Samantha has *conceptual understanding* of crystals because the illustrations are linked to the text (later sections of the report describe how the writer grew crystals). Samantha uses a mix of *scientific language* (e.g., "axis of symmetry" and "geometric shapes") and conventional English appropriate in an explanation. She provides *accurate and sufficient information* to inform a reader (e.g., "Well-formed crystals have symmetrical features. Features have parallel edges"). The information is written in such a way as to be accessible to readers.

Crystal means krystallos in Greek. (Kryos means icy cold.) People used to think that crystals were ice that was frozen so hard that it would never melt! But over the years, people learned that crystals are solid materials in which the atoms are put into a regular pattern. <u>Atoms form</u>

The text contains technical vocabulary and everyday language to explain a concept.

The illustration represents the concept articulated in the last sentence of the text.

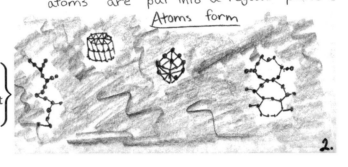

2.

Some crystals grow in characteristic geometric shapes with smooth surfaces. Plane surfaces are called faces. Some crystals form from hot watery solutions within the earth. Conditions have to be just right for crystal growth to occur.

The information is accurate and accessible to the reader.

3.

Well formed crystals have symmetrical features. Features have parallel edges. On many crystals, a face and a parallel face are on opposite sides.

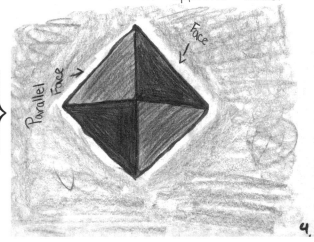

The illustration maps to the text and provides the reader with a sense that Samantha has a conceptual understanding of crystals.

If you spin a crystal around a line and you see the same shape several times, then that line is called an "axis of symmetry." If you cut a crystal in half and the top half looks just like the bottom half then the line where you cut it is called a "Plane of Symmetry." The most important thing about crystals is that they all have an axis of symmetry!

The explanations of the axis of symmetry and the plane of symmetry mix technical language with conventional English. There is sufficient information to inform a reader.

The Rhinoceros and the Cattle Egret/Threats to the Grasslands

Fifth Grade, Informational—Science

The two following excerpts come from a chapter book produced by Hank, a fifth-grade writer. This first selection, "The Rhinoceros and the Cattle Egret," is about mutualistic connections in the grasslands. Hank organized it to illustrate the relationship shared by the cattle egret and the rhinoceros.

Hank's *explanation of the relationship* is accurate and complete. His *illustration* (3-D Mutualistic Concept Chart) *represents the concept.* He uses *domain-specific vocabulary* correctly (i.e., mutualistic connections, predation). Hank's *conceptual understanding* of the grasslands and its inhabitants is obvious.

In the second excerpt, Hank explains five kinds of threats to the grasslands. He demonstrates his *understanding of the concept* of an ecosystem and of threats to the grassland ecosystem. As he explains the various threats, Hank offers a *balanced perspective* on several of them. For example, he explains that poachers who kill for money are a threat because some of the animals they kill are in danger of becoming extinct. On the other hand, he points out that thinning out the animal population increases the food supply for the animals left alive. Fire is another threat that also has some side benefits. Fire destroys the grasses that animals eat, but fire also produces ashes that provide nutrients to roots so that plants will "grow richer." Throughout this selection, Hank provides *definitions of terms* that might confuse a reader and uses *scientific terminology* in such a way that the reader can tell he understands what these terms mean. The excerpt is accurate.

Hank uses domain-specific vocabulary correctly

The Rhinoceros and the Cattle Egret

There are many mutualistic connections between a rhino and a cattle egret. The cattle egret helps the rhino by warning the rhino of danger. The cattle egret has good senses so when the cattle egret senses danger, it screams. If that doesn't work, the cattle egret pecks the rhino on the head until he and his young run away from the danger. In return for saving the rhinos and its young's life, the cattle egret gets an endless feast of grasshoppers.

A rhino wouldn't survive as well without a cattle egret because the rhino wouldn't be able to sense danger as well as having the cattle egret there because the rhino doesn't have good senses like the cattle egret. A cattle egret would survive better with a rhino because, since the cattle egret saved the rhinos life, the rhino will scare up grasshoppers for the cattle egret to eat.

The title and the first sentence announce the topic. The remainder of the paragraph explains the relationship between the egret and the rhino.

Using a cause–effect structure, the second paragraph explains how the relationship contributes to their survival. The explanation is clear and concise.

3-D Mutualistic Concept Chart between a Rhino And a Cattle Egret

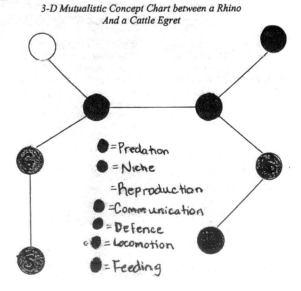

= Predation
= Niche
= Reproduction
= Communication
= Defence
= Locomotion
= Feeding

Threats to the Grasslands

Hank defines the central concept, using domain-specific vocabulary.

There are many threats to the grasslands. If one animal in the **ecosystem** dies, the entire **ecosystem** crashes because the animals need food. An **ecosystem** is a food web in a grassland or any kind of biome.

One of the threats to the grasslands is fire. Fires are bad to the grasslands, but they also can be good. Fires are bad because they destroy the grasses and sometimes the food that animals eat. Fires are good for the grasslands because when there is a fire, there are always ashes. Even though the top of the **soil** is destroyed, the ashes give **nutrients** to the roots to make them richer.

Hank introduces the topic by explaining that the survival of the ecosystem as a whole depends on the survival of its individual organisms.

Another threat to the grasslands are poachers. Poachers go into the grasslands and kill elephants, zebras, and other animals for their tusks, horns and skins to sell for money. Some of the animals they kill are in danger of being **extinct**. Now this helps some of the animals because they have food, but it's bad because the animals get closer to extinction.

Another problem in the grasslands is drought. When the grasslands don't get much rain, there is very little water available. The animals don't have as much water as they need, so they end up dying of dehydration. Then when the animals die they are also killing part of the ecosystem.

The next problem in the grasslands is hunters. Hunters are a lot like

poachers. They do the same thing except that hunters don't hunt for money; they hunt for the meat of the animals for food.

Last, alien **species** can wipe out all the animals in part of the grassland. Alien **species** are animals that come from a different biome or habitat. These can wipe out all the animals because they will need food and they might have a huge appetite. If that happens all the animals might become **extinct**.

In the two sections of the text, Hank uses a compare–contrast strategy to explain the complex, "two-edged" effects of some threats of the grasslands. This helps clarify what could be a confusing concept for a reader.

WHAT WE CAN LEARN FROM THESE SAMPLES

Both of these examples reflect their writers' conceptual understanding of the topics addressed. Such deep understanding takes time to acquire. Therefore, providing sufficient time, experience, and resources to develop an adequate knowledge of the topic is the primary requisite to good science writing.

Both Samantha and Hank provide detailed illustrations to guide the reader's understanding of the concepts. Moreover, each writer uses both technical and everyday language to further accommodate a possible lack of background knowledge on the part of the reader. Finally, and perhaps most importantly, both samples are accurate and complete. Multiple opportunities to discuss the concept, direct vocabulary instruction, and firsthand experience are all strategies used by teachers to help students produce good science writing.

Oula'dah Equiano

Fourth Grade, Explanation/Argument—History

When Mary wrote this piece, she was enrolled in an inner-city school involved in a university–school collaboration. The work presented here was highly scaffolded. Students were told to address specific issues in the first paragraph and other issues in the second paragraph.

Mary provides a *generally coherent argument* that Equiano's writing should be included in the study of American history because of the firsthand insights he provides about the experience of Africans in the triangle of trade. (There is, however, a certain amount of redundancy in the piece.) She supplies information the reader may not have; for example, she explains the triangle of trade. She *organizes evidence* chronologically. Mary uses pronouns and names to maintain *coherence* in reference to Equiano and his sister. She chooses words carefully but provides few *details*. The details she does provide are clearly *relevant*. As necessary, she *uses specialized vocabulary* appropriate for the topic (e.g., *triangle of trade, African, captured, chained, West Indies, British colonies, Atlantic coast*).

Ouladah Equiano

Equiano's writing tell about thee experience: of Africans as a part of the triangle of trade. This triangle started from Britian. They took guns and cloth to Africa to trade for men, women, and children to take to the west Indies and the British Colonies along the Atlantic Coast. He was separated from his family forever. He and his sister were kidnapped together and they were later Separated, never to see each other again. This was the tragedy caused by the triangle of trade. Equiano's writing is evidence of the horrors that Africans suffered as a result of the triangle of trade.

Equiano should be included in the study of American history because he left a written record. He and his sister were captured at a young age. They were taken to a ship where they were chained to other Africans. He was separated from his sister at this time and never saw her again. He was sold in to slavery where he remained for a long time. He eventually bought his freedom and went to England where he spent the rest of his life. In England, he wrote about his experiences as a kidnapped African, placed into slavery. His writing was explicit. It should be included in the study of American history because of the first-hand details that he left behind.

In developing the piece, the writer claims that Africans suffered as a result of the triangle of trade, citing Equiano's writing as evidence.

In support of this claim, the writer provides details about some of those horrors: the capture and subsequent separation of Equiano and his sister at a young age, their being chained in the ship, and their being sold into slavery.

The writer argues that Equiano's writing should be included in the study of American history and provides reasons. The writer's reasons suggest she has learned that primary-source documents provide important information about the experiences and perspectives of individuals of the time—an important first step toward understanding that present perspectives may differ from past, and that different participants in an event may hold very different perspectives on it. She cites directly the relevant documentary evidence, referring to the point of view it represented.

Equianos Writing

Fifth Grade, Explanation/Argument—History

Like Mary, Matthew, the fifth-grade boy who wrote the following piece, was enrolled in an urban school involved in a university–school collaboration. The project took place during the summer and was designed to develop students' understanding of reading (and writing) about history. The assignment for this final draft was highly structured: Students were told to address specific issues in the first paragraph and other issues in the second paragraph.

Matthew provides a fairly *well-developed and coherent argument*. He provides *specific, detailed examples* from Equiano's experience that evoke empathy, and he *supports his claims with evidence*. He comments on the importance of having an *alternative perspective* and on the *validity of the source* as a *firsthand participant*.

Matthew explicitly *cues the sequence* of Equiano's experiences with signal words (*first, next, last*). He also uses phrases like "for example" *to signal details presented as evidence*.

The errors that do exist, such as "he remembers confused," are likely owing to carelessness given the overall correctness of the piece, although some instruction on comma use is probably in order.

Paragraph 1

Matthew claims that Equiano's writing provides insights about what it felt like to be enslaved.

Matthew presents a clear sequence of Equiano's experiences.

Equianos writing tells what it feels like to be seized taken from his home in Africa and brought to the Americas where he was enslaved

First Equiano wrote about what it was like bein captured at the age of 11 years old. Next he wrote about the sight of the slave ship that made him think he would die, Last, he remembers confused while he was on the ship because noone spoke his language, therefore, he couldn't as anyone anything.

Equianos writings are important, because you here information about someone who was a slave themselves.

Matthew provides details to support his claim.

Matthew comments on the validity of the source from a person who has experienced the historical events described.

Paragraph 2

Equiano is included in American history because his writings tell how hard it was for Africans from their point of view. For example he expressed how they would rather jump overboard and drown than be treated like animals, He told how much African suffered when being chained down on a ship, Finally he said what it was like to be apart of the nasty Triangle of Trade where he and other slaves were traded for things like molasses. Equiano is one of the few people who wrote the things that happened during slavery from his and other Africans points of view. Without his writings we would only here the slave owners point of view.

> Matthew comments explicitly about the Africans' point of view and illustrates that point of view with specific examples drawn from Equiano's writing.

> Matthew explains the importance of having Equiano's writing as a primary source because it provides an alternative perspective, revealing an emerging understanding that different participants in an event may hold very different perspectives on it.

WHAT WE CAN LEARN FROM THESE SAMPLES

These two examples illustrate the age-appropriate differences between students in grades 4 and 5 taking on the same topic and experiencing the same instruction. Both pieces illustrate the development of an argument. When students are taught to write effective arguments, they learn the importance of providing evidence for claims and citing sources that are reliable.

Summary

What have we learned from examining all the examples of student writing in this chapter?

1. In writing, as in reading, background knowledge plays an important role. To create effective texts, writers use knowledge gained from lived experience and reading, viewing, or hearing information about particular topics.

2. They also use their knowledge about genres and expectations for writing in particular disciplines, such as English language arts, history, and science.

3. Young writers can use knowledge from their personal experience to great advantage in writing personal narratives, but they need focused instruction on genre features to organize their writing and make their stories come alive.

4. When they write informational texts in history and science or interpretive texts in English language arts, students depend more heavily on knowledge gained from reading.

5. When they respond to literature, students must, at a minimum, read to understand the plots of the stories and the motivations of characters they write about.

6. When they write informational texts in history and science, students must apply background knowledge gained from instruction and reading in these disciplines. But even good comprehenders need instruction in the text features and rhetorical strategies of genres that are new to them. Young writers benefit from focused instruction in the text features and rhetorical strategies that experienced writers use to create, develop, and organize genres in the disciplines.

7. When writers intentionally employ strategies such as signal words, midlevel structures, and paragraphing, they help readers build a textbase.

8. When writers employ strategies such as the effective use of detail, establishing a context for the piece, and incorporating visuals, they help readers construct a mental model.

8

Reading and Writing Together

One must be drenched in words, literally soaked with them to have the right ones form themselves into the proper pattern at the right moment.

————HART CRANE (quoted in Fisher, *Hart Crane: A Life*)

Learn as much by writing as by reading.

————LORD ACTON, "Inaugural Lecture on the Study of History"

Read, read, read. Read everything—trash, classics, good and bad, and see how they do it. Just like a carpenter who works as an apprentice and studies the master. Read! You'll absorb it. Then write.

————WILLIAM FAULKNER (quoted in Merriwether and Millgate, *Lion in the Garden*)

Throughout this book, we have noted parallels between the processes and habits of readers and writers. We know that strong readers read every day, read many different kinds of texts, and read deeply on particular topics. They may read to escape into a story, find specific information about a topic, or follow directions. Strong readers choose texts that interest them, take pleasure in their reading, and talk about books with others. In classrooms, schools, and communities, books give readers a shared knowledge that serves as a wellspring for writing, learning, discussion, and community building.

Like reading, writing is a self-sustaining skill. Accomplished writers read on a regular basis, just as strong readers do. Writers read to gain ideas, inspiration, and information for their writing. And just as readers can get lost in the world of a book, writers can get lost in the language of their ideas. Strong readers talk about the books they are reading; strong writers discuss the writing they are doing. And just as strong readers revise their understanding of the text as they read, so too do strong writers revise their writing to reflect their changing understandings about the topic and their audience.

The habits of accomplished readers and writers are the habits of literate people. As students develop the habits of literate people, they become excited to talk about books, to write about what they are reading and learning, and to use their reading as inspiration for their own writing. The classroom becomes a community of readers and writers with a shared knowledge about the world gained from reading stories, textbooks, trade books, and the writing of other students. And students develop habits that will benefit them for their rest of their lives.

The fact that strong readers and writers share many habits and practices indicates that there is a strong relationship between reading and writing, and research supports this premise (e.g., Tierney & Shanahan, 1991). Specifically, for the fourth and fifth graders who are the focus of this book, reading and writing are closely connected endeavors for these reasons:

- Reading and writing require related—but distinct—cognitive processes.
- Upper elementary students face similar challenges in reading and writing.
- Writing can support reading.
- Reading can support writing.
- Reading and writing together support learning.

Let's take a look at each of these assertions in turn.

Reading and Writing: Similar but Distinct Cognitive Processes

The relationship between reading and writing is a complex and dynamic one. In many ways, the processes of reading and writing are remarkably alike. Like readers, writers set out to achieve purposes and create mental representations of meaning, and they reread and rethink to revise these representations. Like readers, writers use general, specialized, and linguistic knowledge to compose meaning. And in both processes, effective readers and writers actively manage and monitor what they are doing.

In the past 20 years, there have been many different theories about the relationship between reading and writing. In years past, reading was considered by some to be a mostly passive, receptive process, while writing was believed to be an active, generative process—very different mental efforts, in other words. Now, scholars believe both reading and writing alike are active, meaning-making processes. In fact, some have even argued that reading and writing are so similar that reading instruction should automatically benefit students as writers, though that assumption has been hard to prove.

We now know that reading and writing are similar, but they are not exactly the same. While readers and writers may call upon the same general, specialized, and linguistic knowledge to build meaning when they read and write, their purposes—understanding a text versus creating a text—demand that they apply this knowledge in different ways. The cognitive and linguistic patterns of thinking for reading and writing are distinctive even when students are reading and writing about the same topic. That's one reason students don't automatically know how to write when they learn how to read. What's more, each individual has unique processes for reading and for writing and these processes vary, depending on the task at hand.

Despite their differences, reading and writing are closely intertwined. For instance, writing often accompanies reading. Writers take notes about their reading, synthesize what they read in written responses, and paraphrase the words of others in their own texts. And writers invariably read their own texts—just as others might read them—to see if they make sense, plan what to write next, assess the potential effects of particular choices, and anticipate the reactions of the audience. When writers do this, they have to pay attention to these perceptions of what their writing communicates. They also have to consider factors that will shape readers' understanding, such as the knowledge and needs of the intended audience, the purpose for writing, the coherence of the presentation, and so on. Reading and writing, then, draw upon similar knowledge and raise similar questions and issues in people's minds. The two processes can be mutually supportive.

When students understand that reading and writing are connected, they learn to draw on what they know as readers to help them as writers and to draw on what they learn as writers to help them as readers (Murray, 1990). Strong readers know how to read like writers and write for readers. In this way, reading and writing intersect.

Reading and Writing: Shared Challenges With Complex Texts

As we discussed in previous chapters, students in fourth and fifth grades are expected to read longer, more complex, and more challenging texts than in the early years of elementary school. They encounter new and more complex words, sentences, and organizational structures. They grapple with detailed information and explanations of complex ideas and concepts, expressed in vocabulary relevant to specific academic subjects.

Student writers in these grades face similar challenges. Building on the knowledge of genres and the writing process that they learned in the primary grades, fourth and fifth graders are expected to develop well-organized, coherent pieces that include details, observations, and facts that develop the ideas that students express. They need to be more thoughtful and deliberate not just about *what* they write but about *how* they write.

Writing Can Support Reading

As students master the structures and techniques of effective writing, their practice as writers can benefit their performance as readers. For instance, research shows that familiarity with genre and text structures, gained in part through writing, helps students comprehend text. By practicing writing in different genres, students learn the structures and features that characterize various texts they read. Writing helps readers recognize and understand genres when they read them (Langer, 1986).

When they write about what they are reading and learning in school, students have the opportunity to express ideas in their own words, organize information to fit their own purposes, and share their knowledge with others. Writing about texts they read requires students to recall, reproduce, select from, restate, generalize, reorganize, elaborate on, and integrate their understanding—the same kinds of cognitive processes that make up comprehension (NICHD, 2000; Palincsar & Brown, 1984; Pearson & Fielding, 1991).

In short, writing helps students better understand what they read by engaging them actively in practicing comprehension. Students must understand what they are reading to present their ideas about texts effectively in writing. This requires students to go back to the text, reread, monitor their understanding, and clarify misunderstandings. Again, writing about texts pushes students to practice the habits of effective reading.

Reading Can Support Writing

As students read, they acquire knowledge of the vocabulary, sentence patterns, and genre features typically used in written discourse. They become familiar with the language and knowledge structures of texts in the subject areas—history, science, mathematics, and literature. Experienced writers use an array of rhetorical devices to shape their texts, influence readers, and achieve particular aesthetic or emotional effects. Effective readers who are attuned to writers' choices can, in turn, use these devices in their own writing.

Students learn about writers' intentions by responding to reading, then thinking or talking or writing about the choices that authors make in texts to create these responses. Readers can learn to focus on the author's craft, asking such questions as Why is the author telling me that? Why did she choose those words? Why does she use that example? Questioning the text and probing authors' designs helps students become familiar with writer strategies that can help them achieve their own goals in writing. Students also learn about authors' intentions by making and getting feedback about choices of their own.

The strong connections between reading and writing cannot be dismissed. A thoughtful, purposeful literacy program that emphasizes both reading and writing, together, can help students improve in both.

Reading and Writing Support Learning

Practitioners and researchers alike know that writing is an invaluable way for students to learn (Pearson & Fielding, 1991; Tierney & Shanahan, 1991). As scholar A. D. Van Nostrand (1979) says, "The nature of writing makes learning inevitable." Students should be encouraged to write about what they are reading and learning in their academic subjects, transforming their knowledge into their own words. Such writing benefits reading comprehension, facilitates content area learning, develops reasoning skills, and increases the likelihood that students will remember the material they learn (Langer & Applebee, 1987).

As students develop their pieces of writing, they must select, reorganize, and integrate information. Proficient writers organize the information they want to present within the constraining structures of sentences, paragraphs, and paragraph sequences (Goldman & Rakeshaw, 2000; Taylor & Beach, 1984). They build relationships between ideas at the paragraph level, move from old information to new information, and order details. What students actually are doing in this challenging cognitive process is revisiting, rethinking, and rearranging facts, observations, and ideas to make sense of them in their minds. They are taking ownership of the content, melding it with their own knowledge. They are *learning* (Graham & Perin, 2007).

From this creative process, students can produce a piece of writing that brings together their writing knowledge, the academic content, and their own thinking about the content. As a result, students who write about what they learn are better able to understand, use, and remember the new information. Students also become more invested in their learning because writing requires them to engage deeply with the materials.

For example, a student who decides to write about the role of Native Americans in the California missions has to gather a great deal of information about mission life and Native American culture. She has to learn enough about the topic to be able to decide what information to include in the report and how to organize this information. She also has to learn about elements of historical writing, such as using primary sources and thinking about the situation from different perspectives. To produce a polished piece of writing, she must revise the piece, seeking comments from her teacher and peers, returning to her sources to add or clarify information, and editing for grammar, punctuation, and spelling. Writing the report develops the student's learning about California's history, her understanding of historical writing, her facility as a writer, and her sense of herself as a historian.

By writing about what they are reading and learning in literature, history, science, and mathematics, *students begin to think of themselves as active, engaged learners*, a mindset that fosters motivation and sets the stage for a lifetime interest in learning.

Abu-Rabia, S. (1995). Attitudes and cultural background and their relationship to English in a multicultural social context: The case of male and female Arab immigrants in Canada. *Educational Psychology, 15*(3), 323–336.

Abu-Rabia, S. (1996). Druze minority students learning Hebrew in Israel: The relationship of attitudes, cultural background, and interest of material to reading comprehension in a second language. *Journal of Multilingual & Multicultural Development, 17*(6), 415–426.

Abu-Rabia, S. (1998a). Attitudes and culture in second language learning among Israeli-Arab students. *Curriculum and Teaching, 13*(1), 13–30.

Abu-Rabia, S. (1998b). Social and cognitive factors influencing the reading comprehension of Arab students learning Hebrew as a second language in Israel. *Journal of Research in Reading, 21*(3), 201–212.

Acton, J.E.E. (Lord Acton). (1906). Inaugural lecture on the study of history. *Lecturer on Modern History, 2,* 1–24, 26–28.

Alexander, P.A. (1998). The nature of disciplinary and domain learning: The knowledge, interest, and strategic dimensions of learning from subject-matter text. In C. Hynd (Ed.), *Learning from text across conceptual domains* (pp. 263–287). Mahwah, NJ: Erlbaum.

Andersen, E.S. (1990). *Speaking with style: The sociolinguistic skills of children.* London: Routledge.

Atwell, N. (1987). *In the middle: Writing, reading, and learning with adolescents.* Upper Montclair, NJ: Boynton/Cook.

Atwell, N. (1998). *In the middle: New understandings about writing, reading, and learning.* Portsmouth, NH: Boynton/Cook.

Au, K.H.-P. (1980). Participation structures in a reading lesson with Hawaiian children: Analysis of a culturally appropriate instructional event. *Anthropology and Education Quarterly, 11*(2), 91–115.

Au, K.H.-P., & Mason, J.M. (1981). Social organizational factors in learning to read: The balance of rights hypothesis. *Reading Research Quarterly, 17*(1), 115–152.

August, D., & Hakuta, K. (1997). *Improving schooling for language-minority learners.* Washington, DC: National Academy Press.

August, D., & Shanahan, T. (2006). *Developing literacy in second language learners: Report of the National Literacy Panel on Language Minority Children and Youth.* Mahwah, NJ: Erlbaum.

Bakhtin, M.M. (1986). *Speech genres and other late essays* (V. McGee, Trans.). Austin: University of Texas Press.

Bazerman, C. (1988). *Shaping written knowledge: The genre and activity of the experimental article in science.* Madison: University of Wisconsin Press.

Beck, I.L., McKeown, M.G., Hamilton, R., & Kucan, L. (1997). *Questioning the author: An approach for enhancing student engagement with text.* Newark, DE: International Reading Association.

Beck, I.L., McKeown, M.G., & Gromoll, E.W. (1989). Learning from social studies texts. *Cognition and Instruction, 6*(2), 99–158.

Beck, I.L., McKeown, M.G., & Kucan, L. (2002). *Bringing words to life: Robust vocabulary instruction.* New York: Guilford.

Beck, I.L., McKeown, M.G., Sinatra, G.M., & Loxterman, J.A. (1991). Revising social studies text for a text-processing perspective: Evidence of improved comprehensibility. *Reading Research Quarterly, 26,* 251–276.

Beers, K.G. (2003). *When kids can't read, what teachers can do: A guide for teachers, 6–12.* Portsmouth, NH: Heinemann.

Bereiter, C., & Scardamalia, M. (1982). From conversation to composition. In R. Glasner (Ed.), *Advances in instructional psychology* (pp. 1–64). Hillsdale, NJ: Erlbaum.

Berkenkotter, C., & Huckin, T.N. (1995). *Genre knowledge in disciplinary communication: Cognition, culture, power.* Hillsdale, NJ: Erlbaum.

Berkenkotter, C., Huckin, T.N., & Ackerman, J. (1988). Conventions, conversations, and the writer: A case study of a student in a rhetoric Ph.D. program. *Research in the Teaching of English, 22,* 9–44.

Biber, D. (1988). *Variation in speech writing.* Cambridge, England: Cambridge University Press.

Biemiller, A., & Boote, A. (2006). An effective method for building meaning vocabulary in primary grades. *Journal of Educational Psychology, 98*(1), 44–62.

Britsch, S.J. (2002). *Beyond stories: Young children's nonfiction composition.* Larchmont, NY: Eye on Education.

Britton, J. (1997). The spectator role and the beginnings of writing. In V. Villeneuva (Ed.), *Cross-talk in comp theory: A reader* (pp. 129–151). Urbana, IL: National Council of Teachers of English.

Britton, J., Burgess, T., Martin, N., McLeod, A., & Rosen, H. (1975). *The development of writing abilities.* London: Macmillan.

Calderón, M., August, D., Slavin, R., Durán, D., Madden, N., & Cheung, A. (2005). Bringing words to life in classrooms with English language learners. In E.H. Hiebert & M.L. Kamil (Eds.), *Teaching and learning vocabulary: Bringing research to practice.* Mahwah, NJ: Erlbaum.

Calkins, L.M. (1994). *The art of teaching writing.* Portsmouth, NH: Heinemann.

Calkins, L.M., & Bleichman, P. (2003). *The craft of revision.* Portsmouth, NH: FirstHand.

Capps, R., Fix, M., Murray, J., Ost, J., Passel, J., & Herwantoro, S. (2005). *The new demography of America's schools: Immigration and the No Child Left Behind act.* Washington, DC: Urban Institute.

Carlsen, G.R., & Sherrill, A. (1988). *Voices of readers: How we come to love books.* Urbana, IL: National Council of Teachers of English.

Carlo, M.S., August, D., McLaughlin, B., Snow, C.E., Dressler, C., Lippman, D., Lively, T., & White, C. (2004). Closing the gap: Addressing the vocabulary needs of English language learners in bilingual and mainstream classrooms. *Reading Research Quarterly, 39*(2), 188–215.

Chall, J.S., Jacobs, V.A., & Baldwin, L.E. (1990). *The reading crisis: Why poor children fall behind.* Cambridge, MA: Harvard University Press.

Chandler-Olcott, K., & Mahar, D. (2001). A framework for choosing topics for, with and by adolescent writers. *Voices From the Middle, 9*(1), 40–47.

Chapman, M.L. (1995). The sociocognitive construction of written genres in first grade. *Research in the Teaching of English, 29*(2), 164–192.

Conner, A., & Moulton, M.R. (2000). Motivating middle school students to revise and edit. *English Journal, 90*(1), 72–79.

Cope, B., & Kalantzis, M. (1993). *The powers of literacy: A genre approach to teaching writing.* Pittsburgh, PA: University of Pittsburgh Press.

Cox, B.E., Shanahan, T., & Sulzby, E. (1990). Good and poor elementary readers' use of cohesion in writing. *Reading Research Quarterly, 25*(1), 47–65.

Derewianka, B. (1990). *Exploring how texts work.* Sydney: Primary English Teaching Association.

Derewianka, B. (1998). *Exploring how texts work.* Newtown, Australia: Primary English Teaching Association.

DiPardo, A., & Freedman, S.W. (1988). Peer response groups in writing classroom: Theoretic foundations and new directions. *Review of Educational Research, 58*(2), 119–149.

Donovan, C.A. (2001). Children's development and control of written story and informational genres: Insights from one elementary school. *Research in the Teaching of English, 35*(3), 394–447.

Donovan, C.A., & Smolkin, L.B. (2002). Children's genre knowledge: An examination of K–5 students' performance on multiple tasks providing differing levels of scaffolding. *Reading Research Quarterly, 37*(4), 428–464.

Donovan, M.S., & Bransford, J.D. (Eds.). (2005). *How students learn: History, mathematics, and science in the classroom.* Washington, DC: National Academies Press.

Donovan, M.S., Bransford, J.D., & Pellegrino, J.W. (Eds.). (1999). *How people learn: Bridging research and practice.* Washington, DC: National Academy Press.

Downing, S.O. (1995). Teaching writing for today's demands. *Language Arts, 72*(3), 200–205.

Duke, N.K., & Bennett-Armistead, V.S. (with Huxley, A., Johnson, M., McLurkin, D., Roberts, E., Rosen, C., & Vogel, E.). (2003). *Reading and writing informational text in the primary grades: Research-based practices.* New York: Scholastic.

Duke, N., & Kays, J. (1998). "Can I say 'once upon a time'?": Kindergarten children developing knowledge of information book language. *Early Childhood Research Quarterly, 13*(2), 295–318.

Dyson, A.H. (1997). *Writing superheroes: Contemporary childhood, popular culture, and classroom literacy.* New York: Teachers College Press.

Echevarría, J., & Short, D. (2006). School reform and standards-based education: A model for English language learners. *Journal of Educational Research, 99*(4), 195–210.

Fang, Z., & Cox, B.E. (1998). Cohesive harmony and textual quality: An empirical investigation. In T. Shanahan & F.V. Rodriguez-Brown (Eds.), *47th yearbook of the National Reading Conference* (pp. 345–353). Chicago, IL: National Reading Conference.

Fillmore, L.W., & Snow, C.E. (2000). *What teachers need to know about language.* Washington, DC: Center for Applied Linguistics.

Fisher, C. (2002). *Hart Crane: A life.* New Haven, CT: Yale University Press.

Flower, L., & Hayes, J.R. (1981). A cognitive theory of writing. *College Composition and Communication, 32,* 365–387.

Freadman, A. (1987). Anyone for tennis? In I. Reid (Ed.), *The place of genre in learning: Current debates* (pp. 91–124). Geelong, VIC, Australia: Deakin University, Centre for Studies in Literary Education.

Fredericks, J., Blumenfeld, P., & Parks, A. (2004). School engagement: Potential of the concept, state of the evidence. *Review of Educational Research, 74,* 59–109.

Freedman, A., & Medway, P. (1994). *Learning and teaching genre.* Portsmouth, NH: Boynton/Cook.

Friedrich, P. (1986). *The language parallax: Linguistic relativism and poetic indeterminacy.* Austin: University of Texas Press.

Friedrich, P., & Dil, A.S. (1979). *Language, context, and the imagination: Essays.* Stanford, CA: Stanford University Press.

Fung, I.Y.Y., Wilkinson, I.A.G., & Moore, D.W. (2003). L1-assisted reciprocal teaching to improve ESL students' comprehension of English expository text. *Learning and Instruction, 13,* 1–31.

Gillet, J.W., & Beverly, L. (2001). *Directing the writing workshop: An elementary teacher's handbook.* New York: Guilford.

Goldenberg, C. (1991). *Instructional conversations and their classroom application* (Educational Practice Report 2). Santa Cruz, CA: National Center for Research on Cultural Diversity and Second Language Learning.

Gómez, R., Jr., Parker, R., Lara-Alecio, R., & Gómez, L. (1996). Process versus product writing with limited English proficient students. *Bilingual Research Journal, 20*(2), 209–233.

Graesser, A.C., & Person, N.P. (2002). Discourse: Cognitive perspective. In J.W. Guthrie (Ed.), *Encyclopedia of education.* New York: Macmillan.

Graves, D.H. (2003). *Writing: Teachers and children at work.* Portsmouth, NH: Heinemann.

Graves, D.H., & Kittle, P. (2005). *Inside writing: How to teach the details of craft.* Portsmouth, NH: Heinemann.

Graves, M. (2006). *The vocabulary book.* New York: Teachers College Press.

Gundlach, R.A., McLane, J.B., Stott, F.M., & McNamee, G.D. (1985). The social foundations of children's early writing development. In M. Farr (Ed.), *Advances in writing research* (pp. 1–58). Norwood, NJ: Ablex.

Guthrie, J.T., & Cox, K. (1998). Portrait of an engaging classroom: Principles of Concept-Oriented Reading Instruction for diverse students. In K. Harris (Ed.), *Teaching every child every day: Learning in diverse schools and classrooms* (pp. 77–131). Cambridge, MA: Brookline.

Guthrie, J.T., Hoa, A.L.W., Wigfield, A., Tonks, S.M., Humenick, N.M., & Littles, E. (2006). Reading motivation and reading comprehension growth in the later elementary years. *Contemporary Educational Psychology, 32*(3), 282–313.

Guthrie, J.T., & Wigfield, A. (2000). Engagement and motivation in reading. In M.L. Kamil, P.B. Mosenthal, P.D. Pearson, & R. Barr (Eds.), *Handbook of reading research* (Vol. 3, pp. 403–422). White Plains, NY: Longman.

Guthrie, J.T., Wigfield, A., Barbosa, P., Perencevich, K.C., Taboada, A., Davis, M.H., Scaffidi, N.T., & Tonks, S. (2004). Increasing reading comprehension and engagement through concept-oriented reading instruction. *Journal of Educational Psychology, 96*(3), 403–423.

Hakuta, K., Butler, Y.G., & Witt, D. (2000). *How long does it take English learners to attain proficiency?* (Policy Report 2000–1). Santa Cruz: University of California Linguistic Minority Research Institute.

Halliday, M.A.K., & Hasan, R. (1976). *Cohesion in English.* Oxford, England: Oxford University Press.

Halliday, M.A.K., & Hasan, R. (1989). *Language, context, and text: Aspects of language in a social-semiotic perspective.* Oxford, England: Oxford University Press.

Halliday, M.A.K., & Hasan, R. (1992). *Cohesion in English.* London: Longman.

Halliday, M.A.K., & Martin, J.R. (1981). *Readings in systemic linguistics*. London: Batsford Academic & Educational.

Halliday, M.A.K., & Martin, J.R. (1993). *Writing science: Literacy and discursive power*. Pittsburgh, PA: University of Pittsburgh Press.

Hannon, P., & McNally, J. (1986). Children's understanding and cultural factors in reading test performance. *Educational Review, 38*(3), 237–246.

Hasan, R. (1989). *Linguistics, language, and verbal art*. Oxford, England: Oxford University Press.

Heard, G. (2002). *The revision toolbox: Teaching techniques that work*. Portsmouth, NH: Heinemann.

Heller, R., & Greenleaf, C.L. (2007). *Literacy instruction in the content areas: Getting to the core of middle and high school improvement*. Washington, DC: Alliance for Excellent Education.

Hillocks, G. (2002). *The testing trap: How state writing assessments control learning*. New York: Teachers College Press.

Hirsch, E.D. (2003, Spring). Reading comprehension requires knowledge—of words and the world. *American Educator, 10–29*, 44–49.

Hirsch, E.D. (2006). *The knowledge deficit*. New York: Houghton Mifflin.

Holum, A., & Gahala, J. (2001). *Critical issue: Using technology to enhance literacy instruction*. Retrieved June 13, 2006, from www.ncrel.org/sdrs/areas/issues/content/cntareas/reading/li30.htm

International Reading Association. (2002). *Integrating literacy and technology in the curriculum* (Position statement). Newark, DE: Author.

Jenkins, C.B. (1999). *The allure of authors: Author studies in the elementary classroom*. Portsmouth, NH: Heinemann.

Jiménez, R.T. (1997). The strategic reading abilities and potential of five low-literacy Latina/o readers in middle school. *Reading Research Quarterly, 32*(3), 224–243.

Juzwik, M.M. (2004). The dialogization of genres in teaching narrative: Theorizing hybrid genres in classroom discourse. In *Across the disciplines: Interdisciplinary perspectives on language, learning, and academic writing*. Retrieved June 1, 2006, from wac.colostate.edu/atd/articles/juzwik2004.cfm.

Kamberelis, G.A. (1993). Tropes are for kids: Young children's developing understanding and use of narrative, scientific, and poetic written discourse genres. *Dissertation Abstracts International, 54*, 4379.

Kamberelis, G. (1999). Genre development and learning: Children writing stories, science reports, and poems. *Research in the Teaching of English, 33*(4), 403–460.

Kamberelis, G. (2004). (Re)reading Bakhtin as poetic grammarian and strategic pedagogue. *Journal of Russian and East European Psychology, 42*(6), 95–105.

Kamberelis, G., & Bovino, T.D. (1999). Cultural artifacts as scaffolds for genre development. *Reading Research Quarterly, 34*(2), 138–170.

Kamberelis, G., & de la Luna, L. (2004). Children's writing: How textual forms, contextual forces, and textual politics co-emerge. In C. Bazerman & P. Prior (Eds.), *What writing does and how it does it: An introduction to analyzing texts and textual practices* (pp. 239–277). Mahwah, NJ: Erlbaum.

Kenner, C. (1999). Children's understandings of text in a multilingual nursery. *Language and Education, 13*(1), 1–16.

Kenner, C. (2000). Biliteracy in a monolingual school system? English and Gujarati in south London. *Language Culture and Curriculum, 14*(1), 13–30.

Kent, R.B. (1997). *Room 109: The promise of a portfolio classroom*. Portsmouth, NH: Boynton/Cook.

Kinneavy, J.L. (1980). *A theory of discourse: The aims of discourse*. New York: Norton.

Kintsch, W. (1974). *The representation of meaning in memory*. Hillsdale, NJ: Erlbaum.

Kintsch, W. (1982). *Memory and cognition*. Malabar, FL: R.E. Krieger.

Kintsch, W. (1988). The role of knowledge in discourse comprehension: A construction-integration model. *Psychological Review, 95*(2), 163–182.

Kintsch, W. (1998). *Comprehension: A paradigm for cognition*. Cambridge, England: Cambridge University Press.

Kintsch, W., & van Dijk, T.A. (1978). Toward a model of text comprehension and production. *Psychological Review, 85*(5), 363–394.

Kress, G.R. (2003). *Literacy in the new media age*. London: Routledge.

Kress, G.R., & Van Leeuwen, T. (2006). *Reading images: The grammar of visual design*. New York: Routledge.

Kuhlthau, C.C. (1993). A principle of uncertainty for information seeking. *Journal of Documentation, 49*(4), 339–355.

Langer, J.A. (1986). *Children reading and writing: Structures and strategies*. Norwood, NJ: Ablex.

Langer, J.A. (1984). The effects of available information on responses to school writing tasks. *Research in the Teaching of English, 18*(1), 27–44.

Lasisi, M.J., Falodun, S., & Onyehalu, A.S. (1988). The comprehension of first- and second-language prose. *Journal of Research in Reading, 11*(1), 26–35.

Leinhardt, G. (1997). Instructional explanations in history. *International Journal of Educational Research, 27*(2), 221–232.

Levie, J.R., & Lentz, R. (1982). Effects of text illustrations: A review of research. *Educational Communication and Technology Journal, 30*, 195–232.

Levstik, L.S., & Barton, K.C. (2005). *Doing history: Investigating with children in elementary and middle schools*. Mahwah, NJ: Erlbaum.

Martin, J.R. (1989). *Factual writing: Exploring and challenging social reality*. Oxford: Oxford University Press.

Martin, J.R., & Rothery, J. (1980). *Writing project report 1980* (Working Papers in Linguistics No. 1). Sydney: Department of Linguistics, University of Sydney.

Martin, J.R., & Rothery, J. (1981). *Writing project report 1981* (Working Papers in Linguistics No. 2). Sydney: Department of Linguistics, University of Sydney.

McCarty, T.L. (1993). Language, literacy, and the image of the child in American Indian classrooms. *Language Arts, 70*(3), 182–192.

McGinley, W. (1992). The roles of reading and writing while composing from sources. *Reading Research Quarterly, 27*, 227–248.

McGinley, W., & Tierney, R.J. (1989). Traversing the topical landscape: Reading and writing as ways of knowing. *Written Communication, 6*, 243–269.

McKeown, M.G., & Beck, I.L. (1990). The assessment and characterization of young learners' knowledge of a topic in history. *American Educational Research Journal, 27*(4), 688–726.

McKeown, M.G., Beck, I.L., Sinatra, G.M., & Loxterman, J.A. (1992). The contribution of prior knowledge and coherent text to comprehension. *Reading Research Quarterly, 27*(1), 78–93.

McMackin, M.C., & Siegel, B.S. (2002). *Knowing how: Researching and writing nonfiction 3–8*. Portland, ME: Stenhouse.

McNeill, K.L., Lizotte, D.J., & Krajcik, K. (2004). *Supporting students' construction of scientific explanations by fading scaffolds in instructional materials*. San Diego, CA: American Educational Research Association.

Merriwether, J.B., & Millgate, M. (Eds.). (1968). *Lion in the garden*. New York: Random House.

Meyer, B.J.F. (1975). *The organization of prose and its effects on memory*. Amsterdam: North-Holland.

Michaels, S., & O'Connor, M.C. (2002). *Accountable talk: Classroom conversation that works* (CD). Pittsburgh, PA: University of Pittsburgh.

Miller, C.R. (1984). Genre as social action. *Quarterly Journal of Speech, 70*, 151–167.

Miller, G.A. (1978). Semantic relations among words. In M. Halle, J. Bresman, & G.A. Miller (Eds.), *Linguistic theory and psychological reality* (pp. 61–118). Cambridge, MA: MIT Press.

Mirzoeff, N. (1999). *An introduction to visual culture*. London: Routledge.

Moats, L.C. (2001). When older students can't read. *Educational Leadership, 58*(6), 36–40.

Moffett, J. (1968). *Teaching the universe of discourse*. Boston: Houghton Mifflin.

Moffett, J., & Wagner, B.J. (1976). *Student-centered language arts and reading, K–13: A handbook for teachers* (2nd ed.). Boston: Houghton Mifflin.

Murray, D. (1990). *Shoptalk: Learning to write with writers*. Portsmouth, NH: Heinemann.

National Institute of Child Health and Human Development. (2000). *Report of the National Reading Panel. Teaching children to read: An evidence-based assessment of the scientific research literature on reading and its implications for reading instruction* (NIH Publication No. 00-4769). Washington, DC: U.S. Government Printing Office.

National Writing Project & Nagin, C. (2006). *Because writing matters: Improving student writing in our schools*. San Francisco: Jossey-Bass.

Nelson, J., & Hayes, J.R. (1988). *How the writing context shapes college students' strategies for writing from sources* (Center for the Study of Writing Technical Report No. 16). Berkeley: University of California.

Neuman, S.B., & Koskinen, P. (1992). Captioned television as comprehensible input: Effects of incidental word learning from context for language minority students. *Reading Research Quarterly, 27*(1), 94–106.

New London Group. (1996). A pedagogy of multiliteracies. *Harvard Educational Review, 66*, 60–92.

Newell, G.E. (1984). Learning from writing in two content areas. *Research in the Teaching of English, 18*, 265–287.

Newkirk, T. (1987). The non-narrative writing of young children. *Research in the Teaching of English, 21*(2), 121–144.

Newkirk, T. (1989). *More than stories: The range of children's writing.* Portsmouth, NH: Heinemann.

Newkirk, T. (2005). *Misreading masculinity: Boys, literacy, and popular culture.* Portsmouth, NH: Heinemann.

Nystrand, M. (1982). *What writers know: The language, process, and structure of written discourse.* New York: Academic.

Nystrand, M. (1986). *The structure of written communication: Studies in reciprocity between writers and readers.* New York: Academic.

Paillotet, A.W., Semali, L., Rodenberg, R.K., Giles, J.K., & Macaul, S.L. (2000). Intermediality: Bridge to critical media literacy. *The Reading Teacher, 54*(2), 208–219.

Palincsar, A.S., & Brown, A.L. (1983). *Reciprocal teaching of comprehension-monitoring activities* (Technical Report No. 269). Washington, DC: National Institute of Child Health and Human Development.

Palincsar, A.S., & Brown, A.L. (1984). Reciprocal teaching of comprehension-fostering and comprehension-monitoring activities. *Cognition and Instruction, 1*, 117–175.

Pappas, C.C. (1993). Is narrative "primary"? Some insights from kindergarteners' pretend reading of stories and information books. *Journal of Reading Behavior, 25*(1), 97–129.

Pappas, C.C., & Brown, E. (1987). Learning to read by reading: Learning to extend the functional potential of language. *Research in the Teaching of English, 21*, 160–184.

Pappas, C., Kiefer, B.Z., & Levstik, L.S. (2006). *An integrated language perspective in the elementary school: An action approach.* Boston: Allyn & Bacon.

Partnership for 21st Century Skills. (2002). *Learning for the 21st century: A report and mile guide for 21st century skills.* Washington, DC: Author.

Pearson, P.D., & Fielding, L. (1991). Comprehension instruction. In R. Barr, M.L. Kamil, P.B. Mosenthal, & P.D. Pearson (Eds.), *Handbook of reading research* (Vol. 2, pp. 815–860). White Plains, NY: Longman.

Pearson, P.D., Roehler, L., Dole, J., & Duffy, G. (1992). Developing expertise in reading comprehension. In S.J. Samuels & A.E. Farstrup (Eds.), *What research has to say about reading instruction.* Newark, DE: International Reading Association.

Perfetti, C.A., Rieben, L., & Fayol, M. (1997). *Learning to spell: Research, theory, and practice across languages.* Mahwah, NJ: Erlbaum.

Portalupi, J., & Fletcher, R.J. (2001). *Nonfiction craft lessons: Teaching information writing K–8.* Portland, ME: Stenhouse.

Prater, D.L., & Bermudez, A.B. (1993). Using peer response groups with limited English proficient writers. *Bilingual Research Journal, 17*(1/2), 99–116.

Pressley, M. (2006). *Reading instruction that works: The case for balanced teaching.* New York: Guilford.

Prior, P.A. (1998). *Writing/disciplinarity: A sociohistoric account of literate activity in the academy.* Mahwah, NJ: Erlbaum.

Prior, P.A. (2006). A sociocultural theory of writing. In C.A. MacArthur, S. Graham, & J. Fitzgerald (Eds.), *Handbook of writing research* (pp. 54–66). New York: Guilford.

Proctor, C.P., Dalton, B., & Grisham, D. (2007). Scaffolding English language learners and struggling readers in a multimedia hypertext environment with embedded strategy instruction and vocabulary support. *Journal of Literacy Research, 39*(1), 71–93.

Reznitskaya, A., Anderson, R.C., McNurlen, B., Nguyen-Jahiel, K., Archodidou, A., & Kim, S. (2001). Influence of oral discussion on written argument. *Discourse Processes, 32*(2/3), 155–175.

Rogoff, B., & Gardner, W. (1990). *Adult guidance of cognitive development in everyday cognition: Its development in social context.* Cambridge, MA: Harvard University Press.

Routman, R. (2005). *Writing essentials: Raising expectations and results while simplifying teaching.* Portsmouth, NH: Heinemann.

Rozin, P., & Gleitman, L. (1977). The structure and acquisition of reading II: The reading process and the acquisition of the alphabetic principle. In A. Reber & D. Scarbourough (Eds.), *Toward a psychology of reading: The proceedings of the CUNY conferences* (pp. 55–141). Hillsdale, NJ: Erlbaum.

Saddler, B. (2003). "But teacher, I added a period!": Middle schoolers learn to revise. *Voices From the Middle, 11*(2), 20–26.

Santman, D. (2005). *Shades of meaning: Comprehension and interpretation in middle school.* Portsmouth, NH: Heinemann.

Saunders, W.M. (1999). Improving literacy achievement for English learners in transitional bilingual programs. *Educational Research & Evaluation, 5*(4), 345–381.

Saunders, W.M., & Goldenberg, C. (1999). Effects of instructional conversations and literature logs on limited- and fluent-English proficient students' story comprehension and thematic understanding. *The Elementary School Journal, 99*(4), 277–301.

Scardamalia, M., & Bereiter, C. (1986). Research on written composition. In M.C. Wittrock (Ed.), *Handbook of research on teaching* (3rd ed., pp. 778–803). New York: Macmillan.

Schank, R.C., & Abelson, R.P. (1977). *Scripts, plans, goals, and understanding: An inquiry into human knowledge structures.* Hillsdale, NJ: Erlbaum.

Schleppegrell, M., & Colombi, C. (Eds.). (2002). *Developing advanced literacy in first and second languages: Meaning with power.* Mahwah, NJ: Erlbaum.

Schwartz, L.S. (1996). *Ruined by reading: A life in books.* Boston: Beacon.

Semali, L. (2002). *Transmediation in the classroom: A semiotics-based media literacy framework.* New York: Peter Lang.

Shelton, N.R., & Fu, D. (2004). Creating space for teaching writing and for test preparation. *Language Arts, 82*(2), 120–128.

Smith, C.B. (1996). Encouraging young students to use interesting words in their writing. *The Reading Teacher, 50*(3), 268–269.

Sowers, S. (1985). The story and the "all about" book. In J. Hansen, T. Newkirk, & D.H. Graves (Eds.), *Breaking ground: Teachers relate reading and writing in the elementary school* (pp. 73–82). Norwood, NJ: Ablex.

Stanovich, K.E. (1986). Matthew effect in reading: Some consequences of individual differences in the acquisitions of literacy. *Reading Research Quarterly, 21*(4), 360–407.

Stein, N., & Glenn, C. (1979). An analysis of story comprehension in elementary school children. In R.O. Freedle (Ed.), *New directions in discourse processing: Multidisciplinary perspectives* (pp. 53–120). Norwood, NJ: Ablex.

Strunk, W., & White, E.B. (1999). *The elements of style.* Boston: Allyn & Bacon.

Swan, E.A. (2003). *Concept-Oriented Reading Instruction: Engaging classrooms, lifelong learners.* New York: Guilford.

Sweet, A.P., & Snow, C.E. (2003). *Rethinking reading comprehension.* New York: Guilford.

Tannen, D. (1989). *Talking voices: Repetition, dialogue, and imagery in conversational discourse.* Cambridge, England: Cambridge University Press.

Tierney, R.J., & Shanahan, T. (1991). Research on the reading–writing relationship: Interactions, transactions, and outcomes. In R. Barr, M.L. Kamil, P.B. Mosenthal, & P.D. Pearson (Eds.), *Handbook of reading research* (Vol. 2, pp. 246–280) White Plains, NY: Longman.

Torgesen, J.K., Houston, D.D., Rissman, L.M., Decker, S.M., Roberts, G., Vaughn, S., Wexler, J., Francis, D.J., Rivera, M., & Lesaux, N. (2007). *Academic literacy instruction for adolescents: A guidance document from the Center on Instruction.* Portsmouth, NH: KMC Research Corporation.

Toulmin, S.E. (2003). *The uses of argument.* Cambridge, England: Cambridge University Press.

Van Den Broek, P., Young, M., Tzeng, Y., & Linderholm, T. (1999). The landscape model of reading: Inferences and the on-line construction of memory representation. In H. Van Oostendorp & S.R. Goldman (Eds.), *The construction of mental representations during reading* (pp. 71–98). Mahwah, NJ: Erlbaum.

Van Nostrand, A.D. (1979). Writing and the generation of knowledge. *Social Education, 43*(3), 178–180.

VanSledright, B. (2002). *In search of America's past: Learning to read history in elementary school.* New York: Teachers College Press.

Vygotsky, L.S. (1986). *Thought and language* (A. Kozulin, Trans.). Cambridge, MA: MIT Press. (Original work published 1934)

Wang, M., & Walberg, H. (1983). Adaptive instruction and classroom time. *American Educational Research Journal, 20,* 601–626.

Whitin, P., & Whitin, D.J. (2000). *Math is language too: Talking and writing in the mathematics classroom.* Urbana, IL: National Council of Teachers of English.

Williams, C., & Hufnagel, K. (2005). The impact of word study instruction on kindergarten children's journal writing. *Research in the Teaching of English, 39*(3), 233–270.

Williams, J.M. (2003). *Style: Ten lessons in clarity and grace* (7th ed.). New York: Longman.

Wineburg, S.S. (1994). The cognitive representation of historical texts. In G. Leinhardt, I.L. Beck, & C. Stainton (Eds.), *Teaching and learning history* (pp. 85–135). Hillsdale, NJ: Erlbaum.

Wolf, S., & Wolf, K.P. (2002). Teaching *true* and *to* the test in writing. *Language Arts*, 79(3), 229–240.

Wollman-Bonilla, J.E. (2000). Teaching science writing to first graders: Genre learning and recontextualization. *Research in the Teaching of English*, 35(1), 35–65.

Wollman-Bonilla, J.E. (2004). Principled teaching to(wards) the test? Persuasive writing in two classrooms. *Language Arts*, 81(6), 502–511.

Wood, D.J., Bruner, J.S., & Ross, G. (1976). The role of tutoring in problem solving. *Journal of Child Psychology and Psychiatry*, 17, 89–100.

Yolen, J. (1999). Foreword. In K.M. Pierce (Ed.), *Adventuring with books: A booklist for pre-K–grade 6* (12th ed., pp. xvii–xx). Urbana, IL: National Council of Teachers of English.

Zecker, L.B. (1996). Early development in written language: Children's emergent knowledge of genre-specific characteristics. *Reading and Writing: An Interdisciplinary Journal*, 8, 5–25.

Zinsser, W.K. (1985). *On writing well: An informal guide to writing nonfiction* (3rd ed.). New York: Harper & Row.